Father, Forgive Us

A Christian Response to the Church's Heritage of Jewish Persecution

FRED WRIGHT

OLIVE PRESS

Church's Ministry Among Jewish People

MONARCH
BOOKS

Mill Hill, London & Grand Rapids, Michigan

First published by Monarch Books in the UK 2002,
Concorde House, Grenville Place,
Mill Hill, London, NW7 3SA.

Distributed by:
UK: STL, PO Box 300, Kingstown Broadway, Carlisle,
Cumbria CA3 0QS;
USA: Kregel Publications, PO Box 2607
Grand Rapids, Michigan 49501.

ISBN 1 85424 605 4

British Library Cataloguing Data
A catalogue record for this book is available
from the British Library.

Book design and production for the publishers by
Bookprint Creative Services
P.O. Box 827, BN21 3YJ, England.
Printed in Great Britain.

CONTENTS

Acknowledgements

I would like to express my appreciation to the many scholars whose work I have drawn from in the production of this work. With special recognition to the late Christian historian and philosopher Friedrich Heer, the late Lucy Dawidowicz, Bernard Lewis, and in particular to Franklin Littell of Temple University whose work inspired me to begin writing following the 1988 'Remembering for the Future' Conference.

Regarding Section II, I would like to express my indebtedness to MEMRI, the Middle East Media and Research Institute whose translations of articles from the Arabic media have proved invaluable.

My thanks also to CMJ who initially asked for some material on the subject of antisemitism that could have a wide application. Finally, special thanks to my wife Maria for her help in numerous ways, and also to David Scott in the preparation of this work.

PREFACE

Every Christian knows about the Holocaust. But many are unaware of the extent of antisemitism, in countries including England, over the centuries before that horrific event. They are unaware of how antisemitic the church has been and of the fact that Christians laid the foundation upon which the Nazis built their creed. If they are told about such Christian antisemitism, many conclude that it must have been perpetrated by nominal Christians. It comes as a shock to hear that the great reformer Martin Luther became a leading antisemite.

I myself have seen audiences gripped and disturbed when the wider story is told. Fred Wright's book will spread this message and will play a major part in awakening Christians to the enormous damage the church has done in its dealings with the Jewish people. Readers will come to appreciate the massive emotional barriers against the gospel that Jewish people have erected as a result of Christian antisemitism. As a consequence they will see that dismantling those barriers through sharing the love of Jesus the Messiah with Jewish friends needs to be a vital priority.

In Part 1, Fred draws from his extensive knowledge of the subject and gives a most helpful but disturbing account of the history and causes of antisemitism.

In Part 2 he examines a modern form of antisemitism: anti-Israelism. As the Chief Rabbi of Great Britain and the Commonwealth has said: "Tragically, of course, antisemitism has not died. It has merely travelled, and today exists in the form of an Islamic anti-Zionism no less demonic than its Christian antecedents." I would add, Christian anti-Zionism too.

This is not to say that all criticism of Israel is antisemitic. On the contrary, some of it is valid. But the frequent serious imbalance and vitriolic antagonism which is associated with such criticism bears all the marks of (perhaps unconscious) antisemitism. This section of the book contains helpful material about the Israel-Palestinian conflict.

Finally, in Part 3, the author outlines a theological response to the Holocaust, wrestling with the implications it has for belief in God.

This is an important and timely book which will help to combat antisemitism and to remove ignorance and bias in understanding the situation in the Middle East.

Tony Higton
General Director, CMJ

INTRODUCTION

*"Come," they say, "let us destroy them as a nation
that the name of Israel be remembered no more."*
Psalm 83:4

The Jewish people have been the subjects of hatred, libel, slander, repression, conflict, exile, dispossession, expulsion, pogrom, mass murder, genocide and ethnocide. One is tempted to wonder why any particular group should be the subject of universal animosity, particularly when they are a relatively small group and have been disempowered and without a homeland for over half of their history.

The hatred of the Jewish people is generally referred to as antisemitism and has been described by the noted scholar Robert Wistricht as "The Longest Hatred". The hatred of the Jewish people knows no geographical boundaries and even in Japan, where there are probably no more than one thousand Jewish people, antisemitic literature is produced in abundance.

The animus is expressed in numerous ways: in the popular press, literature, art, political theory, philosophy, theology and folk law, and it has a history as old as time. The conflict between the Jewish people and the world has been articulated in both religious and racial terms and reached its climax during the Holocaust that cost the lives of over six million Jewish men, women and children. Whilst the Nazis prosecuted the Holocaust, the world stood by largely indifferent to it, and made little or no attempt to help. This book attempts to offer a Christian response to the matter.

9

There was little response to the problem of antisemitism both before and after the Holocaust, especially from the evangelical wing of the Christian church. The only published books on the subject that were generally available were those of James Parkes (one pre-war and one in the early sixties), Harry Cargas (1992), Franklin Little and Roy and Alice Eckhart (1980s), along with Father Edward Flannery, Rosemary Radford Reuther (1972) and David Tracey on the Roman Catholic side. In the 1990s the present author's *Words From the Scroll of Fire* (1994) and the shorter work by Michael Brown, *Our Hands Are Stained With Blood*, made new contributions. The antisemitism of the Crusaders was investigated by the present author in *The Cross Became a Sword, the Soldiers of Christ and the First Crusade* (1995). Since 1995 there have been a number of articles in journals and at least one new book on the subject. For many readers, however, it will seem there has almost been a secret pact within the church that has imposed a silence concerning its role in the destruction of the Jewish people from its earliest days.

This book will attempt to explain why the age-old hatred of the Jews, generally referred to as antisemitism, differs from all other examples of hatred, genocides and mass killings. The Holocaust, complete with its racial science and mechanised killing, remains unprecedented and is, to date, the climactic event in the history of antisemitism. When one compares the Holocaust with other major historical offences against defined people groups, looking for parallels or precedents, it soon becomes obvious that there is a clear distinction. Recent attempts to place the tragedy in a continuum, either to draw comparisons, or to illustrate the problems of genocide, do not do justice to any of the subject groups and belittle the uniqueness of the Holocaust.

The close of the nineteenth century, and the twentieth century saw genocide rise to be a constituent feature of conflict. Comparative research generally uses three categories of comparators:

1. Historical incidents involving persecution, deportations, mass murder and genocide prior to the rise of Nazi Germany

The most frequently employed sources are:

- The witch trials of medieval Europe, where at least one hundred thousand, mostly female lives, were lost in a systematic quasi-legal offensive against perceived witches. The figure might be considerably higher than this due to local non-recorded actions without the benefit of legal process. In some areas the so-called "witch craze" left some villages in Germany and Central Europe almost devoid of females.

- The destruction of the native North American Peoples, which included both passive and active elements, some of which were repeated in Australia against the Aborigines. A particularly interesting case is that of Standing Bear, where the essential question was: "Is a native North American Indian a human being?" A difficulty in including this as a comparative source is that numbers deliberately killed as a sponsored government action were relatively low. The higher numbers of deaths are better classified as massacres undertaken by settlers, or developmental movements.

- Examples from the slave trade. Many lives were lost in the process of capture, incarceration, transportation and through labour conditions in the colonies. A leading question that arose in America was: "When a master kills a slave – is it illegal to kill your own property?"

- The genocide of the Armenians by the Turks. This has received much attention and aspects that are convergent with the Holocaust have been sought. In particular the proto-mechanised killing and the death marches which were observed and noted by German military leaders have been noted.

- Stalin's de-khulakisation programme in the Soviet Union is the best known genocide of the pre-war years. This is cited as a mega-death genocide motivated by a powerful individual's desire to punish his perceived enemies or the enemies of his movement.

2. The Nazi offensive against other groups:

Gypsies (both *Roma* and *Sinti*), perverts, prostitutes, homosexuals, Jehovah's Witnesses and Communist officials. To these could be added those considered to be imperfect or offensive physically, and those displaying antisocial or asocial behaviour, including habitual criminals. Hitler's plans for the Slavic people, who were to be reduced in numbers by several millions and to become perpetual slave labour, could also be put into the equation. That the Jews were selected for an all-out assault can be illustrated from the lists submitted by Einsatzgruppen A (mobile) killing squads operating on the Eastern front. The "Einsatz" situation report of that date states that as of 25 November 1941 they had executed 136,421 Jews, 1,064 Communists, 56 partisans, 653 mentally ill people, five gypsies and 73 unspecified others. The Einsatzgruppen were responsible for 1,400,000 Jewish deaths in the Eastern theatre of war, which was not fought under the terms of the Geneva Convention. The four Einsatzgruppen units submitted daily reports of their activities, all of which were carefully recorded without comment.

3. Post-Holocaust atrocities and genocides

The massacres of the Matabeli by Idi Amin; the mass killings of the Ibo in Biafra; the Mitsika Indians in Nicaragua; the Cambodian massacres at the hands of Pol Pot's Khmer Rouge "Year Zero" programme, known as "auto-genocide"; the slaughter of the Awami League and of intellectuals in Bangladesh by Pakistan; the mass killings of East Timorian non-Muslims by Muslims; and of Sudanese black Christians by the Sudanese Government from 1955 to 1992 are but a few examples. The atrocities of the Balkan conflict, now referred to as "ethnic cleansing", and the Rwandan massacres are two of the recent examples under consideration. The largest post-war death toll of death by government belongs to Mao-Tse Tung under whom millions died through denunciation or famine during the "Great Leap Forward" and the "Cultural Revolution".

We need not spend any longer studying comparative materials: they can be put aside when attempting to reach an understanding of the dynamic with the simple empirical truth that: **the Holocaust exceeded all other persecutions, genocides and mass killings, as it was worldwide in its intention and merciless in its implementation.**

The Holocaust was not a war in its true sense as the subjects were powerless, neither was it a part of a war – it was a war crime. Nor does there appear to have been any utilitarian purpose whatsoever in the annihilation of the Jewish people. It is considered that the Nazis regarded the extermination of the Jews as being of far greater importance, than the need to win the war. (Hannah Arendt, "Social Science Techniques and the Study of Concentration Camps", Ch 18 in *Echoes from the Holocaust*, p. 366)

The Holocaust was a novum *in the history of evil.* (Emile L. Fackenheim, "The Holocaust and Philosophy", *The Journal of Philosophy,* October 1985.)

Its defining uniqueness was in its intentionality, where the planned, total annihilation of an entire community and a quasi-apocalyptic, religious component [and] the death of the victim became an integral ingredient in the drama of salvation. (Yehuda Bauer, *The Holocaust in Historical Perspective*, Seattle: University of Washington Press, 1980)

The extermination and also maximum prior humiliation and torture, to "punish" the "Jewish devil" was part of "Aryan" salvation, perhaps it was all of it. (Emile L. Fackenheim, "The Holocaust and Philosophy", *op. cit.* p. 508)

In any such study, the Holocaust will be a central motif, as it is central in Jewish perception, and in many ways up to the time of writing has been the greatest manifestation of the antisemitic impulse. Abba Eban remarked that Jewish history and conscious-ness would be dominated for many generations by the traumatic memories of the Holocaust. No people in history has undergone an experience of such violence and depth. Jewry came out of the war orphaned. Six million of its people – over one third of the pre-war total – had perished. Utterly extinguished were the hundreds of Jewish communities which had represented the centres of national consciousness and creativity, its cultural and spiritual resources. The trauma of the mass slaughter and attendant destruction has instilled itself deeply into the national psyche. To combat antisemitism is not simply to be aware of the phenomena but is to work towards its eradication and elimination, and to comfort the Jewish people (Isaiah 40:1).

Part 1 concerns the Western World and, rather than catalogue lists of atrocities, or parade records of incidents, its purpose is to enable the reader to understand and identify antisemitism and, it is hoped, be a part of its eradication. Chapter 4, entitled *Christian Responsibility*, however, does give an overview of the Christian church's role in setting the stage for what Raul Hilberg described as "the world's first completed destruction process", and the move towards positivist or racial antisemitism. When considering National Socialist racism, one should remember that the racism of the Nazis stemmed from their antisemitism. The virtual absence of moral support for the Jews, and the ambivalent or positive atti-tude to their destruction by Christians, has been catalogued and documented. Generally, it has not been reflected on and analysed at any great depth, particularly in the areas of moral complicity.

Part 2 is included as the Arab-Islamic-Palestinian conflict contin-ues to raise tensions in the Middle East and questions in the church. Rather than indulge in polemic or dig trenches, the material dealing with Islamic matters has been selected largely from non-Jewish, or non-Israeli sources and, in matters dealing with the State of Israel, the material has deliberately been deployed from pre-14 May 1948 sources as far as possible. The work of the so-called "New Historians" in Israel is dealt with in Part One in the chapter dealing with the post-modernist approach to Israel and the Jewish people.

Part 3 attempts to draw some conclusions and asks if it is possible to maintain or develop theology after Auschwitz. As the traditional theological category of Theodicy seems to worsen, rather than help the situation, some suggestions are offered to develop an authentic response, which is termed "the Theology of Catastrophe".

Appendix I contains a suggested liturgy for Yom Ha Shoah, which may be used as a liturgical addition for Passover Seders, or as a prayer for the conclusion of teaching on antisemitism in the church.

Further appendices contain extracts from relevant documents to enhance the materials throughout.

Fred Wright
July 2002

Part 1

Antisemitism

CHAPTER ONE

SOME MODELS FOR THE UNDERSTANDING OF ANTISEMITISM

The Jew is the enemy of the human race.
One must send this race back to Asia
or exterminate it!
Pierre Joseph Proudhon

Hatred for the Jewish people can be understood generally as hatred without cause. The phenomenon has existed from the earliest recording of history. Although sometimes given different terms of reference, it is generally known as antisemitism.

Antisemitism is a recent term for an age-old phenomenon. The term is thought to have originally been coined by August Ludwig von Scholzer (in J. Eichorn, *Repertorium für Biblische und Morgenladische Literatur*, Leipzig pp. 177–80) but was brought into general usage by the journalist Wilhelm Marr (1819–1904), founder of the League of Anti-Semites in his much reprinted work, *The Victory of Judaism over Germandom,* (Vienna, 1873; but the 1879 edition attracted the most attention). The term was drawn from the methodology employed by a branch of pseudo-anthropological social science that flourished in mid-nineteenth century Western Europe.

This "science" is generally considered to have commenced with the studies of Gottfried Wilhelm von Leibnitz who, in 1704, had identified a group of cognate languages that included Hebrew, Syriac, Ethiopic, Carthaginian and Old Punic. These languages, he suggested, formed a family group to which he gave the nomen-clature "Arabic". Leibnitz's suggestion was initially slow to be taken up, as naming a family group after one constituent part was considered to be confusing.

The "science" was a direct result of the challenges of the Enlightenment that considered that Judaeo-Christianity was a retardant on the development of man's progress, destiny and self-improvement. In the desire to be free of the shackles of Judaeo-Christianity there commenced what became known as the search for the "New Adam". The races were divided into three groups, ironically using categories based upon the three sons of Noah. Using comparative philology as the basis of their studies, the investigators further divided the groups into those employing Indo-German and those using Aryan languages. Sanskrit, Greek, Latin and German were considered to be Aryan, ie. infinitely superior. Semitic languages considered inferior included Hebrew, Syriac and Arabic and a few others. The term "antisemitism" in the modern era is something of an anachronism as some of the leading practitioners of active antisemitism are the Arab nations who, according to the above classification, are of course "Semites" themselves. A better term for the phenomenon is the German term *"Judenhass"*, which simply means hatred of the Jews and all that they represent.

Why one race of people should be the focus of universal ani-mosity is a problem that has continued to perplex the enquirer. Why should a minority race, generally without a national home-land until the late nineteenth century, largely disempowered, and without political or national aspirations, be the focus of such hatred? This animus came into sharp focus following the extermi-nation of European Jewry by Nazi Germany. Nevertheless, public response to the Holocaust and the phenomenon of exterminatory antisemitism was slow to appear. There was some early secular response, but it was not until the 1960s that Jewish scholars began to produce significant works. There has been little Christian response at all. The inability of Christendom to respond to the news of the fate of Europe's Jewish communities during and after the Second World War illustrates a continued line of general apathy. The conclusions that some leading philosophers have reached about this phenomenon are given below.

The French philosopher **Jean-Paul Sartre** made an early response to the phenomenon in his work *Antisemite and Jew* (Paris, 1948, tr. G. J. Becker). Sartre reviewed various observable categories of the way that antisemitism manifests itself. He suggested that antisemitism is illogical and is derived from mirrored negative self-image. Petty chauvinism, personal insecurities and social snobbery are projected upon the Jew. A further suggestion of Sartre's, which possibly mirrors his view of National Socialist antisemitism, is that it is a form of Manicheanism or radical dualism where ultimate goodness and ultimate evil are engaged in mortal combat. In such a view the antisemite is the *knight-errant of good; the antisemite is a holy man.* Sartre's dictum, whereas it challenges the casuistry, is insufficient, as the categories could be projected against any individual or group of individuals of any race, colour, religion or other arbitrarily designated group. Sartre, as in his other works, presents a gloomy outlook, in common with Albert Camus and the other existentialist thinkers of the twentieth century. His theory also falls prey to their overarching theory of the worthlessness of life in society. It therefore follows that the antisemite would, as a consequence of his findings, commit suicide. I. S. Weschler's theory of individual and group neurosis would sit comfortably alongside Sartre's theory.

Count Heinrich Coudenhove-Kalergi (1894–1977), the father of Richard, a founder of Pan-Europeanism, suggested that antisemitism arises from an extreme form of religious fanaticism (*Das Wesen des Antisemitismus,* Vienna, Leipzig and Paris, 1929, Eng. trans. London, 1935). Certainly Nazi Germany may be viewed as a religious system, with Adolph Hitler as an occult Messiah. The massive rallies, torch processions and military, Volkish pageants, all resembled religious gatherings. Nazi paraphernalia all carried religious motifs such as swastikas and runes.

Similarly, Communism, where the state is the object of worship, may be viewed as being religiously structured. Fundamentalist Islam likewise is an obvious example today. Coudenhove-Kalergi's model may be put aside because, although containing elements that are helpful, it is incomplete because it fails to recognise the anti-God elements. We could usefully categorise the theory as anti-true religion, or a manifestation of the spirit of Antichrist.

Richard Coudenhove-Kalergi reported a comment of Sigmund Freud in which the latter contended that antisemitism was the product of infantile prejudice learned at the parents' knee from scornful and prejudiced comments. It seems that both Richard Couldenhove-Kalergi and Freud also believed that Sunday school teaching on the death of Jesus implanted the notion of Jewish wickedness. Even if not stated implicitly, infantile, pliant minds made the assumption. Although not a direct causation, it is an interesting comment on transmission (in Hugo Valentin, tr. A. G. Chater *Antisemitism,* Uppsala, 1935).

Nicholai Alexandrovich Berdayev (1870–1948), the Christian philosopher and apologist writing in the last years of the Tsarist Empire and the early years of Communism, postulated the view that antisemitism is a political technique to provide a scapegoat when the need arises (*Christianity and Antisemitism*, New York, 1954). Whereas this has often been true in the case of the Jewish people, a simple review of genocide in the twentieth century, particularly in the revolutionary context, reveals that the technique has been applied to any number of minority groups or political opposition groups. During times of political upheaval, a political device can be to invent an enemy to focus and promote animosity or to keep the revolutionary impetus at fever pitch. The Jews as a perpetual alien nation, or a nation within a nation, have generally been at hand to provide the scapegoat required. Berdayev's suggestion is useful in the study of genocide but is inadequate, as it looks at manifestations and impetus rather than casuistry proper. A secondary consideration put forward by Ronnie Landau is that it is inappropriate to use the scapegoat motif of the situation in National Socialist Germany after the early days. Hitler used the Jews as a unifying motif between the left and right wings of his party. He distinguished between "Marxist" (Jewish) and "Nationalist" (Aryan) socialism and between "rapacious" (Jewish) capital and "creative" (Aryan) capital. The term "scapegoat" for the phenomenon is inappropriate as the process invariably revolves around blame shifting or the production of an artificial animus, and is thus devoid of its theological and liturgical understanding. Instrumentalism would be a preferred term.

F. Bernstein and Arnold Zweig both considered that the phenomenon arose from an instinctive feeling of hostility towards social groups other than the self-defining group. Zweig (*Caliban*, 1927) defines polarised emotions as the "centrality emotion" and the "difference emotion". The title of Bernstein's book sums up the theory neatly (*Der Antisemitismus als Gruppenerscheinung*, 1926). The animus may lie passive for long periods until a single unpleasant experience or incident causes it to erupt. In common with most attempts to explain the phenomenon, its inherent weakness is that the theory can be applied to any "other" group.

Albert Einstein (1879–1955), the well-known physicist, proposed in an American magazine article in 1936 that antisemitism was a psychological defence mechanism against dangers that emanate from within the person or from the outside world. Einstein's view is comparable in many ways to that of both Sartre and Berdayev and, as such, it suffers from the same deficiencies as it may easily be applied to any number of situations.

Leon Pinsker was an early Zionist thinker who was based in Odessa in the time following the great pogroms of the 1880s. Pinsker came close to producing a useful model when he stated that antisemitism was a psychic aberration that produced a form of demonopathy. Had Pinsker referred to spiritual aberration that affects the individual and corporate psyche, rather than psychic aberration, he would have been much closer. Pinsker has the distinction of being one of the first Jewish thinkers to realise that antisemitism was "here to stay". It could not be overcome by assimilation and reasoned argument. Pinsker posited that the Jew is:

> ... A dead man; for natives an alien and vagrant; for property holders a beggar; for the poor an exploiter and a millionaire; for patriots, a man without a country; for all classes a hated rival.

Pinsker concluded that the only antidote to antisemitism was a national homeland for the Jewish people.

Theodore Herzl in *Der Judenstaat* stated that the Jewish question is a misplaced piece of medievalism which the civilised nations do not even yet seem able to shake off. The Jewish question persists wherever Jews live. Their appearance there gives rise to persecution. This is the case and it will inevitably be so everywhere.

Ber Borochov, the theoretician of Poalei-Zion (Workers of Zion), offered a Marxist interpretation of the antisemitic phenomenon. He considered the baseline to be the national problem of the declining Jewish petit bourgeoisie, with no territory and no market of its own, which was powerless against the antisemitic menace. In addition, *"antisemitism is closely tied with the social unrest of the lowest elements of the working class"*. Therefore, the impoverished Jews are unable to access the normal process of proletarisation; as a result the Jewish people became Luftmenschen who live a parasitic existence out of the process of production. *"The Jewish problem migrates with the Jews"*, precisely because of these reasons (see A. Hertzberg, *The Zionist Idea*, New York, 1981).

Jules Isaac, whilst not looking for an underlying cause, suggested that the teaching of contempt was so deeply entrenched that it had become a given. As such, we may suggest that black propaganda against the Jews was, and continues to be, readily received as it is rooted deeply in the psyche. The teaching of contempt is based upon traditional antisemitic motifs and may be expanded as follows:

Deicide

This motif is frequently found in the writings of the Early Church Fathers and passed down through the ages. The Jews are the murderers of the vehicle of their own salvation: the Jews killed God. This is the ultimate manifestation and exercise of wickedness. If the Jews are capable of such an action against the Divine, what are they capable of doing to me as an individual and to the society of which I am a part? During the time of the Crusades, in particular the First Crusade (1096–99), the motif of Deicide was widely accepted as just cause for the extermination of the Jewish presence wherever it was to be found. In her autobiography, Golda Meir recalls as a five-year-old, how she was taunted as a "Christ killer" whilst attending school. The Second Vatican Council rescinded the motif of Deicide in the 1960s after great opposition (see Friedrich Heer, *God's First Love*, London, 1970). The legend of the "Wandering Jew" also finds its roots in the story of the Passion. A certain Jew, named variously according to the country the tale is related in, struck Jesus on his way to the cross. God cursed him never to find rest and to wander the earth until the final judgement. The grotesque figure is considered a harbinger of doom and has been reported as being sighted prior to every major disaster. The first records of the figure date to the time of the Crusades and have been reported by all categories of persons, including senior clergy.

Blood libel

This is also known as ritual sacrifice. The accusation is that at Passover, the Jews kidnap a Christian male child and, in a profane mockery of the passion, the child is castrated, crucified and his blood drawn off to make matzot. The earliest cases of the blood libel are in England and took place in Lincoln and Norwich in the twelfth century. The incidences of this accusation are numerous and, although the charges were never proven and the Papacy opposed such accusations throughout Europe, tens of thousands of Jewish lives were lost, whole communities being accused and burnt alive at the stake as a result. Possibly the most famous case is that of Menachem Mendel Beiliss, which took place in Kiev in 1911 and gained worldwide attention during the trial in 1913. Although the accusation still finds frequent currency in the Islamic world, the last case known to the writer was in Moscow in 1993 as the result of an accusation made in *Pravda*, concerning the supposed ritual sacrifice of two members of the Orthodox novitiate. The guilty parties were deemed by *Pravda* to be the Lubavich Habad movement. The charges were proved to be false by the rival independent newspaper, *Isvestia*. The fact that the accusation could appear in such a major publication illustrates how deeply rooted the idea is in the national psyche. An extension of the blood libel is that Jews drink Christian blood as an efficacious remedy for the wounds of circumcision, the congenital haemorrhoids that all Jews suffer from, perpetual menses in both men and women, and to destroy the distinctive odour that all Jews carry. The idea of the Jew as a vampire found popularity in the last century and was often used by the Nazis. The latest notion promulgated in the USA is that Jewish doctors appropriate Christian or even Aryan blood from either their unfortunate patients or from blood banks in hospitals.

Profanation of the host

This idea owes much to folk religion and witchcraft but has been transposed upon the Jews. The charges, in common with the blood libel, date largely from the time of the Crusades (1099f.) and are more frequent in the thirteenth century, but the earliest example is recorded by Gregory of Tours in the mid-sixth century. He describes how the Jews steal, or pay agents to steal, the communion wafer. The host is abused, urinated upon, trampled underfoot, stabbed or tortured. Supposed testimonies include several fantastic attestations to blood spurting out of the wafer, screams issuing forth from it, a flock of butterflies emerging from it, or it taking the form of a child. Once again there is no substantial proof of such events ever taking place but the motif became entrenched in popular thought and remains to the present time. Once again, many Jewish communities and individuals lost their lives on account of this charge. Up until the Reformation (1517), with a few fringe exceptions, all Christians held the doctrine of transubstantiation where the wafer is the real body of the real Jesus during the Eucharistic celebration. One can, therefore, imagine the public outrage such a charge would occasion.

Profane ceremonies

It was popularly held in some parts of Europe that the Jews keep statues or images of Jesus in their synagogues. It was believed that during profane ceremonies the statue or image was taken out and held up to congregational disdain, and that it was crucified after being spat upon, urinated upon or subject to other disgusting practices. It may be that some people were aware of the Birkat ha Minim or twelfth benediction against the minim (generally supposed to be early Christians) pronounced in the synagogue. It is easy to see how this could be elaborated upon in the vulgar imagination of the time, which was more fuelled by paganism than by faith, largely because of illiteracy. Accusations of insulting Christ were the cause of many Jewish deaths. A prime example is that on 25 April 1017 a storm ravaged Rome, causing widespread death and destruction of property. Pope Benedict VIII received intelligence that the storm was the result of the local Jews insulting the image of Christ that they kept in their synagogue. Benedict responded by immediately ordering the arrest and execution by decapitation of several members of the local Jewish community. Contemporary records report that the storm was stilled immediately.

Demonic activity

The Jews were believed to be in league with the devil and be his servants on earth. There are reasons for this motif developing.

Firstly, among the educated, it was a part of the charge of Deicide and arose from the writings of the Early Church Fathers such as Melito of Sardis, Hippolytus, Cyprian and many others. Martin Luther was to echo similar sentiments during the Reformation. On the vulgar level it was observed that Jewish doctors were particularly skilled and it was noted that Jews generally did not succumb so quickly to epidemics. The reason, although not generally known, was that Jewish primary hygiene was more advanced and, because Jews drank only from running water, they avoided many of the infections caught from contaminated or stagnant water.

The motif surfaced from the early medieval period in art and church architecture. In works of art, Jews were shown to be horned. Initially the horns were only applied to Moses due to a mistranslation of Exodus 34:29 by Jerome in the Vulgate. When Moses came down from the mountain instead of reading "the skin of his face shone", it read "the skin of his face had horns". Gradually, the horning was applied to all Jews as were tails and pincered feet – all demonic attributes. Jews were portrayed as cavorting with scorpions, snakes or unclean animals, being suckled by swine or engaging in acts of bestiality with them. Examples of horning may be found at the Cathedral of Auch and, amazingly, in a large statue of Moses in a commanding position outside the public library in Burnley, UK. The motifs of Ecclesia and Synagoga also appeared in the medieval period, Ecclesia being represented as a beautiful young woman, and the synagogue (the Jews) being represented as blind, deformed, stooped or dressed as a whore. The Cathedrals of Reims, Bamberg, Freiberg and Strasbourg are examples, with the most vivid representation being at the Cathedral of Notre Dame, Paris. The only exception known to the writer that gives a more positive portrayal is a window at the Abbey of St Denis, which shows Christ crowning the church and lifting a veil from the synagogue. A similar representation is found in an illustration of the tree of Jesse in the Lambeth Bible (MS 3 folio 198), where Mary is crowning the church and a disassociated hand is either lifting or lowering the veil on the synagogue.

The Victorines were an order of canons formed in 1108 by William of Champeaux, a retired Chancellor of the Cathedral of Notre Dame. In the same period, the Victorines studied the Hebrew Scriptures and held dialogues regarding biblical interpretations, with Jewish exegetes, Andrew of St Victor and Hugh of Bosham being the leading exemplars. The cartularies of St Victor have not revealed any antisemitic writings from the periods of the Crusades. Sadly they were an extremely small island in a raging antisemitic ocean.

Other antisemitic types that identify the Jews by a grotesque representation of hooked and crooked noses in the medieval period include:

- The grotesque nose as Jewish stereotypical image found in church art;
- *The Brunner Chronicle* 1474–1483. Picture no.13 is an illustration of a Jewish ritual murder;
- *The Florentine Chronicle* of Giovanni Villani. In an illustration of the desecration of the Host, the torturer of the wafer is identified in this manner;
- A French chronicle of 1321 illustrates the expulsion of the Jews by Philip Augustus. The deportees are represented as ugly, with hooked noses;
- Rheine Codex Balduini – a Jewish deputation seeking an audience with Heinrich VII is similarly depicted;
- The Fountain of the Child Devourer was erected in 1540 in Berne, where the Jews were either killed or expelled in 1294 on a charge of ritual murder. The Fountain depicts a Jew with a sackful of Christian children, one of whom he is swallowing;
- During the Reformation, art forms did not improve. Pigs suckling piglets and Jews decorate choir stalls, pillars and eaves of Protestant churches, Wittenberg, Regensburg and

Basle being but a few examples. Wittenberg Cathedral has an image of a Rabbi lifting up a sow's tail, which was described by Martin Luther as "The Rabbi Looks into the Talmud".

Conspiracy theories

In their basic form, conspiracy theories proclaim that there is a Jewish plot to take over the world. In the modern period, the motif is manifest in the common coinage that Jews control the world's banking and finance, and the media. Many Jewish lives were lost on charges of "coin clipping" in the medieval period. However, a more serious charge was levelled against the Jewish people. In the late eighteenth century, the only Jewish mint master in Prussia, Veital Ephraim, was ordered to strike debased foreign coinage, ostensibly as a measure to undermine the trading abilities of his adversaries. In the event, the Emperor used the debased coinage in his own lands in order to amass a huge personal fortune. As can be easily imagined, the initiative soon led to an economic crisis. The Prussians held the Jewish people collectively responsible for the disaster and demanded reprisals. The conspiracy theories are a development in some ways of the demonisation process.

The earliest manifestations of conspiracy theories were during the Black Death which ravaged Europe between the late twelfth and fourteenth centuries, and in which over two-thirds of the population of Europe perished. The Jews were accused of poisoning wells in order to destroy Christendom and take over the world. As with all the other elements of the teaching of contempt, there is no trace of truth in any of the accusations. Nevertheless, many thousands of Jews lost their lives, often including whole communities, on the charges of well poisoning. Confessions were extracted from hapless victims when, under unimaginable torture, they would sign a confession in order to be dispatched from their sufferings.

Conspiracy theories are best exemplified by the second most famous Christian forgery, *The Protocols of the Learned Elders of*

Zion. This spurious document was forged by elements of the Tsarist Secret Police at the turn of the century. Briefly, the action commences in a graveyard in Prague at midnight. The Twelve Elders of the tribes of Israel are gathered together and they raise the devil, who gives them the blueprint for world domination. The opening of the First Protocol sets the scene by proclaiming that political freedom is not a fact but an idea; that the power of gold has replaced the power of liberal rulers; that their motto is power and hypocrisy; and that a new aristocracy has been established [by them], based not upon heredity, but on power and wealth. The Second Protocol claims the overwhelming success of Darwinism, Marxism and Nietzschism, for all of which they claim credit for engineering to demoralise the minds of the goyim. The Third Protocol declares that hunger gives to capital greater power over the worker than legal authority: through misery and the resulting jealous hatred we can manipulate the mob and crush those who stand in our way. The Third Protocol concludes by glorying in the triumph of the French Revolution which, of course, the Elders engineered.

In 1917 the Protocols made their worldwide début as they were distributed by the White Russians. Fantastic as it may seem, the *Protocols* were accepted as authentic. *The London Times* produced a lengthy article about the document, which was subsequently published under the imprimatur of HM Stationers. Subsequently, *The Times* published a series of articles in 1921, proving the document was a forgery. However, the damage was already done by this time and the *Protocols* had found a place in the hearts of many. Tsar Nicholas II was an avid supporter of the document, and when the Bolsheviks took him and his family into captivity the two books beside his bed were the Bible and the *Protocols*. The *Protocols* are widely distributed today and were observed for sale in churches in Warsaw during the 1980s and early 90s and in Red Square, Moscow in 1993 alongside the *Black Octopus*, another well-known antisemitic tractate. In 1990 there were no more than 1,200 Jews living in Poland. The Protocols are freely distributed in the Arab nations and are often presented to foreign visiting dignitaries.

In conclusion, we concur with Jules Isaac that the teaching of contempt is the medium of antisemitism, but once again it is a causal effect not the cause in itself.

Jacques Maritain probably offers the best model when he considers that antisemitism is Essential Christophobia. Without wishing to expand on the nuances of the term, we may for our purposes define Essential Christophobia as a fear of the challenges of salvation, attendant judgement and the afterlife. ("Anti-Semitism", transcript of lecture given in Paris on 5 February 1938 at the Théâtre des Ambassadeurs, under the auspices of the Groupes Chrétienté, and later at the Cosmopolitan Club, New York on 14 December 1938, with additions due to the unfolding events.)

We can expand Maritain's suggestion by adding a paraphrased comment from Karl Barth:

> The continued existence of the Jewish people despite over two millennia of their attempted destruction is the only concrete evidence of the existence of God that has any veracity.

Fallen man, in his rebellion, cannot stand the thought of an interventionist God or a God who must be honoured. Man cannot kill God or dethrone him, therefore he attempts to remove the physical evidences of his existence. The Jewish people are God's representative people, a better term than "chosen" as "representative" carries a more intentional quality. The term "chosen" can imply superiority, which is not of course the intention (Deuteronomy 7), and can fuel an antisemitic response. The election of Israel was to illustrate God's character: his mercy and forgiveness, but also his righteousness and judgement. Paul understood this clearly as illustrated in the Epistle to the Romans (1:16 cf. 3:1ff.).

The existence of the Jewish people is God's *via media* to illustrate to all mankind:

1. The unsatisfactory condition of the human heart and spirit and mankind's need for redemption;
2. God's willingness to forgive, reconcile and redeem;
3. The way he has provided salvation for all mankind through the Jewish Messiah;
4. His character and qualities – especially his loving kindness, faithfulness and constancy.

In agreement with Maritain, we conflate his dictum and offer the following model for understanding antisemitism:

> The dynamic of antisemitism is the spirit of Antichrist, which is best understood as the spirit of anti-salvation. Fallen man cannot bear to be reminded of God and his responsibilities towards him. As man cannot kill, dethrone, or physically remove or destroy him he attempts to remove the evidence of his existence. The desire may only be achieved by the removal of the physical evidence, namely the Jewish people.

Many are also perplexed by the role of physical Israel. Why should a small country the size of Wales be the focus of international animosity? The answer is simple and connected to the above dictum. The Jewish people are God's representatives and Israel is the stage that he has chosen for the drama of salvation history to be played out upon (Psalm 105 *et al*). Hence the reason for the everlasting element of the Abrahamic covenant (Genesis 15).

CHAPTER TWO

THE OPERATION OF ANTISEMITISM

"It is sad not to see any good in goodness."
Gogol

Antisemitism, in common with most demonic incursions, frequently commences in a subtle manner. Generally, the primary thrust is accompanied by the statement that measures taken are for the public good. The impetus essentially moves through three phases which will be expanded on but may be simply classified as:

1 **Covert** – exemplified by social exclusion and antilocution (usage of derogatory terminology)
2 **Overt** – exemplified by public denouncement followed by sanctions and violence
3 **Exterminatory** – genocide or ethnocide

Further it may be:

1 **Passive** – usually the first stage is the curtailment and subsequent removal of the means of sustaining life along with the introduction of contaminated water or of disease, overcrowding and exposure to climatic extremes which speed the process. Enforced labour of excessive hours with little or no nutriment and sleep may be included. General reduction of food supplies leads to death by starvation.
2 **Active** – execution by manual, mechanical or scientific means.

34

Raul Hilberg in his magisterial work, *The Destruction of the European Jews* (1961), neatly sums up the process:

> Christian missionaries have said, "You have no right to dwell among us as Jews"; Secular rulers had proclaimed "You have no right to live among us"; The German Nazis at last decreed, "You have no right to live."

Despite the protestations of Leonid Kravchuck, former President of the Ukraine, that antisemitism is dead, the various nationalist groups are violently antisemitic. Likewise, Barbara Amiel's statement that worldwide organised antisemitism has been eliminated is tragically naïve (*Daily Telegraph,* London, 19 Feb 2001). Even Japan, where there are estimated to be less than one thousand Jews, produces a prodigious amount of antisemitic literature.

To help gain an understanding of the process that leads to exterminatory antisemitism, which can usefully be termed "ethnocide" – the extinction of a people group and all traces that they ever existed, as was the desire of Nazi Germany – it is worth mentioning that the Holocaust (if that is the right term to use) has exceeded all other genocides. All other genocides have concentrated on a subject group, as defined by the perpetrators, on a local geographical scale. The Nazi impetus was worldwide, not only against a people group but against those associated with it and descendants of that group who had "married out" or assimilated.

The expression "Holocaust" (Gk. *Holocaustos*) refers to a whole burnt offering. In the Septuagint it is simply a burnt offering. As such, the term carries sacrificial connotations. We, therefore, concur with Walter Lacquer that it is not a suitable term to use of the Jewish people as they were not ritual victims (*The Terrible Secret, The Secret Suppression of the Truth About Hitler's Final Solution,* Boston, 1980). If the destruction of the Jews by Nazi Germany was a Holocaust then it was a sacrifice to Adolph Hitler. As Emil Fakenheim contends, through the ashes of the Holocaust, God commanded that the Jewish people should survive and that we should not accord posthumous victories to

Adolph Hitler. Alternative terms such as "Shoah" and "Churban" have been suggested, but as Uriel Tal has pointed out, as the terms also carry religious connotations, they are to be considered at the least to be inappropriate (*Excursus on the Term Shoah*, Ithaca, 1978). Possibly the German term "*Endlösung*" (final solution) is to be preferred.

The following model is designed to help identify the process of the development of exterminatory antisemitism and carries the pre-supposition that a totalitarian state is either nascent or established. The earlier points can also be applied to any racially fuelled oppression.

Antipathetic attitudes and sentiments

We may paraphrase Elie Wiesel's comment that the opposite of love is not hate, it is indifference, and Edmund Burke's statement that it only takes a few good men to do nothing, for evil to triumph. Antisemitic sentiments can be observed when, for example, a misfortune falls upon a Jewish person and the comment "he is only a Jew" is passed. The comment illustrates a devaluation of that particular individual's worth and the group he is part of or associated with. Ignoring the plight of a Jewish person involved in an accident or who is the victim of assault, or even ignoring the presence of a Jewish person, are the primary symptoms of the spiral. Ian Kershaw, reflecting on the Nazi period, stated:

> Popular opinion, largely indifferent and infused with latent anti-Jewish feeling, further bolstered by propaganda, provided the climate within which the spiralling Nazi aggression toward the Jews could take place unchallenged . . . The road to Auschwitz was not paved with hate but with indifference.

Defamation

The defamatory process may start with seemingly harmless humour that plays on stereotypical motifs. A gradual process of defamation soon finds its way into the collective psyche and can in turn produce the negative stereotype. Comments such as "the Jews are mean"; "all the Jews are interested in is money"; "the Jews will rob you blind if you let them"; "the Jews hate everyone who is not Jewish"; "the Jews are always quarrelling with everyone else", are stereotypical motifs that appear with nauseating regularity. The production of the negative stereotype is foundational to the progress of the antisemitic dynamic. Once the stereotype becomes established, thought patterns generally will tend to address the negative stereotype rather than the reality.

These first two categories may be either passive or active. Those exercising them may not be aware of the underlying spiritual and political dynamic they are involved in. The third category marks the commencement of a more active form of manifestation, but can still be carried on without some of those being involved having an active animus or even being aware of the dynamic in the earlier stages.

Withdrawal and avoidance

In its primary form this may involve the avoidance of so-called Jewish areas, or a refusal to sell or rent property to Jewish people. At this stage there may be an informal boycott of Jewish businesses, tradesmen and facilities by those bearing an active animus. From this stage on, the animus takes on a more active and aggressive form and may include the formation of pressure groups or action groups. It may be at this point that the police apparatus is expanded and deployed along with paramilitary or "patriotic" (sometimes overtly nationalist) groups. The movement may begin to actively pursue the politics of polarisation. The process does not allow for any middle ground. Those who would attempt moderation, conciliation, or meaningful dialogue are consigned to a political no man's land. A further impetus is to establish a cleavage between the current political thrust and previously held ideas. A programme is instituted to sever younger people from their heritage and to instil the values and priorities of the new regime as the norm. As the impetus progresses, irregular paramilitary uniformed organisations become official organs of the state and newer ones established, usually with a policing function. In Nazi Germany, the Boy Scouts were co-opted into the Hitler Youth movement. Under the Nazi regime, churches in other countries were constrained to follow suit. Dietrich Bonhoeffer expressed his dismay when the order reached the church he led in London.

Part of the programme of Nazi Germany was to move away from Judaeo-Christianity and to institute neo-paganism, following a motif of Nietzsche, who regarded the former as being weakening and effeminate. A major aspect was the concept of "hardening". Part of what we might term the orientation-reorientation operation is reflected in contemporary architecture, the arts, music and literature.

Denunciation

Particular negative emphases are placed upon the Jewish religion and its practices. Old chestnuts are pulled from the fire, the teaching of contempt is alluded to. In the modern period, circumcision is presented as a primitive and barbarous practice. It is loudly trumpeted that it abuses the child's rights and is particularly cruel as it is generally performed without anaesthetic. In 1933 Hitler banned *shechita* (Jewish ritual slaughter) on the grounds that it was cruel to animals. Observant Jews were faced with two harrowing choices: either to import kosher meat or to abstain from meat. The first choice was not an option for most people as it was prohibitively expensive, in short supply, and the economic sanctions were beginning to bite. Because of the "separateness" of the Jewish people they are accused of having something to hide that is either criminal or disgusting. The dietary laws are lampooned. Following a libel first proposed by the Egyptian Manetho in the third century BCE, the dietary laws are proclaimed to be the result of congenital illnesses. Conspiracy theories have moved from humorous asides into blanket statements that are received as being authentic. In the Third Reich, the ghettoization process was carried out under the auspices of the Health and Hygiene authorities on the contention that Jews were carriers of Spotted Fever.

It is at this stage that the very presence of the Jewish people is presented as being inimically harmful to society in general. The Jews are presented as a sinister presence, an alien nation within a nation, a fifth column for any real or imagined enemies.

Denunciation finds its way into the arts and the media, where Jewish characteristics are grafted upon evil, undesirable characters. Grotesque or demonic images are employed. Dostoyevsky's money lender in *Crime and Punishment*, Marlowe's *Jew of Malta*, Shylock in Shakespeare's *Merchant of Venice*, Fagin in Dickens' *Oliver Twist*, various works by Hilaire Belloc, G. K. Chesterton, poems by Rudyard Kipling, works by T. S. Eliot, John Buchan's *The 39 Steps*, and the Nazi film *The Jew Suess* are but a few examples.

Classical Christian antisemitism played a large part in establishing negative Jewish stereotypes which were eagerly seized upon by both Nazi Germany and Soviet Communism. Denunciation of the creative output of Jews may be included. The composer Richard Wagner for instance, although happy to plagiarise the work of the Jewish composer Jacob Mayerbeer, claimed, in his antisemitic polemic *Das Judentum in der Musik* that the Jews were incapable of originality and were a nation of plagiarists. Wagner initially put out the scurrilous work which insulted Mendelsohn, Schubert and other Jewish composers under the pseudonym Karl Freudian but appended his own name to subsequent editions. According to Wagner, Jewish music was strange, cold, bizarre, mediocre, unnatural and perverse. The effect of Wagner's music and writing must be taken into account in any study of the rise of German National Socialism. To gain an understanding of it, as pointed out by Adolph Hitler, one must know Wagner (Otto Tolichus, *They Wanted War*, New York, 1940).

Primary social exclusion

This involves exclusion from social and leisure facilities, such as clubs and associations, cinemas, cafés, bars and restaurants, sports utilities, and some public utilities, including public transport and parks. Signs begin to appear forbidding Jews access to premises, utilities, services and tourist facilities.

In Nazi Germany, swastikas and other party insignia on both public and private buildings and facilities were a disincentive to entry.

Legislative and statutory exclusion

Jewish people are disbarred from holding public office or practising in the legal or medical professions, higher education, the arts, media, accountancy or banking industries. Industrial and commercial enterprises may be limited in size or higher rates of taxation levied. Likewise, the amount of monies held in banks may be limited. Exclusions from geographical areas and the public services may be enacted. Jewish communities in exile have generally suffered legislative exclusions from geographical locations and from certain employment, sometimes as a result of canon law.

In Nazi Germany, the first governmental law regarding the "Reconstruction of the Civil Service" was passed on 7 April 1933 within a year of Hitler taking power, to be followed by the Nuremberg Laws concerning racial legislation on 15 September 1935. The so-called laws for The Protection of German Blood and Honour forbade German–Jewish marriages, extra-marital intercourse between Jews and Germans, and Jews from employing females under the age of 45 years. Jews were also forbidden to fly the national flag. On 14 November the First Regulation of Reich Citizenship Law was enacted, which effectively removed citizenship and voting rights and prohibited any Jew from holding public office. The legal status of Jewish Communities was removed on 28 March 1938.

It is at around this stage, although it may vary, that a militaristic model of leadership pervades all areas of the society and a vast bureaucratic network with a large policing element is firmly established. Both Nazi Germany and Stalinist Communist states are leading examples of this.

The development of political and/or religious ideology

It is at this stage that the intelligentsia get involved, having "bought into" the impetus. It is certainly one of the most dangerous stages as it begins to formalise the ideology into a respectable alternative ethical system. Elements of the intelligentsia invariably have been involved before this stage, but it is now that they take a visibly active role. Along with the ideology there is a developed apologetic. The ideology will illustrate the uselessness of the people. They will be presented as a "strain on the wellbeing of the society", "useless eaters", and "surplus population", to borrow expressions from Nazi Germany. They will be held to be a redundant population group who serve no positive purpose and undermine the intrinsic values of the host society by their persistent refusal to be of any use or support to that society. As a nation within a nation, they will be seen as Judases, whose sole intention is to betray and stab in the back the host that feeds them. As such they come to be regarded as lice and parasites. As the impetus advances they will be presented as a different form of life: "I don't know what the Jews are but they certainly are not human" (Adolph Hitler). The Jews' desire is believed to be to defile the host nation's women in order to destroy the society by diluting the racial distinctives. The aim, it is thought, may be achieved either by intermarrying, or preferably by rape or violation. Educational materials are developed and become part of the mainstream educational programmes. A revisionist history may also be put in place accompanied by negative propaganda.

In Nazi Germany, Dr Joseph Paul Goebbels, the Minister of Public Enlightenment and Propaganda, employed posters, cartoons, including what has been described as political pornography, film clips, radio programmes and advertisements in publications and on placards to inflame hatred against the Jews. The news-sheet *Der Stürmer* featured rabid antisemitic material including lurid cartoons and stories. The teaching of contempt is, at this stage, in the public domain and widely accepted as the tip of the iceberg. There is an undertone running that suggests we had better destroy the Jews before they destroy us. Learned papers, articles and books begin to appear, describing the racial differences, the social differences and both the political and the genetic threat of the alien race. Antisemitism, at this point, is becoming respectable and the development and implementation of an alternative ethical system is in progress.

Economic sanctions and boycott

Jewish businesses are subject to sanctions, as are those who would wish to trade with them. The ability to raise finance, which has already been in part curtailed by the effects of legislative exclusion, is now removed. The exterminatory process is now slowly taking shape as economic deprivation will reduce the means of sustaining life. Throughout history there have been legislative measures that have prevented the Jews from trading in certain areas, particularly in Tsarist Russia, the Baltics and Eastern Europe. In 1545, Jewish goods produced or traded from Poland were publicly burned and the Jews banned from Moscow. In Nazi Germany, the economic boycott was introduced on 1 April 1933.

Deprivation of primary health care, medical facilities and welfare

Measures such as these generally accompany ghettoisation. The removal of health-related services invariably leads to increased infant mortality rate and associated deaths in mothers, along with a general reduction in life expectancy. A more active approach may begin to be instituted by contamination of water supplies, causing outbreaks of typhoid and cholera. Other types of infection may be deliberately introduced. Measures contributing to increased death rates are referred to as "passive genocide". The prevention of childbirth by a sterilisation programme may be instituted. The effects of overcrowding and exposure to extreme cold or heat also increase the death rate. Limited food rationing and inferior or rotten items within the foodstuffs cause malnutrition, which in turn has a weakening effect.

Removal of legal protection and human rights

The pogrom is the classical example of this. Pogroms in Tsarist Russia were often government sponsored. Acts of violence against the people are not only tolerated but also encouraged. Beatings in the street, destruction of property, forced emigration, the seizure of property, looting and incendiary acts precede deportation to concentration camps, forced labour camps and centres for extermination. At this stage, the propaganda and ideological rationale has rendered the subject group "non-people". The destruction of "non-people" is not considered to be a criminal act but in some cases a necessity and in others a virtuous act geared to the public good. Kristallnacht, carried out by the Brownshirts on 9 November 1938, is a leading example from Nazi Germany. All of the main European countries had their fascist movements and all looked to Nazi Germany for a lead. A few examples are the Rexists in Belgium, the Arrow Cross in Hungary and the Iron Guard in Romania, all of whom were enthusiastic supporters of Hitler's plans for the Jews, as were the Nationalist movements in the Baltics, the Ukraine and Belarus.

Extermination

At first, extermination may be part of a eugenic programme, including invasive surgery, sterilisation, and euthanasia, all dressed up as acts of kindness designed to alleviate suffering both present and future. The initiative is held at a low key until the time is right to bring it gradually into the public domain in order for it to reach the stage of normality.

In Nazi Germany, the first subject group were the insane, those suffering from hereditary illness or deformity, the crippled and habitual criminals. The exterminatory sciences were developed by medical doctors in hospitals (see Robert Jay Lifton, *The Nazi Doctors*, New York, 1986). The gas van and the gas chamber in an early form were both employed. Nazi Germany employed direct means of extermination, initially by mass shootings but, due to the effect on those carrying out the killings, the high costs and for reasons of greater efficiency, indirect mechanised methods were introduced. The Death March is an early example of economic mass murder exampled by the genocide of the Armenians by the Turks, who marched thousands into the desert to die from starvation, thirst and exhaustion. The Turks also used a primitive kind of mechanical extermination by placing Armenians in mines and filling them with smoke. German observers watched appreciatively. After the extermination camps were abandoned in the face of the approaching Allies, the inmates of most of the camps were marched towards Germany under harrowing conditions. Elie Wiesel recalls how on the march from Auschwitz, he and his father nearly killed each other over a morsel of bread (*Night*, London, 1981).

Ethnocide

This term refers to the removal of all evidences that the subject group existed. All artefacts, archives and any materials containing the language, culture, tradition, arts and religion are systematically destroyed. In some cases, items are retained for propaganda purposes.

There is another form of ethnocide which is non-exterminatory, as was evidenced in Nazi Germany and has been seen at times in other societies, where membership of the elite or perpetrating group is defined by outward physical characteristics, i.e. the kidnapping of infants of the subject group who have a strong degree of physical resemblance to the perpetrators. The children are given to adoptive parents or placed in institutions where they grow without any knowledge of their origins and believe that they are part of the perpetrators' society. The Nazis removed children with Nordic characteristics from every theatre of operation, to be brought up in Germany with adoptive parents of the perceived correct racial stock. Himmler held the view that such children had Aryan blood that had strayed or been misappropriated. The activity was seen by the Nazis as restoring children to their rightful racial group rather than stealing them.

To the category of ethnocide has been assigned the concept of psychic death, where as a result of maltreatment, psychological and physical trauma, demoralisation and despair, an individual may die, or society may cease to exist.

CHAPTER THREE

EXTERMINATORY ANTISEMITISM

*No trace of a Jew is to remain. We should erase them
from the face of the earth – when the last Jew
disappears from the face of the earth, then we shall win
the war.*
Extract from a Sunday sermon delivered by a priest in
Kowel, May 1942

The above quotation illustrates the fact that exterminatory antisemitism affects all levels of society and Christian ministers are
not exempt. A leader of one of the Einsatzgruppen units (mobile
killing squads), Ernst Biberstein, was a Protestant pastor and
theologian prior to the war. To understand the exterminatory
process it is useful to examine genocide in a wider context.

Genocide and ethnocide

As Raphael Lemkin first stated, genocide – *genos* (Gk.) = race,
tribe + *cide* (Latin) = killing – is a recent term for an age-old practice in a modern form (*Axis Rule in Occupied Europe: Laws of
Occupation, Analysis of Government and Proposals for Redress,*
New York 1973 edition). The twentieth century has borne witness
to many genocides, and the practice has become such a constant
concern in the wake of the Holocaust that the United Nations has
been constrained to spell out the "right to life". The Universal
Declaration of Human Rights (1948) was an early response to the

concern. The UN Convention on the Prevention and Punishment of Genocide attempted to draw parameters for dealing with mass killing but only succeeded in proffering a woolly definition. The crime of genocide is defined not in general terms as is needed as a starting block but simply as a number of specified, particular acts. The acts can be roughly classified under five headings. The first three deal with acts of physical extermination, the fourth with the prevention of childbirth and the fifth with the transference of people. The fifth was a response to the Nazi programme of kidnapping children with Aryan characteristics from the conquered nations to improve their "breeding stock" of those with Nordic racial definition.

The UN convention is helpful in describing actions that may be considered to be genocidal acts but is no real assistance in defining and delineating responsibility. Genocide should clearly be understood as primarily an act committed by the state. Empirical evidence shows that acts of genocide are not committed without intention.

Michael Ignatieff correctly points out that "genocide" is a worn and debased term, casually hurled at every outrage, and every act of violence, and may even be applied to events where no death, only shame or abuse, occurs. However, it is a word that does mean something, namely the project to exterminate a people for no other reason than because they are a people (Michael Ignatieff, *Blood and Belonging: Journeys into the New Nationalism*, p. 151. London. 1994).

The following are suggestions by social scientists and historians.

Genocide is a form of one-sided mass killing in which the state or authority intends to destroy a group, as that group and membership in it are defined by the perpetrators. (Frank Chalk, *Definitions of Genocide*, in *Holocaust and Genocide Studies* vol. 4:2, 1989)

Genocide in the generic sense is the mass killing of substantial numbers of human beings, when not in the course of military forces of an avowed enemy, under conditions of the essential defencelessness and helplessness of the victims. (Israel W Charny in *Genocide: Conceptual and Historical Dimensions* ed. George Andreopoulos, 1994)

Genocide is sustained purposeful action by a perpetrator to physically destroy a collectivity directly or indirectly, through interdiction of the biological and social reproduction of group members, sustained regardless of the surrender or lack of threat offered by the victim. (Helen Fein: *Genocide: A Sociological Perspective*, 1993/1990)

By our definition, genocides and politicides are the promotion and execution of policies by a state or its agents which result in the deaths of a substantial portion of a group. The difference between genocides and politicides is in the characteristics by which members of the group are identified by the state. In genocides the victimised groups are defined primarily in terms of their communal characteristics, i.e. ethnicity, religion or nationality. In politicides, the victim groups are defined primarily in terms of their hierarchical position or political opposition to the regime and dominant groups. (Barbara Harff and Ted R. Gurr: "Toward Empirical Theory of Genocides and Politicides", *International Studies Quarterly* 37, 3, 1988)

The concept of genocide applies only when there is an actualised intent, however successfully carried out, to physically destroy an entire group (as such a group is defined by the perpetrators). (Steven T. Katz: *The Holocaust in Historical Perspective*, Vol. 1, 1994)

The last clause in Chalk's and Katz's definitions above are important as they emphasise that the subject group and its membership are defined by the perpetrators, not by third parties, international convention, or the self-definition of the group themselves. Hitler's idea of what constituted a Jew differed significantly from that of pre-Second World War mainstream Judaism. It might also be added that there is a danger with the UN convention using genocide to describe any mass killing, or as a "catch-all" expression for any large-scale atrocity. A secondary weakness in the convention's approach is that it could easily include a spontaneous outbreak of genocide. We contend that genocide is primarily a crime of the state and empirically it has not been found to have been enacted without intent.

The United Nations traditionally has not dealt well with genocides and the question remains unanswered: is the UN capable or has it the will, or the power, to take action to prevent future genocidal impulses? The question was brought into sharp relief following the attempts of the UN to plan a future for Cambodia after the genocide, when it was believed that members of the Khmer Rouge were part of the committee. (John Pilger expressed such a concern in the *Weekend Guardian*, 6–7 October 1990.)

Seamus Thompson, a sociologist studying in Northern Ireland in the 1980s, contends that genocide is "inherently a continuous variable". Thompson postulates that from the eighteenth century there have been a series of events that will inevitably lead to a genocide in that country (F. Chalk and K. Jonassohone, *A Reader in the History and Sociology of Genocide*, Montreal, 1984). Thomson and others who hold to the theory of continuous variables are attempting to articulate the idea that the seed for genocide is sown in a series of initial events and actions that repeat themselves. Although the outward signs and manifestations may vary from time to time, they are the building blocks for a potential future genocide. Although the theory of continuous variables has its appeal and possibly may hold good in a very few shorter-term conflicts, there is no empirical evidence to suggest that genocide is a continuous variable. There has been a suggestion that the only possible exception is antisemitism where there has been a variety of repeating manifestations. We have noted that antisemitism is a spiritual phenomenon and, as such, stands outside of continuous variables, as part of the cause of the variability is variable casuistry. With antisemitism, the casuistry is always the same, only the manifestations vary and, on occasion, only the labelling – the effect is always the same. Secondly, as the general theory does not carry geographic, political or ethnic constants, the contention is weak.

Isidor Walliman and Michael Dobkovsky have suggested that the question of intentionality is problematic in itself. They argue that, as the historical process has unfolded, the structure of society and politics has changed dramatically. Society has moved from a structure that was dominated by the will of particular individuals and we have seen the rise of power élites and social progression. Society today is in fact dominated by anonymous forces. These may include market mechanisms, bureaucracies and distant non-consultative bodies, and third-party decision making. Decisions are made by committees and parliaments, most of which are generally non-consultative. The anonymity and amorphous structure of decision making makes intentionality somewhat difficult to identify. Walliman and Dubkovsky's contention adds to the debate as it emphasises that ethical decision making has moved from the realm of the individual to the conglomerate. The weakness is that the theory overlooks individual responsibility within the governing élite, as decision-making bodies are comprised of individuals who make either individual or corporate decisions. Nonetheless, decision making is a process arising from intentionality within individuals who make decisions based upon the criteria they are operating on at any given time, as can be clearly evidenced in Nazi Germany. In the Talmud, tractate *Bava Kama*, it is stated that "in all the Torah there is no agent for transgression". The plain meaning of the text is that one who transgresses cannot justify himself by the claim that he was acting as the agent of another. In a similar vein, the leading statement on the matter remains with the US War Crimes Tribunal where it was declared that "crimes against international law are committed by men and not by abstract entities" (John Fried, Special Consultant to the US War Crimes Tribunals, at the IMT Nuremberg 1947–1949).

Furthermore, in the case of Nazi Germany, Hitler's intentions were well known and his writings were widely available and compulsory reading in many areas. The "First Letter" of Hitler's political career is a letter dated 16 September 1919, addressed to Adolph Gemlich, where he plainly states his objectives:

Antisemitism based on purely emotional grounds will find its ultimate expression in pogroms. But the antisemitism of reason must lead to a planned legal fight and the removal of privileges enjoyed by the Jew, in contrast to the other foreigners living amongst us . . . But the ultimate, unshakeable aim must be the complete removal of Jews.

Genocide may occur in revolutionary contexts. The actions may be exercises in clearing the decks of real or perceived opposition groups, redundant populations, and those considered inimically dangerous to the new society. Revolutions provide the ideal scenario for heightening popular prejudices and producing distractions from real problems by blame shifting. In such situations, it may happen that, if more than one party is vying for power, they may well declare a common enemy in a third party. The reasons may vary but generally it is an expedient measure. In a similar manner, during times of military incursion, small-scale genocides can be part of a pacification programme or a land-clearance programme. There have been many examples of the latter in the twentieth century in Africa, Latin America and, some would believe, in Australia, and in the case of the native American Indians in the nineteenth and to some extent the opening of the twentieth century.

Models of genocide

Helen Fein identified the following four categories of genocides. A number of examples of each category are given (in I. Chaney ed. *Towards the Understanding and Prevention of Genocide: Proceedings of the International Conference on the Holocaust and Genocide,* Westview Press, 1984).

Retributive genocides

Retributive genocides are committed to ensure or restore the domination of one ethnic group or élite within a state to subdue a subordinate class. The Nigerian army's massacre of the Ibo people in

Nigeria 1966–70 and the Pakistani military action against the Bengalis of the Awami League (Bangladesh), which is reckoned to have killed between 1.25 and 3 million people in 1971, would be but two examples.

Developmental genocides

Developmental genocides are committed with the aim of removing indigenous populations who are deemed to stand in the way of, or slow down, colonisation, development or settlement. The German slaughter of the Herreros of West Africa in 1905, the ongoing Indonesian activities against West Papua and East Timor from 1969 onwards, the Pakistani actions against the Chittagong Hill Tract tribes, and actions against indigenous Amazonian tribes in the rainforests are fairly typical examples. The example which reveals the most cynicism is probably the slaughter of 900 Ache Indians in Eastern Paraguay to make way for a road-building project which took place 1968–72. It is believed that around fifty per cent of the total population was destroyed in the name of progress.

Despotic genocides

Despotic genocides are committed to demonstrate power politics in order to establish or consolidate totalitarian rule. In such genocides, physical force is not only employed against perceived enemies but also used as a tool for controlling the general populace. Examples include Idi Amin's actions against the Matabeli 1972–85 and the Argentinean Junta against its opponents in the 1970s. Stalin's purges within the USSR, replete with show trials against perceived enemies and intellectuals and against the Jews in the post-war period, are prime examples.

Ideological genocides

In ideological genocides the subject group is considered "life unworthy of life". Developmental genocides may overlap with this category. The Turkish genocide of the Armenians was certainly an example of both developmental and ideological genocide. The

Ottomans were pursuing a consolidation programme to strengthen the shaky Empire but there was a heavy ideological strand running through it. Stalin's actions against the Khulaks in the wake of the Revolution (1929–33), where between 11 and 14.5 million people were systematically starved to death, were possibly one of the largest-scale genocides examined. If one were to add the other victims of Stalin's nationalist-related genocides and actions against the internal party mechanisms, the numbers would exceed twenty million. To ideological genocide we could add what Gitta Sereny, terms spiritual murder (*Into That Darkness: From Mercy Killing to Mass Murder,* London: Deutsch, 1974 p. 101).

Nazi Germany's genocidal actions against their perceived enemies cover all four of the above but in the case of the Jewish people it was purely ideological genocide. This may be amply evidenced by the fact that the programme was followed through to the end of the conflict at the expense of war aims even when it was clear that total defeat was imminent.

The requisites for operating a genocidal process

Studies of the Holocaust and the antisemitic destruction of Jewish people and communities have generally concentrated more on what happened, rather than why it happened. Claude Lazmann's *Shoah*, (film and transcript) is a masterpiece of narrative history, recording testimonies of most groups of individuals who were involved in the Holocaust. It is interesting that he does not raise the "why question" in any of his interviews with survivors or bystanders. Emil Fakenheim once asked Raul Hilberg, as one who had been a pioneer in Holocaust studies and as one who had thought long and hard on the subject, *"Raul, why did they do it?"* Raul Hilberg sighed and retorted, *"They did it because they wanted to"* (Emil Fakenheim, "The Holocaust and Philosophy", *The Journal of Philosophy* LXXXII, 10). Fakenheim contends that if the statement were amended to *"They did it because they decided to",* it probably would be more acceptable. The more interesting statement of Hilberg in the same discussion, however, is that he has limited himself to small questions for fear of giving too small an answer to the big question. One wonders whether all attempts to interface with the "big question" are doomed to failure when devoid of the spiritual dimension.

A review of the stages that follow the decision to commit genocide or ethnocide is given below. For an exterminatory policy to be implemented there are a number of requisites that must be in place.

Firstly, as may be illustrated in the Armenian genocide by the Turks and the Holocaust, **the subject group must be held within the power of the perpetrators**. The extermination of the Jews gained momentum as the people became increasingly geographically captive.

Secondly, there must be **an obsessive preoccupation with the subject group**, where the group becomes a symbol for all of the manifestations of ill in the society. The dynamic operates more easily in a society with a weak tradition of pluralism overshadowed by a totalitarian, militaristic government. The subject group as an internal enemy is to be feared far more than the external enemies. During the Crusades, Petrus Venerabilis, Abbot of Cluny, challenged the Crusaders to deal with the internal Jewish problem, taunting them by asking them why they were going to distant lands [to deal with Muslims] when there was a far worse enemy at home [Jews]. The subject group became a by-word for disaster and misfortunes, ranging from economic tensions to endemic or epidemic diseases, the crime rate, unemployment and the failure of internal security. Adolph Hitler is the prime example of a deep-rooted obsession with the Jews, as can be illustrated from an early stage. That his obsession blazed like a forest fire through Germany is evidenced by the fact that within nine years of his ascent to power the exterminatory machinery was in place. Even when it was becoming obvious that the war was lost, the genocidal process continued unabated in Hungary. Adolph Eichmann and his staff ensured that the transports of Jews being despatched to their deaths took precedence at times over military considerations. As Martin Brozat remarked:

> The more Hitler sensed that the military confrontation was lost, the more he pushed forward what had become the "real war" for him. (Martin Brozat, *Hitler und die Genesis der Endlösung*).

The obsessive nature of the final solution captivated the whole nation and was pursued relentlessly. No Jew, no matter how young, old or infirm, was allowed to die in their bed, and the action remained sacrosanct even when it was known that the war was lost. As it has been remarked, the Nazis first killed thousands, then hundreds, then tens and then ones. Testimonies of ghetto clearances describe how, when the major action was completed, the soldiers, auxiliaries and police units combed the remains of ghettos with a fine tooth comb, tapping on walls and lifting floorboards. In the countryside, they scoured hedgerows, dug into banks, and searched wells and timber stores, in a determined effort to ensure that not one Jewish person – man, woman or child, young or old, sick or crippled – remained alive.

Hitler's lifelong obsession with the Jews continued right up to his last moments on earth. Despite the death of over six million Jews of Europe, at 4:00 am on 29 April 1945, shortly before he took his own life, he dictated a political last testament to Dr Joseph Goebbels, Martin Bormann, Wilhelm Burgdorf and Hans Krebs, blaming the Jews for starting the war. The document centres on the phrase reproduced below which may be regarded as his final wish:

> But before everything else I call upon the leadership of the nation and those who follow it to observe the racial laws most carefully, to fight mercilessly against the poisoners of all the peoples of the world, international Jewry.

Hitler's last words are an embodiment of the Hebrew saying: "The wicked, even at the gates of Hell, do not repent." In a similar manner, Joseph Goebbels, as the war was reaching its end, concluded that the Jews alone, out of all those involved, were the only ones who had neither made any sacrifice nor suffered from the war, but only made a profit from it.

Thirdly, there must be **the development of an alternative ethic.** For a genocide to operate there must be in place a post Judaeo-Christian ethic or an ethic that recognises the subject group as "entirely other" – an inimical danger to the society. The destruction of the subject group is regarded as cathartic or virtuous. During the First Crusade it was believed that there was a plenary remission of sins for the killing of a Jew. In the medieval period, where fear of purgatory dominated much of general religious thought, it was an appealing notion. Although the idea never found papal sanction, it was widely believed.

In this mindset, the subject group, seen at first as socially irrelevant, and then as a symbol of misfortune, has become a community which can be disregarded as far as normal ethical considerations to fellow human beings go. The subject group is clearly presented as a malignant community against which limitless defensive actions are demanded. Hitler, in Chapter 7 of *Mein Kampf* (1924), played upon the popular fear of Bolshevism and the belief that the revolution was Jewish inspired. He accused the Jews of:

> Killing or starving 30 million people with positive fanatical savagery in part amid inhuman tortures, in order to give a gang of Jewish journalists and stock exchange bandits domination over a great people. He concludes his tirade with the assertion that: We must regard Russian Bolshevism as Jewry's attempt to achieve world rule in the twentieth century.

A special vocabulary is employed when referring to the subject group. In Nazi Germany the Jews were referred to as "parasites", "lice", and "vermin". In *Mein Kampf* Hitler used these and many other such terms including, "maggots in a rotting corpse", "germ carriers", "eternal blood-suckers", "vampires" and "spongers" when referring to the Jews. Hans Frank, jurist and General

Governor of Poland, referred to the Jews as "...a lower species of life, a kind of vermin, which upon contact infected the German people with deadly diseases".

Such terms carried the idea that the extermination of such dangers could only be for the public good. In the death camps the victims were referred to as "pieces" and the exterminations were referred to as "processing". The terms were a way of ensuring that the victims were not considered as human beings.

The medical killings are a prime example of the alternative ethical view that regards the lives of the subject group as worthless. Dr Ella Linens Reiner, a survivor physician, recalls a conversation with the Nazi doctor, Franz Klein. One day she pointed to the smoking chimneys of the crematoria and asked him:

> How can you reconcile that with your Hippocratic oath as a doctor? He responded, "Of course I am a doctor and I want to preserve life. And out of respect for human life, I would remove a gangrenous appendix from a diseased body. The Jew is the gangrenous appendix in the body of mankind." (Quoted in R. J. Lifton, *The Nazi Doctors*, p.16)

Another example of how Jewish lives were regarded as worthless is the treatment of babies in arms arriving at Auschwitz. Although ostensibly fit young women could be used for labour or camp prostitution, those with babies were considered to be a nuisance and were consigned straight to the gas. Shortly before arriving at the gas chambers the babies were snatched from their mother's arms and thrown alive into fires that blazed in nearby pits. The reasons were pragmatic. The cost of gas was considered to be expensive, so much so that towards the end of the programme it was used in shorter measures and more "pieces" were packed into the gas chambers. The cost of killing one average "stick" of 1,500 people cost $6.50 or two-fifths of one American cent per person. In 1944 this paltry sum was considered too much to put one infant out of its misery before being burned as another piece of human garbage. A further example was when the chief of the Gestapo in Zhitomir (Ukr.) decreed that all children under the age of twelve years should not be shot but should be buried alive. Witnesses report that the ground where victims were interred could be seen to move for several days and that blood seeped to the surface (Steven T. Katz, *The Black Book, The Nazi Crime Against the Jewish People*, New York, 1981 ed.).

An element of the development of an alternative ethic which is not obvious, is what we may term an enabling by the progressive development of previous decision-making. Some major decisions are facilitated by previous decisions, which have either contributed to an unfolding shift in thinking or corroded an established pattern of thinking. An example would be the decision to use the atomic bomb. If the need for the decision had been in isolation, the outcome might have been different. In the event, the progressive move from strategic bombing to area bombing through to saturation bombing effectually closed the gap between a campaign of selected, and to some extent, limited damage to the most horrific method of mass destruction. In Nazi Germany, the enabling decision to eliminate the Jewish people was made long before the events, as has already been shown.

Three theories of exterminatory genocide applied to the Holocaust

A manifestation of absolute evil

Theories based around this concept view genocides, and the Holocaust in particular, as periods when evil triumphs, and the perpetrators become submerged in the evil. Exterminatory genocide fuelled by antisemitism does not suddenly appear as a parenthesis or interruptive aberration in any society. Therefore, theories which seek to present this view, usually in an attempt to decriminalise the perpetrating group and especially those who assisted them either directly or indirectly, or tacitly approved of the programme, must be disregarded. It is both naïve and ill considered in the extreme to suggest that a whole nation could suddenly, within a period from one arbitrary date to another, become a nation of active or passive mass murderers, and then suddenly and inexplicably return to normality. It cannot be stated often enough that **for the Holocaust to have worked, it needed the acquiescence of the active majority of the nation perpetrating the deed and its allies** (despite its deficiencies see Daniel Goldhagan, *Hitler's Willing Executioners* London, 1996). The fact that the animus of the perpetrators was clearly delineated and the exterminatory programme was carried out until the last possible moment, evidences that an ethical system was in place to sustain the enterprise unflaggingly. The starkest evidence that supports the position that this was not a parenthesis is that the perpetrators were generally caring and sensitive people in other matters. From a spiritual viewpoint there is, however, a kernel of truth contained within the theory. For the suggested ethical system to operate there needed to be a spiritual dynamic in place that allowed the suspension and disposal of Judaeo-Christian ethics.

The banality of evil

The late Hannah Arendt, well known for her association with Karl Jaspers and her authoritative work on totalitarianism, wrote an account of the trial of Adolph Eichmann (*Eichmann in Jerusalem*, New York and London, 1963), which she subtitled *The Banality of Evil*. The notion of the banality of evil was an essential part of Eichmann's defence. The term implies that ordinary individuals, whether they were involved directly or indirectly in the exterminatory process, were either "under orders" or simply carrying out their activities in a manner that was uninformed or devoid of moral qualities: they were simply going about their daily business. A large bureaucratic system whose servants' only desire and satisfaction is to fulfil their assigned tasks in the best possible way is the best tool of a totalitarian government. It is suggested that Nazi Germany may be seen as a prime example of this theory. In Arendt's own words:

> The phenomenon of evil deeds, committed on a gigantic scale, which could not be traced to any particularity of wickedness, pathology, or

ideological conviction in the doer, whose only personal distinction was a perhaps-extraordinary shallowness . . . However monstrous the deeds were, the doer was neither monstrous nor demonic . . . [Evil] can spread over the whole world like a fungus and lay waste precisely because it is not rooted anywhere . . . It was the most banal motives, not especially wicked ones (like sadism or the wish to humiliate or the will to power) which made Eichmann such a frightful evildoer.

The above statement is a sharp departure from the generally accepted image of the Nazi death machine as sadistic, gratuitous and grossly antisemitic.

Hannah Arendt, a wartime escapee from France, did not receive a good response to her work in many Jewish circles. The Anti-Defamation League (ADL) and the journal *Commentary* both issued angry responses, and the late Barbara Touchman, in "The Final Solution", *New York Times Book Review*, 29 May 1966, accused her of showing a conscious desire to support Eichmann's defence. The ADL pointed out that it was common knowledge that Eichmann deliberately planned the cold-blooded, senseless liquidation of an entire people (ADL Memo to Affiliates, 13 February 1961). As a prime mover at the Wannsee Conference, it is generally considered that Eichmann personally promoted the idea of mass liquidation. It has been suggested that he could have just as easily proposed mass emigration (or deportation), or other methods, but instead chose the gas chamber and the crematorium when mass execution was taking too high a toll both financially and on the members of the killing squads.

Gideon Hausner, the Chief Prosecutor of Eichmann, expressed the following perspective on the accused, which leaves little to add:

The history of the Jewish people is steeped in suffering and tears . . . Yet never down this entire blood stained road travelled by this people, never since the first days of nationhood, has any man succeeded in dealing such grievous blows as did Hitler's iniquitous regime, and Adolph Eichmann as its executive arm for the extermination of the Jewish people.

The thing that Hannah Arendt noted throughout was Eichmann's "ordinariness", which she found in some ways more terrifying than the record of his deeds. Hannah Arendt was not sympathetic to Eichmann, but her work was perceived as undermining the impetus that brought him to justice.

The notion of the banality of evil must be rejected as it decentralises the individual's ability to make moral and ethical judgements. The cry "I was under orders" has been adjudged an inadequate defence. The idea of ignorance simply does not bear any weight. The extermination camp at Majdanek, for instance, is located only a mile or so outside of the city of Lublin which also housed ghettos. The whole city was a centre of Nazi activity in containing and exterminating human beings. The smoking crematoria would have been a daily sight. The vast enterprise of moving the transports involved over forty thousand persons working on the rail networks alone. The theory of the banality of evil is essentially based upon the concept of totalitarianism being the determining factor in exterminatory antisemitism. The thesis does not stand, as **totalitarianism is the enabling framework for the exterminatory process, not the causation**. Secondly, if evil comes to be considered as banal, the Holocaust rapidly begins to lose its relevance for the future.

Moral identity and new or replacement ethics

We have rejected the two theories outlined above on the grounds that they do not fully take into account the world-view of the perpetrators. All societies have a set of ethics. By the term "ethics" we mean a set of understandings that delineate social actions and behavioural patterns as acceptable or not acceptable. However, I personally hesitate to use the expressions "right" or "wrong" or "good" and "bad", as they are too loose and not universally applicable. What is considered right or good in one society may be considered to be totally aberrant in another. The set of standards which mark out the acceptable patterns of behaviour and social action for the purposes of this discussion, will be defined as ethics.

We offer an example. The Judaeo-Christian ethic is based upon love, reconciliation, peace and goodwill. The Islamic ethic is based on honour, power and revenge. An individual within any society, if he is to remain an authentic expression of that society, must of necessity give at least tacit approval to the ethic proposed and practised by that community.

A new or replacement ethic should not be regarded as a deliberate programme that is engineered overnight. Ethical systems grow from divergent sources over a period of time as may be illustrated within the historical process.

The "cold joke" is a constant feature of changing attitudes towards third parties, or subject group identity. Its purpose is three-fold: it enforces lack of respect for the victim or subject group, provides further distancing and exhibits power. An example of a cold joke is when, in the Holocaust, the camp guards referred to the severely emaciated as *Muselmänner* (Moslems) because of their stooped posture. Similarly, in the Gulf War, the Iraqis picked up an old practice of executing young men and then asking the parents for the price of the bullet. Likewise, the tank of battery acid used by the Iraqis to finish off their victims was referred to as the "swimming pool". A further example is from Argentina where the torturers' favourite electronic device was known as "Susan" and the victims were informed they were be taken "for a chat with Susan". The cold joke is a constant feature of repressive regimes and on occasion takes on non-verbal forms such as grotesque caricatures in the press or graffiti. It was believed by the chief architect that the design of the main road around Vorkuta, in the shape of a skull, was Stalin's cold joke (Julian Glover, *Humanity, A Moral History of the 20th Century*, London, 1999).

The primary consideration in this area is that of moral identity. Friedrich Nietzsche, writing towards the end of the nineteenth century, predicted that in the next two centuries morality would gradually perish (*The Genealogy of Morals*). He could little have realised that within fifty years the moral identity of Nazi Germany and that of the Soviet Union would have undergone such a shift as would have delighted even his darkest dreams where cruelty and hardness would be considered virtues. Aristotle, in the *Nichomachean Ethics,* (for an accessible version see various Penguin editions) offers a simple definition of moral identity and the way it is maintained or eroded:

> For the things we have to learn before we do them, we learn by doing them, for example men become builders by building, and lyre-players become lyre-players by playing the lyre, so too we become just by just acts, temperate by doing temperate acts, brave by doing brave acts. This is confirmed by what happens in states, for legislators make the citizens good by forming habits in them.

Aristotle contended that habit forming made the definitive difference in terms of moral perception. The move away from Judaeo-Christianity, the concept of natural law and the insinuation of the virtues of Social Darwinism and Nietzschean hardness towards the subject group(s), provided an alternative ethic and moral identity.

We propose that the Holocaust ethic was not discontinuous with the perpetrating society's norms. In the case of Nazi Germany, several convergent streams flowed together to form a new ethic, complete with a moral identity, that enabled antisemitism to become an exterminatory ethnocide with a worldwide design. The convergent elements may be considered to be representational of both popular and intellectual motifs of the nineteenth century and the causal effects of the German military failures in the acquisition of new territory in the African continent and in the First World War.

Firstly, we may conclude that a high profile must be given to **German Volkish chauvinism** together with music and literature, such as the works of Richard Wagner and his son-in-law, Houston Stewart Chamberlain (*Foundations of the Nineteenth Century*). The yearning for a return to pre-Christian religion featured highly in both the music and writing of Wagner as we can see from the annual Bayreuth festival, where Parzifal was considered a spiritual work and at the end silence, not applause, was considered appropriate in order to show reverence for the religious status of the piece.

Secondly, **racial science** and the categorisation of differing people groups and the allocation of racial strata allocated the Jews to the lowest status. Racial science was a high priority in Nazi Germany as may be illustrated by the infamous Dr Joseph Mengele's medical experiments at Auschwitz. Mengele studied both medicine and philosophy and held doctorates in both disciplines. Declared medically unfit to serve at the front in the Second World War, he was, at his own request, appointed doctor of the Auschwitz camp from 1943 to 1945.

He became something of a symbol of the selection process at Auschwitz, by his own choice meeting the arriving transports and with an indication of his hand consigning most arrivals to the gas and the remaining few to slave labour. He conducted a large number of medical experiments, and his particular interest was in twins and dwarves whom he collected for dissection.

Mengele was not alone in his work and was joined by many eminent doctors and scientists in his investigations. Christian Wirth, who started as a bureaucrat in the police service, promoted the euthanasia programme and other medical crimes. His success led to his being put in charge of exterminations at Chelmo, Treblinka and Sobibor. Other experiments included transplanting tumours into healthy limbs, injecting chemicals and substances into healthy people and testing the effects of extreme temperatures.

We noted previously that medical science and particularly the eugenic movement, which found its roots in the USA, was an insidious programme that came to be seen generally as acceptable or virtuous. Between 1940 and 1941, when the "T4" programme concluded, over 70,000 men, women and children had met their deaths at the hands of those who were supposed to preserve life. The eminent scientist, Professor Kranz, is an example of the confidence that existed that there would be no public reaction when such information was brought into the public domain. In an article in the National Socialist Journal, *N.S. Volksdienst,* he contended that it would be desirable to "remove" one million German people. It does not require a feat of mental gymnastics to arrive at the conclusion that, if such a view was propounded in a Nazi journal in Germany during a time of war, when all publishing was subject to censorship, that it was a view that would be readily accepted. As Rubenstein and Roth point out:

> If the National Socialist ideologues were willing to contemplate the murder of one million of their fellow Germans, many of whom were merely handicapped, they would be entirely free of scruples when it came to murdering Jews and non-Germans. (*Approaches to Auschwitz,* London, 1987)

We could say that that **racial science declared the Jewish people to be a form of life unworthy of life**.

Thirdly, we must mention the element of **transferable motifs.** The initial proposal that the new ethic was not discontinuous may be shown in the fact that classical religious antisemitism (see the next chapter) sat comfortably within the new ethic.

Thus far we have examined the broader picture of exterminatory genocide in its societal context. We now turn to individual considerations. G. M. Gilbert stated during the Eichmann Trial that the most challenging question posed to him by Attorney-General Gideon Hausner was, what kind of mentality the mass murderers of the SS possessed in order to be able to carry out the atrocities that they did. The first consideration concerns personality type. Is there a particular type of individual that is inextricably drawn to such activities, or are they created by artificial organs like the SS who gather the raw material by racial selection and then psychologically process them? Gilbert, a prison psychologist who interviewed most of the leading prosecutors of the destruction of the Jews of Europe, concluded that the SS developed a new personality type which he described as "the murderous robots of the SS". Gilbert postulated that there are discernible personality traits that render individuals malleable in certain circumstances and that facilitate the development of murderous activities as routine.

Firstly, an exposure to extreme authoritarianism in younger years makes the individual prone to "blind" obedience which comes to be regarded as virtuous. The consequence is a surrender of conscience in which ethical decision making is not considered to be a part of the individual's world: it is the province of the dominant, authoritarian third party.

Secondly, there is little doubt that constant exposure to propaganda or "conditioning" can produce certain personality types. In Romania under the Ceausescu régime, certain orphans were placed in special facilities and brought up in the belief that they were specially selected to be children of the ruler and must show blind obedience to him. The schools produced fodder for the Securitate (interviews with author 1987–9).

Thirdly, a deviant personality that is lacking in sensitivity is another predisposing factor.

Gilbert's contentions are helpful but they ignore the spiritual dynamic that underlies the ethnocidal impulse and do not take into sufficient consideration the widely held support for the programme by the general public. The data are not specific to antisemitism. The Jesuits are an example of fixed loyalties and the Crusading Military Orders were another example of the three elements that Gilbert mentions. We could add more phenomena to the list, not least the individuals involved in Soviet and Chinese extermination programmes this century.

In conclusion we may say that, for exterminatory genocide to arise, there must be an alternative ethic put in place which renders the subject group as "entirely other", "not human", and, ultimately, life unworthy of life and of no intrinsic value. Secondly, their presence must be viewed as an absolute threat to the good of the host society. In the case of the Jewish people, the animus and hatred is not simply against the people group, but is against God himself and the physical, visual evidence of him in his representative people.

CHAPTER FOUR

CHRISTIAN RESPONSIBILITY

The church still owes the Jews the actual proof of Christianity's Truth. Is it surprising that the Jewish people are such an insensitive and barren field for the gospel? The gospel itself has drenched it in blood and then heaped stones upon it.
Franz Delitzsch

It could be contended that there is something akin to a secret history of Christianity's dealings with the Jewish people. It comes as a great shock to many to find that rather than the Jews being the enemies of the cross, the Christians themselves have enthusiastically filled that role. It comes as a further shock to realise that the Holocaust was carried out in the middle of Christian Europe and was by and large carried out by baptised Christians. At the time of writing, Adolph Hitler remains a member of the Catholic Church and the question of his posthumous excommunication has hardly been raised. The trauma increases when it is realised that the Nazi killing machine was not only welcomed in many areas, but it was supplemented and supported by the local church leaders and their congregants.

Gerhard Kittle, the eminent German theologian, revered for his research work, gave a public lecture in Tübingen on *Die Judenfrage* (The Jewish "Problem"), which was published immediately afterwards. Kittle commenced the lecture by laying out the parameters of definition that were needed to approach the "problem".

Rehearsing the fundamentals of the nineteenth-century German perception of the Jews, he proceeded to remind his audience that it was simply a matter of common sense to realise that the Jews were a racially constituted, alien body within the German nation. Emancipation and assimilation were not a remedy for the problem. Instead of rendering the Jews more fit to take their place in German society, in effect the opposite was the case. In reality, what had happened was that such measures had allowed the Jews to infect the German people with their blood and spirit. The consequences were a calamity. Kittle went on to offer the following four models for dealing with the problem:

1   **Zionism** – the settlement of the Jewish people in the land of Palestine. This must be rejected as impractical.

2   **Assimilation** – this must be rejected as it is a great evil in itself: it allows the pollution and corruption of the racial stock.

3   **Extermination** – Kittle contended that "one can try to exterminate the Jews". In 1933 hardly anyone would have considered that this was even a possible measure. Extermination was rejected on pragmatic grounds.

4   **Fremdlingschaft** – this probably best translates as "guest status". It would seem that Kittle had in mind something more drastic and higher up on the scale of eliminationist thought. The Jews should be separated from people of the host nation.

That a respected theologian could contemplate extermination as an answer to the Jewish problem, publicly and without going into detail, and furthermore did not feel any need to justify the suggestion is illustrative of how pervasive and developed the eliminationist impulse was that was rapidly incubating within the nation.

Christian activity in the destruction of the Jewish people was neither new nor peculiar to the Holocaust. There are three basic approaches to studies of antisemitism, usually taking the Holocaust as the point of explication. Before considering them it would be useful to undertake a brief review of Judeo-Christian

relations. The development from animosity to exterminatory genocide can be considered to have developed in the following phases:

1   The ancient animus
2   The rift between Jewish and Gentile Christians and the estab-
    lishment of the church and Rabbinic Judaism
3   The development of mytho-demonological Jewish stereo-
    types
4   Developed religious Antisemitism and increased demonopa-
    thy
5   The Medieval period institutionalised religious antisemitism,
    both refined and vulgar
6   The Renaissance, the Reformation, Humanist anti-religious
    antisemitism
7   Racial antisemitism
8   Anti-Zionism, including what we shall term anti-Israelism –
    the Islamic–Arabic response to Zionism and Israel
9   Post-modernist thought

(For a fuller view of these categories, the reader is referred to
Words From the Scroll of Fire, F. Wright, Jerusalem, 1994.)

A review of Christian antisemitic thought follows. The initial
process is referred to as the demonisation of the Jews. The exterminatory impetus probably starts at the third stage listed above.

The ancient animus

Before reviewing the history of the Christian contribution to
Jewish suffering it should be pointed out that hatred without
cause towards the Jewish people reaches back into the mists of
time. The first incident is the mocking of Sarah by Hagar. The
next is the attempt of Pharaoh Seti (r. 1308–1290 BCE) to limit
the Jewish people as recorded in Exodus. The well-loved feast of
Purim celebrates Haman's thwarted attempt to destroy not only
Mordechai, but also all of the Jewish people (Book of Esther).

Egyptian apologists justified the Exodus as an expulsion necessary on sanitary grounds, and the priest Manetho (third century BCE), contended that Moses was not Jewish at all, but a renegade Egyptian priest from Heliopolis who led a revolt of lepers, slaves and negroes. Manetho's notion of Moses was to be recycled later by Karl Marx in his work against the Jews. In the classical period, antisemitic sentiments were expressed by Cicero, Juvenal, Tacitus and Plutarch. To which we may add Posidonius, Democritus, Apion, Apploynus Molon, Chermon, Lysimachus of Alexandria and Pompeius of Trogus.

The apologists and Early Church Fathers

The difficulties between Christians, by which term we should emphasise we are speaking about Gentile Christians, began at an early date. Until recently, the generally held view that Jewish Christianity was a short-lived insignificant movement has been severely challenged (see F. Wright, *The Journal of the Centre for Biblical and Hebraic Studies* vol. 1:1 and 1:2 *Orthodoxy and Deviancy in Jewish Christianity to the 4th century*). The cleavage came during the bar-Kochbah revolt (137 CE) when Rab Akivah (50–135 CE) pronounced Shimon bar Kochbah to be the Messiah. It is not known whether Shimon regarded himself in this way. Although Eusebius contends that he claimed the title, coins minted during his rule are simply inscribed Shimon Nasi (Prince). The aftermath of revolt led to a widespread scattering of the Jewish people, of whom the Jewish Christians were but some of many.

The earliest apologetic writer of the church is Justin Martyr who wrote in the mid-first century following the second Jewish revolt. His *Dialogue with Trypho the Jew* has the distinction of being the first written example of Replacement Theology which maintains that the Jews have forfeited the Scriptures, and the prophets are now the property of the church (chapter 16). The Gospel of Barnabas (*c.* 130 CE) warns its audience against the Jews and states that the Jews have "lost" the covenants.

An early accusation of deicide was put forward by Melito of Sardis (d. 190 CE), who accused the Jews of sending Jesus to the cross, and therefore of being directly responsible for the death of God. Ignatius of Antioch (martyred *c.* 117 CE) contended that the Jews were in league with the devil and warned his readers to be on their guard against their evil practices. Hippolytus (160–236 CE) in his *Expository Treatise Against the Jews* once again placed the charge of deicide at the door of the Jews. He proclaimed that the Jewish people were a perverse race as could be seen in the way that they gloried in the sufferings and death of Jesus. Tertullian, born in the mid-second century, was a distinguished lawyer and Christian scholar. He claimed that the Jews were victims of their own impiety and that their sin was compounded by their refusal to acknowledge that they were in error. In his *Answer to the Jews* he presented the Jews as having a propensity to idolatry and claimed that their mindset predisposed them to the practice. Cyprian, Bishop of Carthage (248–258 CE), wrote three books of *Testimonies Against the Jews.* He claimed that the Jews were blind to their errors and said that, because they had worshipped idols, they were under the wrath of God. Cyprian lived in a time when the church was suffering persecution. He blamed the Jews for conspiring against the Christians and the authorities. The charge would be repeated by some of his contemporaries, notably Sozomon in 341 CE, who accused the Jews of conspiring with the Magi. Around 306 CE a council was held at Elvira Beatica in Spain. The canons that were instituted prohibited the marriage of Christian girls to Jewish men (16) eating with Jews (50) and gave a warning against allowing Jews to pray for crops (29).

Eusebius (263–339 CE), the great church historian, considered that the fall of Jerusalem was due to the divine retribution for the murder of James, brother of Jesus (see F. Wright, *The Priesthood of James the Brother of Jesus in Roots and Branches, Exploring the Jewish contour of the Christian Faith, Essays in Honour of David Forbes*, London, 1998). Eusebius may be credited with the notion that the heroes of the Old Testament were not Jews but in fact, proto-Christians. Mohammed picked up this idea when he claimed that the Patriarchs were not Jewish but were *hanif* or proto-Muslims. Eusebius played a leading role, along with the Emperor Constantine, at the Council of Nicea (325 CE) which was attended by 318 bishops, none of whom were Jewish believers. The definition of the Trinity arrived at by the council was viewed as firmly establishing the motif of Jewish deicide. A further measure was the separation of Easter from Pesach. Constantine considered it was unbecoming beyond measure that Christians were following the practices of this "most odious" people and were unable to celebrate their festival(s) without the aid of their rules. Ephraem Syrus (306–373 CE) considered that the condition of the Jews was a result of their just punishment. He stated that one only had to read the accounts of their dealings as revealed in Scripture to understand that their level of perversity made it inevitable that they would eject the vehicle of their own salvation. Ephraem's invective knew few limits and he used language that became common coinage when referring to the Jews. He described the Jewish people as harlots and prostitutes, concluding that "Israel is wanton between the legs". Gregory of Nissa (d. 394 CE) once again used the common coinage of invective, describing the Jews as murderers, rebels, and detesters of all that was good. He furthermore proclaimed the commonly held view that the Jews were companions of the devil and were a Sanhedrin of demons. Hilary of Poitiers (315–357) claimed that before the giving of the law the Jewish nation was possessed by an unclean spirit which returned as a result of their rejection of Christ. He declared that the enormity of their sin was compounded by the way they gloried in their wickedness.

Another fourth-century leader and formulator of creeds, Athanasius of Alexandria, considered that the Roman Empire should take up the "Sword of Judgement" against the Jews. He contended that tolerance of the Jews was treason against Christ and should be treated accordingly.

The apex of antisemitic outpouring came from the renowned

and much admired bishop of Constantinople, John Chrysostom (345–405). John was, and still is, considered to have been one of the greatest Christian orators of all time, hence his sobriquet Chrysostom (golden mouth). In a well-known series of eight popular sermons entitled *Against the Jews* he referred to the Jewish people along with the synagogue and its practices in the most graphic defamatory manner (for a full treatment see *Words From the Scroll of Fire*). John contended that if one were to refer to the synagogue as a brothel, or a criminals' hangout, or a resort of demons, or a citadel of the devil, the ruin of souls, or a cliff or a pit of complete destruction, or by any name a refuge of brigands, or a meeting place for the assassins of Christ, one would be speaking more kindly than the place deserved. He described the Jewish people as being grossly lewd and no better than lusty goats and hogs. At the end of the series he encouraged his listeners to make an active response against the enemies of Christ. He said that he had made an investment in them and that now he was calling for the interest. He further contended that "God has always hated the Jews [and] it is incumbent upon all Christians to hate the Jews".

To the list may be added Ambrose of Milan (339–397 CE), who viewed the Jews as enemies of Christ and instigated riots and acts of destruction against Jewish communities. Following an arson attack on the synagogue of Callinicium in 338 inspired by the local bishop, the Emperor Theodosius called for an investigation into the matter. Upon examining the evidence he demanded that the bishop and the incendiaries be brought to justice. He was stoutly opposed in this measure by Ambrose on the grounds that the act met with his approval; in fact it could be considered to have been carried out at his instigation. The truth of the matter, contended Ambrose, was that the blaze should be regarded as a judgement of God. Cyril of Alexandria was a colourful character who was not opposed to acts of extreme violence against perceived enemies, amongst whom the Jews were significant. He considered the Jews to be on the same level as pagans and had them expelled from the city. Although Jerome (331–419) lived for a while in the Holy Land and had mastered Hebrew and met with Jewish believers, he had no time for either Jews or Jewish Christians. He contended that the Jews had tampered with the Scriptures to remove any evidence of the Trinity. He further contended that they were incapable of understanding the Scriptures and should be severely prosecuted until they confessed the true faith. Jerome's comment in his *Tractate Against the Jews* has been understood by some to have been the grounds for forced conversion. A few major examples of forced conversions are: Spain in general, 1148, 1391, 1411 and 1482; Claremont 576; Arles and Marseilles 591; Paris 629; Limoges 1010; Worms 1096; Ferrara 1584 and 1817; Ancona 1735; Rome 1543 and 1783; Cracow 1407; and throughout the Ukraine 1648–58. In the Byzantine Empire there were four major enforced conversion campaigns, in 640, 721, 873 and 930.

Augustine of Hippo (354–430) considered that the true image of the Jew was Judas Iscariot, who sold the Lord for silver. He believed that the Jews were incapable of understanding the Scriptures and would therefore eternally bear the responsibility for the death of Jesus. He said that the Jews bore the mark of Cain and were allowed to remain on the earth to serve as a visual reminder of what the consequences are of turning from God. He also believed that their punishment was just and their suffering progressively increased. In a series of sermons to baptismal candidates on the Lord's prayer he explained that the Jews were the "earth" in the following manner: "O, church of God, thy enemy is the heathen, the Jews, the heretic, he is the earth." (included in *Sermons to Savanarola*, eds. Clyde E Fant Jnr. and William Pinson Jnr., Waco, 1971.

Augustine's Manichean background is evident here, as he believed that the Jews were completely evil. The conclusion drawn by antisemites from his pronouncement is simply that the Jews are dirt under your feet.

Julian, Archbishop of Toledo and Primate of Spain in the seventh century, was a prolific author. In his work *On the Advent of the Messiah* he pointed out the Jewish errors in rejecting Jesus as the Messiah. He is believed to have been the instigator of the Council of Toledo, remembered for its antisemitic measures that included the proscription of the observation of Pesach and Shabbat, the proscription of circumcision and the ban on Jews possessing Christian slaves.

Avitus, Bishop of Clermont, took a reactive stance against the Jews in his area in 576 by setting the synagogue to the torch and offering the Jews a choice between baptism and exile. A similar action was taken by Ferriol, Bishop of Uzes, fifteen years previously.

The medieval period to the Reformation

The medieval period witnessed institutionalised antisemitism, and the emergence of what would lead to exterminatory antisemitism. The Crusades, called in the name of Christ, remain one of the darkest stains in the history of the church. The Crusades were called by Pope Urban II at a general assembly called for the purpose at Clermont Ferrand, on 27 November 1095. The Council of Piacenza in March earlier that year had been marked by a request from the Byzantine Emperor Alexius IV Comnenus for help in freeing the holy places from the infidel and in relieving the sufferings of Eastern Christians at the hands of the Muslims. The plea was in reality a request for mercenary soldiers because the infrastructure of the Empire meant that the military resources were insufficient to maintain a defence against the marauding Seljuk Turks. Urban seized the opportunity to channel the aggression of the warring magnates of Western Europe and to re-establish the superiority of the church over secular authority. He also envisaged an attempt to re-unite the Eastern and Western churches. (For a full treatment see F. Wright, *The Cross Became A Sword, the Soldiers of Christ and the First Crusade*, Harpenden, 1995).

The First Crusade was marked by its ferocity against the Jewish communities of the Rhine and the Danube, most of which were destroyed, particularly by the contingent led by Count Emich of Leiningen. Before departing on the Crusade, Godfrey de Bouillon, who was to become the first Crusader king, proclaimed that he would avenge the blood of Christ on Israel and leave no member of the Jewish race alive. His intemperate language caused him to be rebuked by the Emperor Henry IV. The Crusaders murdered the Jews wherever they were to be found, destroying the long-established Jewish communities of Speyer, Mainz and Worms. The records of the destruction of the communities are recorded in the Chronicle of Solomon-bar-Simpson, The "Anonymous" Chronicle of Mainz and the Chronicle of Eliezer ben-Nathan, all of which were composed in the twelfth century. Along with the chronicles there are a number of elegies, dirges, laments and various *Memorbücher* from various communities. The recitation of these has burned a negative image of Christianity deeply into the Jewish psyche. The final act of infamy was when Jerusalem was taken on 15 July 1099. The Jews were rounded up and locked in the synagogue, the doors and windows barred and those inside were burned alive. The Crusaders, enjoying the spectacle, sang "Christ, We Adore Thee" as their helpless victims perished in the flames. Any who had survived the pyre were mercilessly hunted down and sold into slavery.

Life in medieval Europe was short, violent and fuelled by fear of robber barons, famine, disease, war and natural catastrophe. Few people were literate, and religious life was riddled with superstition and the remnants of folk religion. Common people were in fear of the afterlife, particularly of purgatory, in which they expected to spend up to several millennia. The caricature of the Jew as agent of the devil and a harbinger of doom fitted well into their spiritual world. The Black Death destroyed over one-third of the population of Europe between the twelfth and fourteenth centuries. The "plague" was considered to be either a manifestation of evil, or a judgement of God. Those holding the second view were represented by the Flagellant Movement whose public mortifications ended in attacks on Jews and their property. A notable band of over 300 flagellants were led by the Dominican friar and preacher Vincent Ferrer (1350–1490), who was considered a miracle worker and was met with acclaim wherever he appeared. Ferrer would enter a town during the time of Jewish worship and burst into the synagogue and demand that the congregants accepted conversion. Ferrer was the leading mover behind the Edict of Castile (14 January 1412) which contained 24 articles against the Jews and established the creation of ghettos in all Spanish towns. John of Capistrano (1386–1456) represented the Franciscan order within the Office of the Inquisition. Known as the "Scourge of the Jews", he was prone to evict preachers from pulpits. He insisted that to fight the Jew was the duty of the Catholics: it was not a matter of choice.

The generally held view was that the plague was caused by the Jews poisoning wells in order to destroy the Christians and take over the world. One of the grounds for the accusations was that when the plague struck, it usually struck the cities and towns before the areas outside the towns where the Jewish people lived. The cities and towns had no public health or hygiene measures and raw sewage ran through the streets. The Jewish practice of only drinking running water helped to slow down the outbreaks but Jews died in just the same way and numbers as the Gentiles. Many Jewish communities were accused of well poisoning and burned at the stake.

The image of the Jew as a servant of the devil ran high in the medieval period. The Council of Paris 1212 declared that Christian midwives were forbidden to attend Jewish women in labour. Any found guilty of bringing the brood of the devil into the world would be excommunicated – in medieval Crete, Greek Orthodox clergy compelled the Jews to affix a wooden image of the devil to their doors as a warning to Christians against entering their homes.

The question of Jews converting to Christianity came to the fore in the ninth century. Archbishop Agobard of Lyons instructed the clergy of Lyons to preach in the synagogues on

Saturdays – one assumes that the Jews were constrained to attend. Indications are that this was probably not a unique or localised happening. In the year following the Fourth Lateran Council in 1215 under the auspices of Pope Innocent III and the foundation of the Dominican Order (*Ordo Fratrum Praedicatorum*), conversionist sermons were introduced. The Jews were compelled to listen to them. James I of Aragon in 1242 enacted enforcing legislation throughout his domain to regularise the practice. James saw conversion sermons and public disputations as invaluable and was one of the disputants himself at the Barcelona Disputation of 1263 and, on occasion, even preached conversion sermons himself in local churches. In 1278 the compulsory conversionist sermon became a part of canon law when Pope Nicholas III issued the Bull *Vineam Soreth*. In the case of children who were not capable of making a decision for themselves, Duns Scotus (1266–1308) proved with convincing logic that it was not only a privilege but a duty of the Catholic Church to remove and forcibly baptise children of Jewish parents who would not be baptised themselves. In 1497 King Manuel allowed the Catholic authorities to issue an edict that all Jewish children under fourteen years of age be taken from their parents and distributed by parish priests amongst Christian parents.

In 1577 Pope Gregory XIII (1572–1585) decreed that Jews in Rome, on pain of death, be constrained to listen attentively to a Catholic sermon immediately following their Shabbat service. The sermons were delivered initially in the Church of San Bernadotto alla Regola and subsequently in San Angelo in Pescaria. It should be understood that by and large there was no real desire to see Jewish souls saved from a motive of love. Conversion was seen as a way of eliminating the Jewish people from within the given society by assimilation.

In 1222, in a move to prevent the defilement of churches by the presence of Jews, the Provincial Synod of Canterbury enacted a ruling that forbade Jewish people any entry to Christian places of worship.

The ghetto

There were numerous rulings and enactments to separate Jews from the main communities. The expression "ghetto" in its primary form refers to the Italian word "borghetto" (small town suburb or possibly "quarter"). Although separation of the Jewish community had been a common practice previously, the first usage of the term is considered to be the separation of the Jewish people to a disused canon factory named *La Gheta Nuevo* following a disastrous defeat of the Venetians by the League of Cambrai in 1516, when the Jews were accused of betraying their Venetian hosts. The notion of the Jew as a danger to society, who must be not only easily identified but separated, found official sanction in the Bull *Cum Nimis Absurdum* issued by Pope Paul IV (r. 1555–1559). In this Bull he directed that ghettos should be erected throughout Catholic Europe. Paul's successor, Pius V (r. 1559–62) took the measures one step further and expelled the Jews from the Papal States.

The Office of the Inquisition

The Office of the Inquisition was established by Pope Gregory IX following the procedure instituted by Pope Innocent III (1198–1216) for searching out persons accused of heresy. The Fourth Lateran Council was also responsible for the introduction of the Distinctive Clothing Order. Jews, as a danger to society, must be identified by wearing a variety of badges on their outer garments, as determined by the country of domicile, or specified garments, hats being the most obvious. In Germany, the yellow star was chosen. In 1233, Pope Gregory created the office of inquisitorial judge (*inquisitores dati ab ecclesia*). The lands were allocated between the Dominican Order, who were created for the purpose, and the Franciscans. Those brought forward for trial if found guilty were sentenced either to life imprisonment, if believed to be truly repentant, or capital punishment if they would not recant and repent. As death sentences were considered unseemly to be passed by those in holy orders, who were forbidden to shed blood, the guilty party was handed over to the secular authorities for execution on the charge of treason. The method of execution by burning was to keep the shedding of blood out of the proceedings. At the outset, the Office of the Inquisition only involved itself with the pursuit of Christian heretics, like the Cathar Albigensians and Waldensians against whom internal Crusades were authorised by the Papacy from 1209.

Under the current Canon Law, the Inquisition was not authorised to be involved with the Jews. Part of the problem facing the Inquisition, especially in Eastern Europe, was that the Jews, particularly in the Polish lands, were enjoying positions of favour with some of the rulers. After consideration, the restrictions regarding the Jews were abolished on the grounds that the mere presence of Jews was a direct cause of heresy developing wherever they dwelled in Christian lands.

The opportunity the Inquisition was waiting for to institute the change arose in 1232 with the outbreak of internecine squabbling amongst the Jews regarding the published works of Maimonides. The Inquisition seized the opportunity to become involved in the matter on the grounds that the so-called Maimonides Affair was promulgating heresy. By the end of the thirteenth century the Inquisition had reached its maturity and by 1255 was fully developed in practice. The public spectacle of the auto-da-fé was well established and, by then, heretics were burned publicly at the stake.

The Spanish Inquisition, which was established in 1481, marked the ever-increasing influence of the Office. A distinctive feature of the Spanish Inquisition was that a leading principle was to eliminate any influences of Judaism as well as those inclined towards it, a matter that was considered to be a particularly Spanish problem. One should mention at this stage that Spain, possibly due to the Islamic invasion with its long lasting presence in the south, was particularly concerned with the purity of blood. The Spanish rulers considered that Jews who had converted to Christianity were a high level risk and that their degree of sincerity was always in doubt. At the turn of the fifteenth century, a new wave of persecutions broke out on the grounds that *conversos* maintained too close relationships with their former co-religionists. This clearly evidenced that they were secretly practising their former faith. Legislative attempts to separate them from the Jewish quarters and re-education programmes were fruitless. The Jews, it was loudly proclaimed, simply refused to be persuaded by these measures and would not depart from their own ways.

The anti-converso controversy was inflamed in the mid-fifteenth century by the Franciscan monk Alfonso de Espina in his work *Fortalitium Fidei* (Nuremberg, 1485–98). The converso problem must be addressed, he declared, and a thorough-going programme instituted to seek out all heretics amongst the conversos. Heresy was defined in the thirteenth century by John Grosseteste as "an opinion chosen by the human faculties contrary to the Holy Scriptures, openly taught and pertinaciously defended" (*Haeresis in Greek, Electio*, Latin text).

It is considered that Espina's work was the opening broadside that paved the way for the Office of the Inquisition. His work was greeted with great acclaim and accompanied by outbreaks of violence and vandalism against conversos. Activities against both Jews and conversos increased dramatically with the ascent of Ferdinand and Isabella to the throne of Castile in 1474. Isabella, in particular, was a greatly fanatical Catholic and greatly influenced by the Dominican Alonzo de Hoja, who held a highly developed animus against conversos. Partly from religious fervour and partly because of support from influential figures both in the aristocracy and the clergy, they introduced a series of restrictive measures against both conversos and Jews. Their crowning achievement was a successful appeal to Pope Sixtus IV in 1477, to authorise them to establish an Office of the Inquisition. Papal permission was granted to appoint officers in every part of their kingdom in November 1147.

Two years later the Dominican monks, Miguel de Morillo and Juan de San Maren, were appointed to head the Inquisition, commencing their duties in the new year. The Dominicans began their activities in Andalusia. As it was thought to be the region housing the largest concentration of both Jews and conversos, it was considered to be a hotbed of Judaising. A demand was circulated to the magnates and powerful landowners that they were to hand over to the Office of the Inquisition any conversos under their jurisdiction who had recently arrived or had sought refuge on their lands. As a result, many conversos were arrested, notably those who had established themselves and gained high positions in society. As in most cases, envy or debts owed to them were the reasons behind their denouncement. In the seven years between 1481 and 1488, according to the chronicler Andreas Bernfeldez, 700 conversos were found guilty of Judaising and burnt at the stake, whilst around 5,000 recanted.

The conversos complained about their treatment to the Pope who, as a result of their pleas, initially halted the next stage of expansion into Aragon, but soon gave in to royal displeasure. Thomas d'Torquemada, the head of the Dominican monastery at Santa Cruz, was appointed to the office of Inquisitor General and is generally considered to have formulated what became the ongoing policy. An immediate initiative was the abolition of any privileges or reliefs accorded to the conversos by the Pope.

Between 1483 and 1485, at least 200 cases concerning conversos were brought before the Spanish Inquisition. The result was that 104 were burned at the stake, a further 40 who had escaped were burned in effigy, and the remains of 40 who had been condemned posthumously were exhumed and ceremonially burned. In 1486, 20 autos-da-fé were held in Toledo and 3,327 persons sentenced; in 1488, there were 40 conversos burned alive and in excess of 100 *post mortem*. Two years later the year 1490 witnessed 422 conversos burned at the stake and 11 sentenced to life imprisonment; in 1492, five conversos were burned whilst others were sentenced to imprisonment for life.

Evidence of Judaising would seem ridiculous by today's standards: not lighting a fire on a Friday or being seen washing clothes on a Sunday was sufficient to drag a converso to court. People charged with keeping Jewish festivals, owning Hebrew Scriptures and circumcising children as well as those, usually falsely, imagined to be proselytising a steady stream of unfortunate victims, found themselves brought before the Inquisitors. Conversos were in general contemptuously referred to as "marranos" (pigs). The following is an extract from Bernard Gui, author of one of the manuals of the Inquisition, providing hints on how to spot a Jew or a backsliding convert. The manual also includes methods of extending and intensifying the suffering of the suspect under interrogation, such as by flame, garrotte, rack, whip and needle. Hints for spotting Jewish practices amongst converts included:

- the wearing of clean or festive clothes;
- clean shirts and hair dressed on Fridays;
- arranging and cleaning the house on Friday afternoons;
- lighting new candles with new tapers earlier on Fridays than on other days of the week;
- cooking a double portion of food on a Friday;
- eating food on Saturday cooked on a Friday;
- not eating during the first day of Purim and Yom Kippur;
- Jewish fathers placing their hands on the heads of the children without first signing with the cross;
- Saying Jewish prayers;
- praying with the face turned to the wall;
- moving the head backwards and forwards whilst praying;
- burying or burning nail parings;
- the cleaning of meat, cutting away fat and grease;
- cutting away the nerve in the sinew of the leg after killing a beast;
- covering the blood with ashes, cinders or earth;
- speaking out Jewish blessings over food or wine;

- after a drink being taken from a glass of wine other people sipping a little from the glass;
- not eating pork, hare, rabbit, strangled birds, conger eel, or any other kind of eels, cuttlefish or any scaleless fish;
- not baptising children or, if they have been baptised, scraping off the chrism;
- blessing children by laying hands on them;
- giving Old Testament names;
- women not attending church up to forty days after giving birth;
- someone dying turning towards the wall;
- pouring out water when somebody dies;
- washing a corpse with warm water;
- not adding *Gloria Patri* at the close of reciting a Psalm.

These were to be found amongst the suggestions, all of which could be easily imagined or fabricated, and which rendered every life vulnerable (Dagobert Runes, *The War Against the Jews*, New York, 1968).

Among the prominent trials held by the Inquisition prior to the expulsion of the Jews in 1492 was the blood libel known as the case of the *Niño de la Guardia* (The Holy Child of La Guardia in 1490). There is no evidence to suggest that la Guardia, let alone the child, existed, or was the victim of a ritual killing or even a miscellaneous murder. The Jews were expelled from Spain in 1492. The Turkish Sultan, valuing their expertise, sent several ships to carry the deportees to his lands. Some conversos took the keys to their houses with them, some in the vain hope of a return in the future, some as simply a memento.

During this time, the doctrine of the purity of blood became an important doctrine amongst the ruling classes and senior clergy. This doctrine was known as *limprezia de sangria*. In 1547 Archbishop Juan Martinez of Toledo, which was the home of the Inquisition, expressed concern that the clergy, particularly at senior level, might be polluted by Jewish blood. In tones reminiscent of

Nazi Germany, the archbishop was concerned that Jewish blood might even have infected the upper echelons of society. To tackle the problem, a certificate of purity of blood was issued. The document was invaluable for those wishing to maintain, or improve, their social standing.

The Renaissance and the Reformation brought no relief to the antisemitism within Christendom. Despite a renewed interest in Hebrew and Old Testament motifs appearing in most art forms, in the area of thought things changed little. Erasmus of Rotterdam (1466–c.1536), echoing St John Chrysostom in a letter to the inquisitor of Cologne, declared, "If it is Christian to hate the Jews, here we are all Christians in profusion" (quoted in I. Jonathan, *European Jewry in the Age of Mercantilism,* Oxford, 1985). He further considered that the Jewish people's presence and particularly their scholarship were *adverse and inimical to Christ*, and should be regarded as a plague.

The Reformation is considered to have properly commenced with Martin Luther (1483–1546) on the 31 October 1517. Luther had previously been a member of the Augustinian Order and, as such, was very influenced by St Augustine's writings, which bore remnants of his former Manichean thought. Initially, Luther hoped that the Jews would join the church, as the major stumbling block to their conversion was the Church of Rome and now there was a second option. In 1523 he published a pamphlet entitled *Jesus Christus ein Geborener Jude sei (Luther's Works* 45: 229 tr. W. Brant, Philadelphia, 1962), where he appealed to the Jews in the form of a diatribe against the Catholics. Luther's appeals to the Jews fell on deaf ears. Luther did not realise the effect of antisemitism upon the Jewish people, in whose memory the Crusades, blood libels, accusations of profaning the host, charges of well poisoning, the Armleder riots, the Rindfleisch massacres (1298) led by Johann Zimberlin, the Fettmilch riots and other atrocities committed by Christians, were all part of their collective psyche. Losing patience, as he got older he turned angrily upon the Jews. In 1543 his impatience was aggravated by a polemical tract issued by a Rabbi against another of his works entitled *Against the Sabbatarians*. The content of the tract is no longer extant but was enough to occasion an angry outburst from Luther, who demanded that the Jews be deported to Palestine. He produced a tract entitled *On the Jews and Their Lies* (*Works*, ibid. 47:268–272 – full text). Along with his other tract *Haemaphorus von Shem*, Luther's output has often been regarded as the blueprint for modern antisemitic literature. In brief, Luther contended that:

> We are at fault for not slaying them . . . their synagogues should be set on fire, their homes should be broken down, they should be deprived of their Talmuds and prayer books, their Rabbis prohibited to teach on pain of death, passports and travelling privileges abolished, they should be banned from usury and they should be put to labour.

Julius Streicher quoted Luther in defence at the Nuremberg War Crimes Tribunal. (For a fuller treatment see *Words From the Scroll of Fire*, for the full text *Works*.) Echoing John Chrysostom, Luther vilified the synagogue and its practices, proclaiming the Jews to be the devil's people. In a bitter attack against usury, once again he erupts in an exterminatory mode:

> Since we break on the wheel (execution by being tied to a wheel and having the bones in the body systematically broken with iron bars until the victim dies) and behead, highwaymen, murderers, housebreakers, how much more ought we to break on the wheel and kill . . . hunt down, curse and behead all usurers.

Finally Luther claimed that the Jews' overwhelming hope in their Messiah was that he would "murder and kill the entire world with their sword".

By the sixteenth century, some Jewish people had achieved positions of influence in the Polish lands within the Ukraine. The Cossack brotherhood under the leadership of Bhogdan Khmelnitski, along with the Crimean Tartars, revolted against the Polish land-owning aristocracy, following the seizure by a Polish aristocrat of his lands and the woman he intended to marry. The Cossacks attacked the Polish land-owning aristocracy, any Polish Catholics they encountered, and particularly the Jews, whom they claimed to be in league with the Poles. The sufferings inflicted upon the Jews are some of the most savage on record. Some were flayed alive and their flesh fed to dogs; others had their hands and feet amputated and then were flung into the path of carts, or trampled underfoot. Some had multiple wounds inflicted upon them so they would die slowly. Others were buried alive. The fate of children was no less lacking in excess; some were dashed to death or torn apart; some were nailed to their mother's breasts; pregnant mother's bellies were slashed open and the child flung in the mother's face as she lay bleeding to death. Other children were roasted on lances and their flesh forcibly fed to their mothers. Other women had their stomachs cut open and live cats inserted into the wound; rats were forced into bodily orifices post amputation. Women were raped in front of their husbands before being brutally murdered (F. Wright, *Within the Pale*, due 2003).

In the eighteenth century, within the same lands, the Jews suffered greatly at the hands of the Haidamacks, paramilitary bands who ranged the Ukraine. The main activities of the bands were the ambush of travellers, or raids on small villages or isolated settlements. Jewish travelling merchants were particularly subject to attack. The Haidamacks increased in power, number and confidence, attacking several cities with significant Jewish populations. The height of infamy was in 1788 when for a second time the Haidamacks lay siege to the large city of Uman, a centre of Jewish devotion, and massacred the townspeople when Ivan Gonta, the Cossack Military Commander of the town, defected to them.

The French Revolution and the Enlightenment were accompanied by a wave of post-Christian thought, and liberal theology challenged even the most basic assumptions of the Christian faith. The consequent weakening effects left the church vulnerable to numerous incursions of deviant thought. It is reasonable to conclude that, by the time of the rise of National Socialism the church was ready to assimilate any prevalent Nazi ideology. The Enlightenment was a movement that in its nature was essentially Humanist and, as such, did not subscribe to religious motifs. The Enlightenment brought with it positivist or racial antisemitism. The search for the new Adam and works by Joseph-Arthur Compte de Gobineau; Canon August Rohling, Professor at the Imperial University of Prague (*Der Talmudjude*), based on the earlier work of Johann Andreas Eisenmenger (1654–1704) *Entdecktes Judentum (Judaism Unmasked)* and Ernest Renan's *Life of Christ* represent some of the major antisemitic works of the time.

Eisenmenger was a Protestant theologian from Frankfurt-on-Main who held a professorial post in oriental languages at the University of Heidelberg. Eisenmenger trawled the Talmud for perceived Jewish evils and published his lengthy conclusions in 1699. Before publication, the contents became known and the Jewish community in Frankfurt appealed to their influential co-religionists, Samson Wertheimer and Joseph Suess Oppenheimer (the subject of the grossly antisemitic film, the *Jew Suess* made by Joseph Goebbels in 1940 based on the 1917 novel of the same name by Lion Feuchtwanger who presented Oppenheimer in a sympathetic manner). Because of their positions, these men were known as "court Jews" and the Jewish community asked them to intercede on their behalf and have the publication prevented. The entreaties of Wertheimer and Oppenheimer to the Imperial court gained a measure of success in that the publication was banned in Austria but not in Prussia. The spurious publication soon became a best-seller running into many subsequent editions. Judaism unmasked was the direct cause of an upsurge of resentment and ongoing antisemitism within the Empire, that would become a constant for many decades that followed.

Frankfurt-on-Main witnessed an incident in the winter of 1711 that was not only to have a devastating effect upon the Jewish community in the city but to have wider implications. A fire broke out at the home of R. Naphtali Cohen that quickly engulfed the narrow streets of the ghetto, causing widespread destruction.

Despite the extreme weather conditions, those fleeing the blaze were offered no shelter by their Christian neighbours. Worse was to come when, after the fires had burned out, the officials of the city council refused the victims permission to re-build their homes. The Emperor Franz Joseph was approached by the court Jews and immediately rescinded the ruling, allowing the Jewish community to rebuild their homes. The relief was to be short lived. The Emperor died the following year, and his successor, Charles VI, had hardly ascended the throne when the Christian merchants of Vienna presented him with a petition for the expulsion of the Jews on the grounds that their presence was reducing the city to "beggary". The appeal was met with approval and Charles enacted a series of measures against the Jews. Most of the Jewish community were expelled. Of those allowed to remain, only the eldest was allowed to marry. Those remaining who were employed by a Jew were not allowed to have the members of their families reside in the city. A statute of limitation on the areas that Jews were allowed to move within was enacted and a ban on Jewish people loitering in the vicinity of Christian places of worship was introduced and rigorously enforced. The full range of anti-Jewish enactments was extended to Bohemia in 1727.

Other antisemitic outbreaks from the mid-nineteenth century to the eve of the First World War included massive pogroms throughout the Tsarist Empire and a series of orchestrated campaigns in Romania that led to 70,000 Jews fleeing the country, out of a total population of 125,000.

A contemporary view of the Jewish people may be illustrated in an 1897 work by Pater Constant, a Dominion doctor of canonical law, published as *Les Juifs Devant L'Eglise et L'Histoire*, in which he presents the following statements concerning the Jewish people:

- In the heart of every Jew flows a traitor's blood – a Jewish child over the age of seven can be baptised against its parents' will;

- No Christian may be in the service of a Jew;
- No Christian woman may nurse a Jewish infant . . . it means bringing the devil [Jewish child] into contact with the Holy Ghost;
- A Christian may not eat with a Jew;
- Even in a prayer the Jew must be referred to as perfidious;
- A Jew may not instruct a Christian, in science or out;
- A Jew may not occupy a position of honour or of public office;
- A Jewish physician may not attend a sick Christian;
- A Jew may not be a magistrate because of his perfidy;
- A Jew may not be a soldier; he may only be an old clothes dealer, a ragman, a peddler or a moneylender.

The German church

The role of the church in Nazi Germany has raised many questions. Pre-war Germany considered itself to be a religious country. In 1944 as few as 1.5 per cent considered themselves to be non-believers. The denominational spread was 40 per cent Roman Catholic and 54 per cent Protestant (*Report to Joseph Goebbels on membership and finances in the church* 3 July 1944). During the rise to power of the National Socialists, the church was in a position where it could have exerted great influence, the question remains as to why it took a silent, inept and eventually collaborative role.

The German Protestant Church

The Protestant Church did at times raise its voice but generally any attempts at opposition were inept, poorly organised and shambolic. By the time of the outbreak of hostilities, most Protestants supported the régime. Robert Michael suggests (*The Case of Martin Niemoeller* in *Holocaust and Genocide Studies* vol. 2:1 1987) that there are five reasons for the phenomenon, upon which the following are based:

1   Protestants, along with Catholics, felt that opposition to the régime could destroy the church if it was seen to be a nascent opposition party or banner for dissidents to run to. A similar notion is felt by some to have been held by Pope Pius XII, thus accounting for his silence.

2   There was a hesitation caused by the moral tensions that the *modus operandi* required for effective opposition. Acts of violence, killing and associated activities were not concomitant with Christian activities – members of the Christian clergy were not regarded as military opposition leaders. The converse was manifested during the war, with clergy leading and serving in exterminatory groups.

3   The doctrine of Theological Disability – The Lutheran conception of two kingdoms – stated that the secular kingdom was the domain of the rulers. They had no rights, authority or remit to criticise the Nazi government which enjoyed exclusive rights in the secular and political arena.

4   The Protestants were very nationalistic – in a state with a poor historical record of pluralism accompanied by a historiographic understanding of the superiority of the German race, they generally approved of the Nazi policies. One should also add that Hitler's internal reconstruction programme was considered an outstanding success along with the restoration of national pride.

5   Possibly the most significant reason, was the antipathetic attitude towards the Jews. It has been pointed out that sympathy towards the Jews was considered a grave symptom of dissent and resistance to the régime. As Eberhard Bethge remarked, the Protestant middle classes may have objected to the Nazis' [brutal] methods but saw little wrong in antisemitism itself (Dietrich Bonhoeffer, Munich, 1967).

The German Catholic Church

It has often been remarked that Hitler lived, died and remained a Catholic, and, to this day, has not been excommunicated. On 26

April 1933, the Catholic bishop Wilhelm Berning met with Hitler to come to an agreement about the Jewish question. During their discussion, Hitler affirmed Nazi ideology to be in continuity with the Catholic Church which had always regarded them as evildoers.

Wolfgang Gerlach suggests that the collaboration and silence of the church should not be understood in ethical terms but in theological terms. Gerlach contends that the overwhelming concept of "theologia gloria" predominated thought at all levels: it was Christian triumphalism not love of the neighbour that was the driving force (Ph.D. dissertation, Hamburg, 1972). The Confessing Church, as exemplified by Dietrich Bonhoeffer, opposed the racial laws. However, over two-thirds joined or voted for the antisemitic Christian Nazi movement, complete with the full antisemitic baggage. The position is best summed up by Hermann Greive:

> Most Christians tolerated the Nazi persecution of Jews largely due to the persistent belief in the profound and obvious guilt of the Jews and that their sufferings were due to divine judgement. (H. Greive, *Theology and Ideology* Heidelberg, 1969).

Recent studies have illustrated that Germany's pre-war leading theologians, Gerhard Kittel, Paul Althous and Emanuel Hirsch, all shared the Nazis' bias against the Jews (e.g. Robert Erickson, *Theologians under Hitler*, Yale University Press, 1985).

The silence of Pius XII has been subject to much controversy. Pinchas Lapide feels that his silence was the most effective tool to employ at the time and suggests that his position helped to preserve 860,000 lives (P. E. Lapide, *Three Popes and the Jews*, 1967, referred to in J. Jocz, *The Jewish People and Jesus Christ after Auschwitz*, Grand Rapids, 1981). On the other hand, Carlo Franconi states that any church worthy of being called Christian cannot afford to remain silent in the face of such provocation. Despite his silence, in Italy both the Pope and some of his clergy helped Jewish people to hide in their premises. In Germany, the Dean of the Berlin Cathedral, Monsigneur Lichtenberg, preached against the persecution of Jewish people. For this he suffered imprisonment and death in Dachau. In the early days, support for the Jewish people also came from Cardinals Galen, Faulhaber and Count von Preysing.

The myth of Martin Niemoeller

One churchman took an apologetic approach concerning the *Bekennende Kirche* during the period of National Socialism. Martin Niemoeller is lauded as an example of a clergyman who opposed the Nazis and suffered incarceration for his pains. He is well known for two often-quoted statements. The better known of the two, which seems obligatory to be included in Holocaust writings is his plaintive cry concerning the escalating removal of those deemed unworthy of a place in society and his moral failure to respond. The exact quotation is varied in its presentation according to the author who is using it. In addition, there are occasional revisions. The exact quotation is:

> First they came for the Communists, but I was not a Communist – so I said nothing. Then they came for the Social democrats, but I was not a Social democrat – so I did nothing. Then they came for the Trade Unionists, but I was not a Trade Unionist. And then they came for the Jews, but I was not a Jew, so I did little. Then they came for me, there was no one left who could stand up for me.

The text is often paraphrased for any political polemic, and other groups are included such as Catholics, and in America, in a speech by Al Gore in which this quotation was used, the Communists were excised. It is interesting to note that often, when the text is quoted, the line concerning the Jews is rendered "so I did nothing". In the original text, however, the wording is "I did little". The "I did little" has been used to underpin the notion that Niemoeller did in fact do something to help the Jews when read in conjunction with the second well-known saying below:

> Christianity in Germany bears a greater responsibility before God than the National Socialists, the SS and the Gestapo. We ought to have

recognised the Lord Jesus in the Brother who suffered and was persecuted . . . *despite* him being a Jew . . . Are we Christians much more to
blame, am I not much more guilty than the many who bathed their
hands in blood.

Martin Niemoeller had been a naval officer in the First World War
and, prior to ordination in 1924, had served in the Freikorps and
supported the Nazis in 1925 (T. Prittie *Germans Against Hitler*,
Boston, 1964). Despite his stand against the Nazis and his defence
of Jewish baptised Christians, he admitted that his defence was
scriptural, ecclesiastical, and theological rather than ethical. He
remarked that it was an act of self-denial to support their cause
(see R. Gutteridge *Open Thy Mouth for the Dumb; The German
Evangelical Church and the Jews, 1879–1950*, Oxford, 1976), and
that the fact that Jesus was a Jew was a painful and grievous stumbling block. In a sermon recorded in a collected work, he uses
eleven traditional negative Christian antisemitic motifs (*The First
Commandment*, 1937, and published the same year in New York
under the title *Here I Stand*. The New York title is a quotation
from Martin Luther's *Apologia*). We can see that in reality the
"little" Niemoeller spoke of in the first quotation was implicitly
referring to baptised Jews and not the Jewish people in general, for
whom, as it is plain from his other writings, he had little regard.

CHAPTER FIVE

POST-MODERNISM AND THE NEW ANTISEMITISM

Political correctness is the disease of the modern age.
Anon

A particularly subtle form of antisemitism has insinuated its way into recent thought and to some extent has found its success in Post-Modernist Post-Zionist thinking (henceforth referred to as PMPZ), much of which is due to a phenomenon which, for convenience, we will term auto-antisemitism or racial self-loathing. In the same way that an individual can experience self-revulsion, particularly because of constant rejection, the same dynamic can appear within a social group. The Jewish people, as the subject of innumerable persecutions, have in some cases reached a point of spiritual and ethnic exhaustion. This is particularly true in Israel due to the tensions of constant militant pressure from the surrounding nations and political pressure from the West.

Historically, the view prevailed, and particularly amongst the *haskalah*, that the only way to escape the dilemma was assimilation. By adopting the societal norms, language, dress, culture, and in many cases, the religion of the host nation, or abandoning his own religion, the Jew sought to end years of hatred, persecution, and disabilities that were the lot of himself and of his family. There were periods when assimilation was viewed as being desirable as it brought rewards, especially if accompanied by conversion. In the Polish-Lithuanian Commonwealth for instance,

Jewish converts and their heirs were enlisted into the upper stratas of society. On other occasions it was a simple choice between conversion and death, with no reward for either choice (See F. Wright, *Within the Pale*, A History of the Jewish people under Kievan Rus, the Polish-Lithuanian Commonwealth, the Tsars, Communist and post-Communist eras, London, 2001). Ironically, Germany was one of the nations where the Jewish assimilationists felt very much at home, and the nation was considered to be the centre of advanced thought and culture. Even when it became clear that the Nazi persecution was an unstoppable juggernaut, many assimilated Jews still could not accept that the death knells of Jewish life had been sounded. Some Jewish men, especially those who had assimilated, went to their deaths on the transports wearing their German Army uniforms from the First World War. Of those who had converted, some stubbornly hung onto their new faith despite being subjects of the ghettoization and deportation process. There was a Catholic chapel in the Warsaw ghetto until the time of the clearance.

Sadly, some of the worst agents of Jewish persecution have been converted Jews. Whether or not they viewed their actions as verifying their new status is debatable. During the debates between Jews and Christians in the High Middle Ages and the occasions when the Talmud was put on trial, the Christian expert was invariably a converted Jew, some of whom were prepared to go to great extremes of exaggeration. At an unspecified date in the 1230s, Nicholas Donin of La Rochelle, a pupil of the yeshiva of R. Jehiel b. Joseph of Paris, was dismissed from the yeshiva and excommunicated for heresy. He converted to Christianity and joined the Franciscan order. Donin, with the assistance of some other apostate Jews, compiled a list of 35 accusations against the Talmud. The charges levied were that the Talmud teaches that the Oral Law is superior to the Written Law, and that it is full of grossness. Within its pages, anthropomorphisms, obscenities, and blasphemies against Jesus, Mary and Christianity abound. In 1240 he was the main counsel, along with Eudes de Chateauroux of the

Sorbonne, at the Paris Disputation, where the reality of the proceedings was that the Talmud was put on trial. At the disputation, four rabbis were called to be the defendants. Only two of them, R. Jehiel and R. Judah b. David of Melun, were given the opportunity to defend the Talmud. The rabbis explained that Judaism was tolerant of Christianity and, using Jewish writings, proved that the charges that Jews believed that Jesus was illegitimate and was consigned to hell to be boiled in semen were fictions. The Talmud was adjudged "guilty" of the charges of heresy and promptly condemned to be burned in public. Upon the result being announced, 24 cartloads of Talmudic works were burned in Paris in 1242. Donin was also said to be responsible for the spread of a blood libel, but the charge is unsubstantiated. From 1240, Jewish people were forced to listen to conversion sermons and testimonies of converted co-religionists, accompanied by the burning of the Talmud along with other Jewish writings.

Donin appears once again in the 1270s as the author of a tractate against the Franciscans. Whether he was a true convert or was full of hate for the faith he was excommunicated from, remains a matter of speculation. Another disputation of a different nature took place in Barcelona in 1263 where the disputants were Paulus Christianus, a converted Jew, and the Chief Rabbi of Spain, Moses Nachmanides. It was contended by Paulus that the Jewish writings were in agreement with Christianity as they carried articles that pointed to the Messiahship of Jesus whilst the Rabbis opposed the view. Nachmanides departed from Spain shortly afterwards.

Tensions within the State of Israel

The creation of the State of Israel brought along with it, as we have noted, a new form of antisemitism which is best described as anti-Israel, the term being preferred to anti-Zionism. An internal problem of a quite different nature arose within Israel and the Jewish people centring on the question of the nature of the state, and the people who are citizens of the state. Further tensions surrounded the role of the Diaspora and international relations. The tensions may be expressed thus:

The State and its relationship to Judaism

This to some extent issues from the consideration below. Is Israel a Jewish state or is it a state that Jews live in alongside others? After all, the state is called Israel and ostensibly is a secular nation. This tension may be considered to be the most important one, as the link between God-land-people is the basic identifying consideration in the historical claim to nationhood.

The nature of the State

Is it:

(i)   A theocracy based on the motive that God has a direct rule within all matters?

(ii) An ethnocracy where ethnic affiliation is the most important distinguishing principle?

(iii) A democracy? This is a question that relates to Israel specifically in a way that it does not relate to other nations theologically.

The relationship of the State to the Diaspora

The central question is, should Israel, and Jerusalem especially, be regarded as the worldwide centre of the Jewish faith? PMPZ would contend that the Jewish people who live in America are Americans, those who live in Germany are Germans, those who live in France are French, yet these people all practise, or have historical associations with, the Jewish faith. The Jews in Israel likewise are Israelis who either practise, or are associated with, the Jewish faith, or have no faith. Ahad Aham ridiculed Herzl for attempting to found a state of mixed nationality. The relevance of the Diaspora to Israel, therefore, is in reality a non-question or a redundant concept.

The State's relationship to the surrounding nations

This question includes its relationship to other faiths. Should Israel's defence and security policy be abolished in order to offer conciliation to the surrounding nations? In the PMPZ view Israel should become a pluralistic society and not insist on Jerusalem being the eternal capital of Israel. The city should be a centre for all religious faiths.

International relations

The tensions have been heightened by the peace process and demographic concerns, both internally and externally. The pace of modernisation and the attendant secularisation, along with post-modernist thought, have thrown the religious contour into sharp relief, not the least in matters concerning its role and relevance. Therefore, the question of Jewish continuity, although not a part of PMPZ initiatives, becomes re-centralised.

In the face of these tensions, post-modernist thought has found fertile ground in the hearts and minds of those who have no real attachment to Jewish continuity, the Bible or the Zionist ideal. Post-modern deconstruction provides a climate which provides a "soft" route to level questions against any historical construction and loudly contends that history is a matter of perception, language and political agenda. An intellectual climate of post-modernism provides fertile ground for revisionist thought to flourish. The post-modern view of history for the purposes of this discussion centres its critique on "modernist history". In this view, "modernist history" provided the framework for oppression. Disenfranchised groups were disempowered, silenced and rendered passive and inert, until post-modern identity politics (IP) by its nature provided subject groups with both dynamic identity and an ability to articulate their own narratives, enabling them to arise and claim their rightful place and role. The major problem with IP is that of "essentialism", namely the component parts of the identity. An example is that white women in the USA who identified with feminist causes were disinterested in the additional tensions appertaining to black women feminists. IP, by its nature, is fragmentary and therefore in many cases is self-defeating. The natural development of essentialism is the question of fixed or fluid identity. The trend is towards fluidity of identity, in which one not only has the inalienable right to choose one's identity but also to change it at will.

Although Zionism was opposed by such luminaries as Martin Buber, Yehuda Magnes and Prof. Yeshayahu Liebowitz, that which we have termed PMPZ fired the opening volley when Baruch Kimmerling of the Hebrew University unleashed a broadside of criticism against the accepted Israeli historiography, claiming that Zionism was an expression of European colonialism. The declassification of certain historical documents under Israel's new Archive Laws in the 1980s provided the impetus for the first academic challenges to the legitimacy of the founding history of the state. *The Birth of the Palestinian Refugee Problem 1947–1949* by Benny Morris is generally regarded as the first work of the PMPZ movement. He coined the term "New Historians" to describe the developing school whilst researching for a book on the Palmach. As Ephraim Karsh points out, there is nothing "new" about the work of the school. They are simply revisionists who fall prey to the usual revisionist shortcomings of using selective and derivative sources: they quote either the same materials or each other. History is a not a sacred cow. Any nation's historiography should always be open to dialogue and debate by legitimate means. The writing of history should at all times be objective and not subjective. It is significant that most of the so-called "new historians" were born after the Holocaust and the foundation of the state. There is little doubt that second generations usually challenge the assumptions of their forebears. No matter how good an historian one might consider oneself to be, the skill of assumed empathetic understanding and working from secondary sources pales alongside the voice of the eyewitness. There are major contentions which, although they appear to be legitimate, as will be illustrated, when taken to their conclusion can only set the stage for a further destruction of the Jewish people.

The tensions of empowerment and disempowerment

Many Israeli PMPZ writers extol historical self-abasement and disempowerment as a virtue. They appear to have a self-destructive desire to pick up and rehash classical antisemitic motifs describing Zionism as being both colonialist and racist. The Israel Defence Force is regarded as no better than the Nazis, Zionist heroes as irrelevant, and the religious communities as being both corrupt and a drag anchor against the democratic process. Post-Zionists appear to have forgotten Frederick Santayana's telling dictum that "those who forget the past are condemned to relive it". A return to disempowerment would surely be an act of national suicide.

The modern Zionist movement was a direct response to persecution and a growing belief that the Jewish people could only escape endemic Western antisemitism in their own land. Disempowerment will certainly come about by erosion of the inner unity of the nation, as Zionism provided the nation's historical consciousness, preserving the continuity of both its culture and heritage. The second strand, which is of a religious rather than Zionist nature, is that PMPZ has no concern for the loss of the ideology concerning the holiness of the Land.

The role of the Diaspora

Along with the "new history" there has appeared a flurry of political correctness (PC). Elissa Gootman points out that even in Jerusalem it is considered inappropriate to speak of the Diaspora, as PC demands that Israel should not be considered to be central to Jewish existence. We may note the anti-Judaism stream at work within this thrust. Bereft of its biblical significance, Israel would indeed become "as the other nations". The Post-Zionist position was articulated quite clearly when the late Yitzhak Rabin referred to the Bible as a "dusty old book of contracts". The implication was that the God–land–people trichotomy was passé, void or irrelevant. PMPZ asserts that Israelis are citizens of a pluralistic democracy situated in a geographical entity known as Israel; this does not imply that they are Jews; and as such there can be no demands for loyalty to or from the Diaspora, which is at the best a redundant concept. An example of the trend is the pressure to change the Israeli national anthem from Ha Tikva to something more acultural.

The founding mythos

As Friedrich Wilhelm Schelling (1775–1854) once remarked, "a country's identity is founded in its mythos". Almost all social groups have an underlying ethos and mythos which provides the glue that holds them together. This is sometimes referred to as collective identity. In the case of the PMPZ the tension holding them together is that of self-loathing. As in the case of most militant minorities they employ their energies on ensuring that they have the right to be heard. Subsequently, upon gaining the right of self-expression and the legitimisation of their views, they have proceeded to inflict their programme in a strident manner upon others, insisting that their view should be the received measure of all truth and wisdom. Those holding a more traditional view are classed as reactionary, fascists or colonialists, or in other derogatory terms.

The "piece" process

One should clearly understand that Israel has been wearied by its wars and by losing some of its finest young men. In this situation of perpetual disquiet, as in Northern Ireland, the peace process has become a jewel in the crown for international statesmen hoping to gain a Nobel Peace Prize and a place in posterity. The tension is the demand that Israel should become the same as other nations by moving forward into a pluralistic society, where Jewish identity is just one of many. The route to achieving this is seen to be agreement with Palestinian Authority demands, ignoring Yasser Arafat's determined stance on a phased plan. That is to say, to take the land one piece at a time until it is all in PA hands (see Benyamin Netanyahu, *A Place Among the Nations,* Haifa, 1981). To understand the PA's real strategy one should read what is said in the Arab press as opposed to the Western press. The election of Arial Sharon saw a more determined stance concerning the land. At the time of writing, Binyamin Netanyahu may well return to lead the Likud in the next elections. If so, a more biblical approach could be expected.

Has Zionism achieved its goals?

PMPZ contends that the Zionist vision reached completion with the foundation of the State of Israel. Others hold that there is still much work to be completed and that the foundation of the State was only the beginning. Israel is now possibly the largest concentration of Jewish people in a single geographical identity, but the Jewish population of the USA, in particular, nearly reaches the same number. However, the Zionist programme will not be complete until the time that as many as are needed to provide the biblical remnant are in the land.

In order to discuss the above question one should initially look at the programme as envisaged by the founders and, in this case particularly, the vision of Theodore Herzl. A significant fact is that Herzl considered the glue that would bind the people together was a national Jewish homeland which would provide the only place that they would be free from the endemic antisemitism of Western society. The notion that the founders' idea was a Jewish state and not a state where people of Jewish blood could safely be domiciled can be easily dismissed. Herzl did not regard the Jewish people in racial terms. He viewed them rather as a group held together by a commonality of heritage and culture. "The Declaration of Independence" pronounced by David ben-Gurion on 14 May 1948 illustrates the intention that it should be a Jewish state, the expression appearing not less than five times. The founding fathers of

Zionism, even though some were not particularly religious, did not divorce the "land"-Jewish faith question. PMPZ adherents who claim the Zionist task is finished do not take this into consideration, as part of their programme is to dislocate the state from its religious foundation. Secondly, it takes far more than fifty years to change a founding ethos, even by today's standards of technology and communications.

An outline of the main PMPZ positions

There is a vast amount of Post-Zionist literature. Rather than commence an extensive trawl of the materials, a synopsis with comments follows:

- Israel forcibly expelled the Palestinians from their homes. Benny Morris first introduced this idea when attempting to write a history of the Palmach;
- A false connection has been made between the Jews and the land (Boas Evron). This view is possibly the most outrageous contention as a simple read through the Bible illustrates;
- The Holocaust is an industry and a cynical motif for political aims (Tom Segev). The category borrows in essence the same line as some of the Holocaust deniers, claiming that the Holocaust has become an industry on the one hand and a tool of political blackmail at the other extreme;
- Zionism was a colonial movement in the sense of Western European colonisation (Ilan Pappe).

The above four motifs have a common ground in that they assault the state from its pre-foundation through to the present day. The work of the chalutzim (agricultural pioneers), the return of the Holocaust survivors, the in-gathering of the exiles, the blossoming of a desolate land, the purity of the centrality of intention when defending the land by arms, are all presented as aggressive, ignorant, cynical and colonialist. The religious contour that defined the land is neglected, ridiculed, lampooned or presented as a medieval, misanthropic spectre that haunts the land.

The ideological war

One of the points that will not be obvious to most readers may be that in a war of ideas there usually is either a conservative wing that resists change or a reactionary wing that violently opposes change. Although Israel could be argued to be one of the oldest nations in existence, this is only true in terms of religion, heritage and culture. Yoram Hazony of the Shalem Centre seminally points out that the nearest thing to a national party in Israel, Likud, and its associates are devoid of "think tanks" or effective media presentation for intellectual discourse. As such, the pro-gression in social thought issues from those who have no desire for Jewish continuity. I suggest that PMPZ is a recent manifestation of auto-antisemitism or Jewish self-loathing.

A further development contingent with the above has been the elevation of victim culture. Whereas those perceiving themselves to be subject to social, national or international disabilities have attempted to assimilate or disguise their differentials, the trend of Post-Modernism has been to exalt victim identification as a tool in the power struggles.

CHAPTER SIX

REVISIONISM AND HOLOCAUST DENIAL

THE NEW HISTORICAL ANTISEMITISM

Darkness hides this vilest crime ever perpetuated by
man against man.
Golo Mann

"Soviet historiography is current politics projected onto the past," declared the Soviet historian M. N. Prokovsky in 1952, a short time before he and the members of his school were purged and subsequently executed by Joseph Stalin. The statement is a useful preliminary warning to anyone attempting to examine histories that issue from totalitarian regimes. In a similar manner, Islamic historiography can be shown to be current theology projected upon the past. One should also be aware when dealing with Islamic historiography that Islam should be understood as a politico-religious system, as it needs a political entity to which to attach itself in order to operate successfully.

Excision of the recollected past from its accepted historical narrative leaves its recipients in a debilitated state. The condition is referred to as "memory without history". Historiography becomes the production line of official history which is iconographic and impossible to enter into dialogue with or challenge. Official histories are manipulated and sanitised to keep out the infection of any truth that is at odds with the position of governmental apparatus at any given moment in time. The corrosive nature of official history renders the society bereft of any motifs of continuity outside of the current political system and is an effective tool in disabling nationalist aspirations.

Whereas it is not true that history is written by the victors, one should also be aware that materials which can in themselves be useful in developing an empathetic approach to the world-view of the society that they are, or were, prepared for, may, nevertheless, have a subjective approach. History has always been a tool in the arsenal of the nation which wishes to defend itself in the face of international criticism. As Lucy Dawidowicz puts it, "History has traditionally been a partisan or accessory to national policy." Polybius remarked that, whilst one should not write untruths in order to promote one's nation, it is a regrettable necessity "that historians must show some partiality to their own countries" (Polybius, *Histories*, Penguin, various editions). The task of the historian is to present objective critical materials which are then open to further research, analysis and debate by integrating the known and frequently contradictory facts into broader systems of interpretation. Where possible, primary source materials should be employed. For those not familiar with the term, primary sources are eyewitness accounts, artefacts employed, the sites, locations and premises where events took place (subject to changes) and autographical writings along with epigraphical and archaeological findings.

There are four main kinds of antisemitic divisions in historical writing and a fifth non-historical category which will be discussed below, all of which promulgate antisemitism. Most of these are known as revisionist. Revisionism is generally the use of selective writings and derivative sources where data is either deliberately ignored, excluded, overwritten, miscontextualised or altered in order to reach a predetermined conclusion. Western thought is prey to revisionism as, rather than employ critical path analysis (starting at the beginning and each time a decision is made analysing all the possibilities), the tendency is to start at the conclusion and work it backwards in procrustean manner. The main divisions are:

Soviet historiography

The Soviet Union in the post-war period refused to acknowledge the uniqueness of Jewish suffering in the tragedy of the Great Patriotic War. As Hitler paid special attention to Communists and Slavonic people who had a role in his genocidal plans for the future, one would have assumed that, as many Russian POWs went through the gas at the extermination camps, there would have been a greater measure of, at least, empathy. The converse was the case. The six-volume official *History of the Great Patriotic War* contains no individual references to Jewish suffering or heroism, despite the fact that at least 150 Jewish fighters were awarded the title Hero of the Soviet Union between 1941–1945, the highest award in the Soviet Union. The index does not carry the terms for antisemitism or Holocaust (*Istoriya Velikoi Otchestevennoi Voine Sovetskogo Soiuza* 1941–1954, Moscow, 1962–1965).

Even the exceptional horrors of Babi Yar (to which one could add Odessa and others) were ignored by the Soviet authorities, who generally refused to acknowledge that "the mass execution at Babi Yar" was a Jewish tragedy. Part of the reason may be illustrated by the Communist position that is generally taken regarding Auschwitz and other sites of Jewish mass death. The position may be seen clearly in *The Great Soviet Encyclopaedia* and *The History of the Great Patriotic War*, where it is implicit that Jews were simply Soviet citizens. Because other nationalities and racial groups as well as Jews lost their lives in the same locations, the sites were designated as being not specific to Jewish interests. Demand for a fitting memorial to this particular manifestation of genocide began to be made by several Soviet writers, including the novelist Victor Nekrasov.

The Soviet poet Yevgeny Yevtushenko brought the problem into the public arena on the eve of the 20th anniversary of the slaughter when his poem *Babi Yar* was published in the *Moscow Literaturnaja Gazetta*. Not only did it cause a stir in the USSR, but it generated worldwide attention.

Yevtushenko reaped a whirlwind, being loudly denounced for his poem in the Soviet media. He had the distinction of being attacked publicly in a most vitriolic way by the then president, Nikita Kruschev. It was only due to the winds of liberalism that were blowing through the USSR at the time that Yevtushenko did not pay a high price for his endeavours.

Whereas it is difficult to ascertain the true number, the slaughter of Jews is an outstanding piece of infamy. The claim of the Holocaust denial lobby that the slaughter of Babi Yar is a fabrication was helped in the early post-war period by the Soviet authorities' refusal to place a monument on the site. In the end, a memorial was erected in 1976 some distance from the site but its emphasis was on Soviet citizens. The bronze tablet bears the inscription: "Here in 1941–1943 the German Fascist invaders executed over 100,000 citizens of the city of Kiev and prisoners of war."

The State of Israel placed a memorial in the shape of a menorah at the authentic site some time later.

As the anti-Zionism movement found its way into official policy in the wake of the Six-day War of 1967, the Soviet Academy of Sciences was in 1971 given the task of investigating "Zionism", in an attempt to legitimise the antagonistic propaganda. In this same year, Vladimir Bolchakov, who had been given the task of producing anti-Zionist propaganda, wrote two articles that appeared in *Pravda*. One of these pieces, operating on the big lie principle and using an anonymous and obviously fabricated letter in support, accused the "Zionists" not only of collaborating with the Nazis but of being responsible for the slaughter at Babi Yar which would:

... forever remain the embodiment not only of the cannibalism of the Hitlerites but also the invisible shame of their accomplices and followers – the Zionists. (*Pravda*, 18th and 19th February 1972)

In the three years between 1975 and 1978 there appeared at least twenty-three articles in the Soviet press claiming that the "Zionists" acted in concert with the Nazis.

In a pamphlet written in both Russian and English in 1972, anti-Communism was presented as the foundation of "Zionism". Some startling accusations appeared in articles by several different writers. Along with accusations that Zionists co-operated with the Hitlerites in prosecuting the Holocaust, the following idea was propounded. Zionist (Israeli) Intelligence purposed to find and capture Adolph Eichmann and take him to Israel for trial and to seek his execution primarily to:

> . . . ensure secrecy over a number of Zionist deals and the collabora-
> tion of their secret services with the Hitlerites during the Second
> World War. (*Soviet Antisemitic Propaganda: Evidence from Books,
> Press and Radio,* Institute of Jewish Affairs, London, 1978)

A pamphlet in 1983 contended that Zionism was the foundation of anti-Communism and that the Jews collaborated with the Nazis during the war. A lengthy pamphlet issued in Kiev in 1984 attacked Zionism in the traditional manner claiming that Zionism:

> [is a] . . .bourgeois-nationalistic ideology, suffused with the poison of
> racism and chauvinism, militarism and extremism, representing a
> threat to all humanity – precisely the characteristics generally asso-
> ciated with Nazism.

When examining the question of the Soviet attitude to the Jews and the Holocaust, several questions arise, but two are of partic-ular relevance. Firstly, why the Holocaust and the role of the Jews as victims and also heroes has been glossed over and, secondly, why there is an equation of Zionism and fascism. In regard to the first question, Zvi Gitleman suggests that when the question is set against post-war Stalinism and the anti-cosmopolitanism campaign launched by A. Zhadanov in the late summer of 1946, a sinister plan may be observed as unfolding.

The first three years of the campaign were marked by increasingly explicit antisemitic content. The campaign was instituted by a wave of mass arrests, the construction of large barracks in Siberia, exiles and executions. This bears the hallmarks of another Holocaust. The arrests and executions of the leaders of the anti-fascist committee and the arrest of Yiddish writers and the Jewish Doctors' Plot of 1952–53 all have a sinister foreshadowing of a larger ranging initiative to come. As the Jews were the recent subjects of an aggressively prosecuted campaign of destruction, it may have been considered that an immediate initiative would have been ill timed without an element of preparation. A subsidiary reason might be that the Holocaust was capable of raising Jewish identity and potentially nationalism. Stalin, who operated a policy designed to eliminate any nationalist sentiments, would have viewed anything that strengthened Jewish identity as a stumbling block to assimilationist policies. As the Soviet Empire was in the process of consolidation, it was not in the leadership's interest to remind those who had collaborated with the Germans in the destruction of Europe's Jews that they had recently served other masters.

In conclusion, Soviet historiography remained antisemitic. As such it denigrated and robbed a people group of an essential part of their history, desecrated the memory of millions, devalued their lives and suffering and sent out the clear message that the Jewish people are of no value. Glasnost and Perestroika brought a new wave of historical interest in Soviet historiography; *Iszvestia* pleaded for the formation of an honest school of history to arise and re-examine the nation's histories. It is only recently however that the bulk of materials for investigation have been made available to both historians of the former USSR and international scholars. It will be interesting to see what shape a new historiography of the years of the Soviet Empire will reveal as the mountain of documents now available are researched.

German historiography

In the immediate post-war period, Germany was faced with a crisis or series of crises in its approach to history. Recovering from a totalitarian regime in which all writing and broadcasting was subject to censorship and a tradition before the National Socialist government that espoused a value-free approach to history, the field was wide open. In chapter 3, prerequisites for the implementation of a genocidal process were examined. An element for reaching the prerequisite of an alternative ethic is what we might term the self-perceived national identity. German historiography played a leading role in preparing the way.

There were two elements that dominated German thought from the mid-nineteenth century. Firstly, the idea that the German nation was not merely essentially different from the other nations but was in fact endowed with superior physical, intellectual and moral qualities. Modern antisemitism in its positivist (racist) form, as opposed to its religious context, is considered to be a Western European phenomenon that became universal. By the end of the nineteenth century the doctrines of racial superiority and particularly that of the Germans were firmly established. The concept can be traced to Johann Gottlieb Fichte (1762–1814), the first Rector of the University of Berlin, who demanded that the State be built upon moral convictions. Fichte had a strange admixture of ideas about Jewish matters. He was a great respecter of the Bible but dismissed the Talmud as being full of childish conjectures. He was also opposed to citizenship for Jews in his essay on the French Revolution, and contended that they held to a dual set of moral laws, one for Jews and one for Gentiles. In his *Address to the German Nation* he contended:

> Throughout almost all of the countries of Europe, there is spreading a hostile minded state that is engaged in constant warfare with all others and that in many countries exerts a terrible pressure upon the citizenry. I speak of Jewry. I do not think it so fearsome because it

forms a cohesive body that holds itself aloof from its fellow citizens, but because this cohesiveness is built upon hatred for the entire human race.

One can detect a element of Juvenal's view of the Jews' universal animus against the goyim (*Satyricon*) and Martin Luther's sentiment that the Jews' main desire was to destroy the Gentile world. In 1816, the philosopher Jakob Friedrich Fries published *On the Endangering of the Welfare and Character of the Germans by the Jews*. Fries suggested that the way to deal with the Jewish problem was "a war on Jewry" and that the Jews should be exterminated "root and branch". Fries' work spawned an immediate stream of imitators. The rise of antisemitic literature and in particular the pamphlet *Der Judenspiegel* (the Jewish Mirror) by Hartwig von Hundt-Radowski, in which he claimed that killing a Jew should not be regarded as sinful but was in reality virtuous as it fell outside of the definition of crime and should be understood as a policing action, led to the infamous Hep! Hep! Anti-Jewish riots. The riots were named after the slogan and battle cry of the rioters "Hep! Hep! Jude verreke!" – vulgarly supposed by some to be the battle cry of the Crusaders as "hep" is an acronym for *Herosolyma Est Perdita* (Jerusalem is lost or has perished). The late nineteenth century saw the emergence of the politician Theodore Fritsch's *Antisemitic Catechism,* later renamed as [the] *Handbook on the Jewish Question* (1883). The work contained the Antisemites' Decalogue which contained such commandments as: Thou shalt be proud of being German (1), Thou shalt keep thy blood pure (3), Thou shalt have no social intercourse with a Jew (5) or business relations (6).

The developing notion of national superiority provided a fertilised seed bed for a state that extolled racism as a virtue. Secondly, there was the notion traditionally ascribed to Wilhelm von Humbolt that the individual found his authentic expression by living in absolute subordination to the State. The doctrine of the centrality of the State became centralised and it came to be thought that the highest expression of spirituality and existence was to be found in the framework of the State and its pursuit of political and military power. One can understand that a generation who grew up under the influence of chauvinism and political centrality was likely to take a deep offence at the conditions of the Treaty of Versailles, which rather than stifling nationalist-expansionist desires only refuelled them, together with a deep-seated desire to exact vengeance. It has been suggested, particularly by Daniel Goldhagen, that one of the explanations for the unnecessary cruelty inflicted upon the Jews by the Germans and others was a deeply felt sense that they were wreaking revenge on the Jews for a complex web of reasons, not the least the "stab in the back" promulgated by Hitler in *Mein Kampf*. The suggestion has merit in that Clemenceau's insistence on large-scale reparations, the standing down of the army and the forfeiture of lands left a bitter resentment. A nation with a doctrine of racial superiority could not effectively hold itself responsible for the humiliating defeat and subsequent international loss of face. The blame could not be applied to the military and the national leadership, so a third party needed to be identified as the cause of the disaster. The Jews perfectly fitted the bill.

Goldhagen's main contention, however, revolves around the equation of Jews with Bolshevism which can be amply illustrated from Hitler's writings. At times it can appear that Jews and Bolsheviks are one and the same. The contention is over-stressed at the expense of the convergence and confluence of other positions and motifs.

With the Nazi rise to power, the history departments at the universities were subjected to the dismissal of Jewish and non-Aryan historians. Once the decks were cleared of the undesirables, the historical profession joined itself, sometimes with great enthusiasm, to the Nazi cause. Very soon the Commission for History was replaced with the Reichsinstitut für Geschichte des neuen Deutschland (Reich Institute for the History of the New Germany), which opened at the University of Berlin on 19

October 1935. A major work of the Nazi historians was the production of *Forschungen zur Judenfrage* in nine volumes. The work remains a defining standard of the prostitution of the historian's craft. Some of the "learned pieces" that appeared included:

- "Jewry as an Element of Decomposition Among Nations – Reflections on World History"
- "The Invasion of the Jewish Spirit"
- "Jewry and Bolshevik Cultural Politics"
- "The Literary Predominance of Jews in Germany 1918–1933"
- "Albert Einstein's Attempt to Subvert Physics"

Another paranoia that ran through German thought was the domination of the British. The Empire was seen as a progressive movement to world domination and *ipso facto* a superior racial group, which was of course the destiny of the cleansed Aryan German people. It should, therefore, come as no surprise that within the volumes is found an essay entitled, *The Penetration of Jewish Blood in the English Upper Class.*

In common with other post-war research, German studies on National Socialism and the Holocaust, and in particular the "big question", were not approached until the 1960s. Most readers will have little experience of post-conflict trauma, let alone that of an action on the scale of the Holocaust, and may find it difficult to understand the time-gap. Traumas caused by involvement in international conflict affect not only the psyche of the individual but also that of the society. One can hardly comprehend the horror, revulsion and feeling of internal condemnation that engulfed many of the German people after the fall of the Third Reich. An initial impetus was simply to deny the events. Some of the initial statements have become stock in trade for the Holocaust deniers. For the historians, the challenge was to attempt not to sully Germany's reputation as the centre of European civilisation.

It seems that the general German populace and its representative historians suffered from an immediate post-war amnesia and selectivity of memory. The impetus to what we might term "neglecting memory" was helped by the confusion of the status of war crimes in the immediate post-war period. Winston Churchill, who had been an early advocate of punishing those responsible for atrocities, in a speech made in Zürich on 19 October 1946, advocated an end to retribution, encouraging his audience to turn their backs upon the past and get on with the future. The reasons were somewhat pragmatic: the necessity of re-building Germany and the threat of Communist consolidation and expansionism that were perceived as a clear and present danger. The almost ludicrous spectacle of Germany dealing with its own war criminals is worthy of mention. Germany had not overthrown the National Socialist government, neither had they mounted any real resistance against them. Therefore, when the legal process was instigated, the first act of the new judiciary was to declare amnesty for themselves for complicity with the National Socialists before they proceeded. Of the relatively low number of 90,921 investigations into war crimes, of which some 10,000 should have carried the death sentence, some forty years later only 6,479 cases had been processed that carried any kind of a sentence. It seems apparent that having cleared themselves from their incriminating past, the judiciary were unwilling to be party to bringing convictions against members of the former élite. The so-called "cold amnesty" accelerated apace when the time came for the military build-up of the Federal Republic. By 1951, as a result of petitioning by Konrad Adenauer, the West German Chancellor, many of those convicted of war crimes, ostensibly with sentences of less than fifteen years, were released to help rebuild the nation. In a similar manner, many scientists and those of the medical profession who had committed crimes were recipients of the cold amnesty in return for the results of the experiments they carried out during the Reich. It is sad to relate that most Germans and the rest of the world thought little of it.

The German nation and the historical profession were awakened somewhat from their post-war historical slumber in 1973 with the screening of the TV mini-series, some nine hours in length, "The Holocaust". The series is credited by Peter Novicks with bringing the Holocaust into focus in the USA some months previously. The series which focuses upon a German family and a Jewish family through the years of the Holocaust was not without its critics. Elie Wiesel thought it was trivialising. The positive effect was that it caused something of an earthquake in German schools of history, who at the time were shaping up for a major internal conflict on the concepts of writing the modern history of their nation.

The challenges faced by German historians brought into sharp relief the polarisation in thought and approach between the schools of history known as the intentionalists and the function-alists, which was to have wider implications. The intentionalists are represented by historians such as Gerald Flemming, Steven T Katz, and the late Lucy Dawidowicz whose *The War Against the Jews* is a fine example of the school.

In a simplified form, following Tim Mason, intentionalists con-sider that genocides may be understood in terms of intentional actions based upon belief. In an intentionalist framework, Adolph Hitler is central to the Holocaust. The underpinning ideology was his, along with the overall strategy and implementation. The destruction of the Jewish people was in his mind from an early stage in his career and the question was not one of feasibility: it was rather one of waiting for the opportune moment. The Holocaust should be considered to be a unique event and not uni-versalised. Intentionalists generally feel that to elucidate an event the centrality of the thought behind it is a key issue.

Functionalist approaches, as represented by Christopher Browning and Martin Brozsat, present the view that actions are influenced by the way that they come about. The Holocaust should be seen as a series of *ad hoc* measures that were improvised following the invasion of the USSR, as bureaucrats vied with each other to win Hitler's attention, knowing all too well his deep animus against the Jews. There was no initial overall strategy or long-term planning. This view is seen to be wanting, as a cursory read through the protocols of the Wannsee Conference of January 1942 will reveal. The Holocaust in functionalist thought tends to find its place in a line of augmented continuum.

The weakness in functionalist thought is that the dynamics of decision-making are subjugated to the events themselves and the areas of individual responsibility may become blurred. In some ways, the functionalist approach can, as exampled in the work of the German historian Ernest Nolte, appear to be degenerating into the apologetics of denial. A weakness in functionalism is that it assumes too much understanding of an individual's self-consciousness and the interplay between individuals in the dynamics of decision making. Intentionalism provides a more realistic framework. However, the approach needs to be augmented with some of the tools of functionalism.

A further problem in constructing models for the exterminatory impulse within Nazi Germany is the lack of written documents relating to the extermination of the Jewish people. At the time of writing there are no known extant written documents relating to the orders to annihilate the Jewish people issuing from Hitler or any other Nazi politician. A congress of historians meeting in Stuttgart discussing *The Murder of the Jews in the Second World War* went over an immense amount of ground, covering many different viewpoints. The significant thing that they did find consensus upon was that an order for annihilation had not been discovered. The eminent historian Leon Poliakov a few years previously stated that in this matter:

> Certain details, however, must remain unknown. The three or four people chiefly involved in drawing up the plan for the total extermination are dead and no documents have survived, perhaps none ever existed. (Leon Poliakov, *Harvest of Hate,* New York, 1979)

CHAPTER SEVEN

IS THE NEW TESTAMENT ANTISEMITIC?

*It is dishonest henceforth to refuse to face the fact that
the basic root of modern antisemitism lies squarely in
the Gospels and the rest of the New Testament.*
James Parkes

The above statement by James Parkes, the pioneer of Christian studies into antisemitism, if true, is something more than merely alarming. It challenges the whole integrity of the Christian message. In the school of Holocaust studies it is generally accepted as a given that there is a line of continuity from the New Testament to Auschwitz. It is grossly irresponsible not to face the challenges raised by such a view and to discuss the question, "Is the New Testament antisemitic?". If the answer is that it is, then we must consider the New Testament bankrupt for the purpose of evangelism and conclude that we should leave the Jews to their own devices. We must also conclude that if the New Testament is antisemitic, then Christianity by its nature must also be so. If this indeed is the case, then we are faced with a problem of gargantuan proportions, as it would seem that hatred of the Jews is God's best, a notion that flies in the face of biblical truth. In one sense both the questions of anti-semitism in the New Testament and Jewish evangelism underlie a mirrored vision of what the real question is, namely, "Is it antise-mitic not to evangelise Jewish people?". The problems are inter-twined but for convenience we will treat them as separate issues.

119

The New Testament – an antisemitic document?

Although the Jewish people seem to have to some degree recovered Jesus, whom they regard as a gifted teacher and a typical sage of his time, they reject the church's claim to his Messiahship on the grounds that the Messiah was expected to re-build the Temple, return the exiles and usher in a reign of peace. Jesus did none of these things. The answer to the above question is probably best phrased thus:

> We, as believers that Yeshua is the Messiah, believe that the church is the continuing ministry of Messiah in the power of the Holy Spirit.

I have been quizzed on innumerable occasions by rabbis and Jewish scholars on this question and its subsidiary, "Could you confirm for me that Paul was an apostate Jew, a rebel, a law-breaker, an antisemite and the inventor of Christianity?" It also seems that this is not a discussion that can normally be held without a great degree of angst all round.

There have been several books and articles that have declared that the founding charter of antisemitism is the New Testament. It is useful to be acquainted with the main streams of the accusation. Rabbi Eliezer Berkovitz sums up the generally held Jewish view of the New Testament, which has also found support in some minority Christian circles.

> Christianity's New Testament has been the most dangerous antisemitic tract in history. Its hatred-charged diatribes against the "Pharisees" and the Jews have poisoned the hearts and minds of millions and millions of Christians for almost two millennia . . . it does not matter what the deeper theological meaning of the hate passages against Jews might be, in the history of the Jewish people the New Testament lent its inspiring support to oppression, persecution, mass murder of an intensity and duration that were unparalleled in the entire history of man's degradation. Without the New Testament,

Hitler's *Mein Kampf* could never have been written. (Eliezer Berkovitz, "Facing the Truth", *Judaism* 27, 1978)

According to Berkovitz, any approach trying to define a New Testament view of Judaism is an inauthentic approach and doomed to failure as it is an antipathetic, antisemitic document.

Legitimate thinking would start by placing the texts in their historical context and not read back later ideas into them. For the purposes of this discussion we will follow the late Bishop J. A. T. Robinson (*Re-dating the New Testament*, SCM, London, 1976) and others by assuming dates for all documents to have reached a completed stage prior to 70 CE with the possible exception of Revelation. But before proceeding it is worth asking the following question: "Is it likely that documents produced by Jewish people for an initially Jewish audience are likely to be antisemitic?"

The best approach to the subject is to set the New Testament documents in their historical and cultural setting. The New Testament is a library of twenty-seven documents in diverse literary forms written by around fifteen authors at various times, in a variety of situations and contingent situational factors. The so-called anti-Jewish polemics need to be examined at the different levels at which they operate. The following is a conflation of headings suggested by the Cardinal of Venice, Carlo Maria Martini (Carlo Maria Martini, Christianity and Judaism, "A Historical and Theological Overview", in *Jews and Christians, Exploring the Past, Present and Future,* ed. J. H. Charlesworth, New York, 1990), with a further category added.

Internecine disputes

As Lester Grabbe has pointed out, it is incorrect to consider Judaism as a homogenous whole in the Second Temple Period. At the time of Jesus, along with the Saduccees, Pharisees, Herodians and Essenes of differing practice, there were several other groups and subgroups, including zealots of various hues. Disputations between the differing groups could be aggressive and filled with invective. In the New Testament we have the example in the book of Acts of the five occasions where the Jews and the Notzrim (emergent church) are in dispute. Four times it concerns the right to preach in the Temple precincts. The Portico of Solomon was of particular significance as it provided shelter for the numerous pilgrims attending the mandatory festivals and hence was a place of gatherings that were intensely charged. The fifth was when Paul caused a dispute between the Pharisees and Sadducees as a device to distract attention from himself (Acts 23:1–10).

Use of the expression "Jews"

It has generally been considered that the use of the term, particularly in the Gospel of John, is pejorative. The expression, as Karl Barth ably demonstrates in his *Epistle to the Romans*, is a general "catch all" term for anyone who is Jewish of any sect who is not a follower of Jesus. The term is not intended to express discontinuity. In the synoptic gospels the term "Jew" (*Ioudaios* pl. *Ioudaioi*) appears 16 times, mostly in the Passion narratives. It is as if the term is coined on behalf of the Romans. As the audience is Jewish it is a fairly superfluous term. In John's Gospel the term appears 71 times. Modern studies have shown that in John the term is invariably, as suggested above, applied as a general term but that it has a specific inference of the ruling élite (U. C. Von Walde, *The Johannine Jews: A Critical Survey* in *New Testament Studies*, 1982). On occasions in John, the expression is applied where the Jewish people serve as surrogate for the world, which is hardly surprising, as the Jewish people were "the world" at the inception of the Gospel.

The eschatological contour

It has been said that Jesus preached the Kingdom of God but the church preached Jesus. Reading a realised eschatology and *theologica gloria* into the biblical texts has resulted in the Jews becoming the opposition on the one hand and redundant on the other. Rosemary Radford Reuther passes the useful comment that the church, through its Christology, attempted to historicise eschatology to bring about the End Times in the present age. The response to the eschatological question is defined by any individual or group's general theological or eschatological position. Do the end times commence at the resurrection as proposed by the outstanding German scholar and proto-liberation theologian Jurgen Moltmann? If this is the case, is the Kingdom of God fully realised or is it unfolding? If either stance is rejected, then is the Kingdom still awaited? In either case a Kingdom devoid of the Jewish people can only be supercessionist. If the eschatological position is that the Kingdom is unfolding, which is more in line with Jewish thought that centres on the Messianic Age rather than the person of the Messiah, the tension evaporates. A template of the unfolding Kingdom is a useful tool in developing any eschatology.

To Cardinal Martini's headings we offer the following consideration:

The tensions of linguistic appropriation

The New Testament was written by a group of individuals who were addressing their respective recipients in language and terms that were readily appropriated by them. One should understand that most of the New Testament, including the Gospels, is of a literary form that was intended to be read aloud in a single session. The Jewish recipients of the Gospels had a repertoire of understanding that enabled the writers to speak to them in a way that did not involve having to explain every motif used. A tension for Bible translators is the use of idioms and the hermeneutic system employed by those who proclaimed the Messiahship of Jesus. A large part of the problem relating to the question of antisemitic polemics within the New Testament is when the commentators are unaware of the idioms employed or the social and cultural milieu and, most of all, of the conventions of the time. A secondary tension today is that terms used in one discipline can carry a completely different meaning in another. Similarly, words can change their meaning in common usage as time passes. Confusion or misunderstanding can very easily be caused if the recent usage of a term is applied. A simple example is the rendering of the word we have in some English language Bibles as "hate". Jesus is not encouraging his listeners to hate their parents. The term simply means to "love less than". Jesus is explaining to his listeners that their discipleship is to be their first priority. Likewise in 1 Corinthians 13 the word translated in the King James Bible as "charity" had a significantly different meaning in 1611 than it had at the turn of the twentieth century, when rather than an expression of divine love it had become something related to the workhouse and its attendant miseries.

The two Gospels that are considered to contain the largest amount of antisemitic polemic are Matthew and John.

The Gospel of Matthew

In common with all other New Testament documents, there are differing opinions on the date and authorship of the Gospel (for an overview of how to handle ancient documents see F Wright, *Understanding Ancient Documents*, PARDES Occasional Paper II, 1998). For the purposes of the following we assume that the Gospel of Matthew was written by Matthew bar Levi and generated from the *logion* (diary) that he kept according to the church historian Eusebius, with conflations from Mark's collection of sayings, which were also used by Luke. Krister Stendahl, one time Dean of Harvard Divinity School and subsequently Archbishop of Stockholm, in a definitive study of Matthew, concluded that the Gospel emerged from a school which interpreted the Scriptures in a similar manner to that revealed in the Dead Sea Scrolls (*School of Matthew*, Philadelphia, 1954 and 1968), and in particular the *pesharim* (commentaries). The Gospel was addressed to his own community and is not biographical but a narrative theological interpretation of the breaking through of the Kingdom of God in the person of Jesus. Contrary to the opinion that the gospel is anti-Jewish, at least six positive affirmations of Judaism can be clearly seen.

1   The players in the drama are all Jewish. There is no sense of third parties being imported to supersede the Jewish people. The concept of the Kingdom of Heaven that dominates the writing was a major theme within the Judaisms of the time (see various works by the late Dr Lindsay, David Bivin, Joseph Frankovic and other members of the Jerusalem School).

2   Continuity with the Jewish Scriptures. Matthew quotes regularly from the Tanakh. There are at least five allusions in the birth narratives alone.

3   The concept of Israel. The mission is directed to the lost sheep of the house of Israel (10:5–6). The anticipated entry of Gentiles is not considered as far as the status of Israel goes.

4   The relationship to Torah. The term "Torah" is used in this discussion rather than law. Torah carries the sense of instruction or teaching. It should not be regarded as a forensic term (5:17–20).

5   Application of Old Testament and inter-testamental titles, i.e. Messiah, Son of God, Son of David. Matthew illustrates an unfolding model based upon continuity.

6   Comparative usage of materials with the Judaism of the day, such as the categories of leadership, the understanding of binding and loosing which relates to rabbinic rulings to allow or disallow practices, and the emphasis on the Lord desiring mercy and not sacrifice. One should bear in mind that there was a growing antipathy against the Temple and its leadership. It was considered by the Essenes and some of the zealot groups as a foreign intrusion.

The Gospel is considered to have four main antisemitic elements:

1   The usage of the expression "their synagogues" or "your synagogues" (4:23; 12:9; 13:54) is generally considered to illustrate a late date for the Gospel and reflects the rift between the church and the synagogue. Keeping to the earlier dating as illustrated above, there were divergent streams within first-century Judaism. When Jesus was addressing a mixed audience or referring to a particular grouping the expressions are appropriate and do not carry any negative emphasis.

2   In Matthew, truth is devoid of any value or content when pronounced by the scribes and Pharisees. In the interpretation of the law only Jesus has true authority. The scribes were not clerks or copyists: they were doctors of the law and some were experts in particular areas. It is thought that they belonged to the priestly caste, which is one reason we do not find Jesus in dialogue with "priests". This view is disproved in 23:2 where Jesus states unequivocally, "The Pharisees sit in the seat of Moses and you must do all that they tell you." Jesus was not against the Pharisees in terms of their authority or their instruction (23:2). He was against the hypocrisy of not practising what was preached.

3   The rejection by God of Israel. The house being left desolate (23:38) and the parable of the wedding feast (22:7) are appealed to as illustrations. It seems clear that Matthew is speaking of judgement on the house of Israel which, as Paul points out in Romans 3 is the cost of being entrusted with the oracles of God. God punished Israel in the Old Testament, and the judgement included the destruction of the Temple and the exile. Even so the judgement did not include abandonment, displacement or supersession. It is hardly likely that a writer who uses the Old Testament as his point of verification would step outside of the Old Testament and inter-testamental parameters of the received understanding of God's relationship with his covenant people.

4   The Passion narrative where the crowds are manipulated by the leaders to demand the death of Jesus. Once again one should be able to discern between what is levelled at a corrupt leadership, hypocritical teachers and the general population. Because the bystanders are addressed in national terms it does not affirm the notion. The expression used merely applies to any number from two upwards.

We now come to examine the most quoted passages to support an antisemitic view.

Matthew 23

The lengthy passage containing the seven woes is a composite of Mark 12:38–40, and a number of sayings in Luke at 11:42–48, 13:34–35 and 20:45–46 which are regarded as antisemitic polemical materials. The placing of the notice comes before the eschatological discourse and the way to Calvary. The blistering denunciation of the spiritual leaders could almost be regarded as Jesus' last earthly testament, speaking in anguish over the fate that awaited his people, and is not without compassion (v. 37b). If understood as such it takes away the antisemitic appropriation.

Matthew 27:25

Tertullian appears to be the first to have committed the idea to writing that this verse spelled self-condemnation on the whole Jewish race for eternity (*Answer to the Jews* 8). Although an eminent lawyer, Tertullian seems to have overlooked several very obvious points. Acts 4:27–28 indicates that Herod, Pontius Pilate, the Romans (Gentiles) and the Jews were all responsible for the death of Jesus, but their actions were committed under the will of God. The traditional church view of deicide, however, places the blame squarely on the shoulders of the Jews and stands as the ultimate act of wickedness in history.

When one engages with the text and places it in its historical setting, a different picture emerges. The precinct where Pilate enacted out the crowd scene did not hold many thousands of people, only a relatively small number in relation to the amount of people in Jerusalem at the time. Even if the curse they spoke on themselves was binding, they did not have the power or authority to place it upon all Jewish people for all time. It is more likely that the cry was a common usage of an Old Testament idiom (Deuteronomy 19:10; Joshua 2:19 *et al*) to denote the acceptance of their responsibility for the decision they had demanded from Pilate. If this is the case it throws more meaning on Pilate's hand washing: Pilate has allowed the crowd to make a decision, they have taken responsibility for that decision and Pilate has accepted that it is their decision. Another suggestion is that as a nation of priests, only the Jews could offer up the perfect lamb as a sacrifice. As such they were victims of God's sovereignty. Another, rather naïve, suggestion is that it is a later antisemitic insertion.

We may conclude that Matthew did not have any antisemitic intent in the inclusion of the verses. It is simply a record of the crowd acting as a decision-making body and the procurator's response to that decision – a soft option on his behalf. It should also be pointed out against the charge of deicide that the crowd did not knowingly call for the death of the Messiah, but that they acted in ignorance (Acts 3:17 cf. 1 Corinthians 2:8). The Acts 3:17 passage is of particular note as, when bringing the event to the attention of the hearers, Peter addresses them as brothers and points out that they were ignorant of what they had done, holding out to them the opportunity of the true knowledge of the one of whose death they had agitated for.

One should also bear in mind that not all priests and Pharisees were opposed to Jesus (John 3:1–21; 19:39; Luke 23:50–51; John 19:38). A notice in Acts 6:7 relates that a great many priests were obedient to the faith. Even among the rulers many believed in him (John 12:42). Luke 23:48 paints a picture of the people who gathered to witness the crucifixion beating their breasts in great mourning.

All three of the synoptic Gospels contain what is generally considered an acrimonious polemic in the parable of the wicked tenants (Matt 21:33ff.). To appreciate what Jesus is saying one should first look at the location and the composition of the audience. The parable is told in the Temple environs and the audience is a mixture of people, including a group who want to arrest Jesus but are afraid to do so because of the crowd. The group is obviously the ruling élite, probably Sadducees. All Sadducees were priests but not all priests were Sadducees. The office of the High Priest at this time was always held by a Sadducee and was corrupt in the extreme. The office was purchased on a yearly basis from the Romans. The Temple, as well as being the religious centre of Judaism, was also the seat of civil and civic government and held the national treasury. It is plain to see that Jesus is addressing the ruling élite, not the general crowd. If one decides to allot a prophetic element to the parable, it was fulfilled in CE 70 with the destruction of the Temple. The saying was not addressed to all Jews for all time. To apply content that is addressed to a particular group at a particular time as being applicable to all Jews is erroneous.

In conclusion, we contend that the Gospel of Matthew is not antisemitic, although materials therein have been appropriated and deployed as such. The supposed anti-Jewish elements are to be understood in their sociological and theological contexts along with other considerations relating to specific passages.

The Gospel of John

The Gospel of John is a strange paradox in being regarded as both the Gospel of love and the Gospel with the most violent anti-Jewish polemical content. The Gospel has found a deep affection in the hearts of believers and is normally the first biblical book studied or read. Eldon J. Epp, commenting on the popularity of the Fourth Gospel, concluded that:

[the Gospel]. . . more than any other in the canonical body of Christian writings is responsible for the frequent antisemitic expressions by Christians during the past eighteen or nineteen centuries, and particularly for the unfortunate and still existent character of the Jewish people as Christ killers. (Eldon J. Epp, "Antisemitism and the Popularity of the Fourth Gospel in Christianity", in *The Journal of the Central Conference of American Rabbis* 22:35, 1975).

One should be aware that the adduced polemical materials in John's Gospel operate at differing levels and need to be differentiated between. One reason is the usage of the term "Jews" dealt with above. J. Christiaan Beker, Professor of New Testament Theology at Princeton Theological Seminary, gives a typical appropriation of the general view. Beker contends that in John the Jews are equated with the fallen world and its darkness and given a satanic genealogy (8:44). Jesus is portrayed as a metaphysical miracle without a concrete relationship to the Jewish community. John's Jesus is a stranger to the Jewish community (10:34). The Jews are displaced as the people of God and the spiritual believers in Jesus are now God's own. He further contends that the reference at 4:22 *"salvation is of the Jews"* is enigmatic and cannot exonerate the basic tenor of this Gospel.

John 8:44

The often-used demonopathic understanding of this passage is that Jesus equates all the Jewish people with darkness and the devil. The verse has been the cause of much animosity against the Jews, particularly in the medieval period. In the modern period, the Roman Catholic theologian Rosemary Radford Reuther, commenting on John 8:40–44, states that John's Gospel:

. . .portrays the Jews as the very incarnation [of the] false, apostate principles of the fallen world. . .because they belong essentially to the world . . .their reaction to the spiritual Son of God is murderousness. (R. R. Reuther, *Faith and Fratricide; The Theological Roots of Antisemitism*, New York, 1974)

If one examines the text and social and cultural setting, the saying is seen in a different light. In the days of Jesus there were two dominant Yeshivot, if that is the correct term for the time, in Jerusalem. The Yeshiva led by Shammai held a rigorist position, whilst the school of Hillel focused upon the centrality of intention. Both Jesus and Paul have a degree of commonality with the school of Hillel. The school of Shammai, when disputing with their opponents, condemned them by ascribing their teaching to the devil whose brood they were. The account of the events portrays Jesus as in discourse with followers of Shammai and he is humorously using their own sayings against them. Once again the common mistake is made of assuming a universal application of a particular saying to a particular group.

John 10:34

It is not clear why Professor Beker (cf. v. 33) feels that Jesus is a stranger to Judaism, as John's Gospel clearly shows distinct lines of continuity, this passage being an example. One assumes that the professor takes a late date for John's Gospel as opposed to the more modern view we have advocated for all the documents being completed in a primary form pre-70 CE. Modern scholarship is tending toward a very early date for the Hebrew sub-document of John, Bishop J. A. T. Robinson contending for a priority (*The Priority of John*, London, 1985). It is also thought that there are Levitical allusions running through the text. The prologue of John is of particular interest. If one takes out the [anti-] John the Baptist polemical insertion, we are left with a clear expression of Jewish creation theology. The traditional ascription of the Logos motif in John to the work of Philo of Alexandria is erroneous in two aspects. Firstly, the usage of the term within the text fits within Hebrew terminology better in the sense of the subject matter and secondly, it forces back a late development of the Logos motif in its neo-Platonist usage which is of a later date. Once again, the expression in John 4:22 is not incidental or enigmatic, it is a clear expression of continuity.

John 16:2

Jesus prophesies that a time is coming when "They will put you out of the synagogue; in fact a time is coming when anyone who kills you will think he is offering a service to God." The Talmud relates that Jerusalem and the Temple were destroyed because of hatred without cause. The above saying of Jesus fits perfectly within this context. Jesus is midway through his farewell discourse and is preparing his followers for the trials and tribulations to come. As such, the passage needs to be viewed through a wider window than the time immediately following the death of Jesus and has a wider application than the internecine strife. The Romans burned and destroyed the Temple and many Jewish lives were lost. The passage almost perfectly describes the ongoing history of the Jewish people, who were indeed banned from the synagogues by other sectarians and by governments, and during the Crusading period it was even considered virtuous to shed Jewish blood.

In conclusion, the subject of "the Jews" in John received scant attention until the modern period. Recently it has been more widely considered, but the subject is still in its infancy. In the areas of exegesis and interpretation, works by Wayne Meeks, Marinus de Jong, Klaus Wengst, Oscar Cullman and the later editions of C. K. Barrett's, *The Gospel according to St John* all illustrate the trend. One of the more helpful discussions in the debate came from N. A. Beck in his 1985 work on the polemical aspects of the gospel (*Recognising and Repudiating the Anti-Jewish Polemic of the New Testament,* Toronto, 1985). Beck makes the suggestion that it would be helpful to replace "Jews" with "religious authorities". The suggestion has met with mixed reactions. D. Moody Smith suggests that to so do would be to pander to political correctness of the type insisted upon by some feminist theologians who demand that sexist comments and paternalistic language in the Scriptures be amended. Along with Smith, the present writer feels that it would not be helpful as such measures can lead to decontextualising. Also those who want to read "Jews" in a negative stereotypical sense would continue to do so (*Jews and Christians, ibid*).

We contend that the Gospel of John, although hailed as the finest example of antisemitism in the New Testament, is not antisemitic. Such an appropriation can only be drawn from erroneous late dating and an absence of understanding of the relationship between Judaism and Christianity and the Jewish contour of the Christian faith. In the other Johannine writing, "Ioudaios" only appears twice and in both instances is indirectly positive.

The Pauline Corpus

Paul is happily referred to as an antisemite and the inventor of Christianity by some Jewish people, and hailed as an abolisher of redundant Judaism by some Christians. The crux of the matter concerning Paul revolves around a single question: was Paul an apostate Jew and a rebel, or did he, along with the other emissaries, demonstrate continuity? The history of Paul remains enigmatic. He appears without a biography and the truncated end of the Book of Acts does not relate the end of his life or the manner of his death. It is considered in some circles that the apocryphal Acts of Paul and Thecla continue the story. Paul does not appear in contemporary non-Christian writings although there are several mentions of James. The relationship of Paul to the Herods and his glorification of Roman citizenship continue to raise questions. The charge is brought that Paul is discontinuous with Jesus in that his emphasis is not on the teaching of Jesus but is focused upon the person of Jesus and his resurrection. Paul's Christocentric emphasis dominates his work as he addresses the leading questions of the time, where developed thought was needed to deal with the polemical confrontations that surrounded the emergent communities. In common with Jesus, Paul is dependent on Apocalyptic thought and Jewish tradition. It is helpful at the outset to see Paul as an interpreter of Jesus and see continuity in that sense. A developing Halakah can also be clearly seen to be developing in Paul's thought.

Paul illustrates his continuity with Judaism. Although the

sponsoring and undertaking of the Nazirite vow of Numbers 6 (Acts 21:17ff.) in all probability was to satisfy a general distrust by the Jerusalem leadership, in his writings he proudly declares: "I myself am an Israelite, a descendant of Abraham, a member of the tribe of Benjamin." He further contends that God has not forsaken his people and that the defining characteristics of God's relationship with them remain (Romans 9:1f.). He describes the advantages of the Jew over the Gentile and the riches that the inclusion of the Jewish people will bring (Romans 11:12), and declares that all Israel will be saved (Romans 11:26).

Paul views Israel as having not only a positive role in salvation history in the past but also as looking forward to a positive role in the future. Israel's proto-salvation will be clearly seen in their forthcoming eschatological salvation. To Paul, the eschatological role of the Jewish people may be defined thus:

1   The eschatological deliverance of mankind awaits the salvation of the Jewish people.
2   The authority, authenticity and the identity of the Gentile church is derived from its Jewish roots and remains contingent upon them. The key expression to understanding Paul's teaching on the olive tree is in Romans 11:24,28, where the phrase "grafted against nature" appears. Paul is pointing out in a way that was readily understandable to his audience that the wild olive branches (Gentiles) will produce cultivated (Jewish) fruit. The reason for the ingrafting is that Israel remains beloved for the sake of the fathers.
3   The promise to the Gentiles has no value unless God's promises to the Jewish people remain true. The issues of God's righteousness and faithfulness are at stake, and these are the determining aspects of the truth of the gospel.

Craig Evans notes that the New Testament does not on any occasion, as opposed to the writings of the Essenes and other sectarians, call upon believers to petition God to damn enemies of the church or to curse its opponents. In conclusion, the accusation that the New Testament is antisemitic holds little water. It only becomes antisemitic when viewed through antisemitic lenses. If we apply the same measures to the text of Psalm 44, which is but one of many examples, we must draw the conclusion that the Old Testament is also antisemitic, a notion which, at best, would be condemned as ridiculous.

Replacement Theology

Replacement Theology is not a new phenomenon and finds its roots in the Second Temple Period in the question of who is the true Israel. Whereas it was, at first, an internecine question as has been shown, with the failure of the Second Revolt and the bifurcation of Jewish and Gentile Christianity, it took on a new dimension. Supersessionist thought has two streams, one based on theological grounds and one on a misreading of history with attendant post-modernism.

The propositions of Replacement Theology

1   The modern State of Israel is a theological aberration, a freak of history or simply irrelevant.
2   Israel has been replaced by the church in the purposes of God. The Scriptures, prophecies and promises are now the exclusive property of the church.
3   Israel and Jewish people are now a theological irrelevancy. One stream of thought contends that the Jewish people were used to prepare the way for the Messiah. With the Christ event, this particular period of salvation history came to an end and the church is a new expression of God's election and saving power. Another stream proposes that the church is the continuation of Israel. Israel in this context loses its geographical, ethnic and spiritual identity and the term becomes a generalisation for the believing community.

4   The extreme right wing of Replacement Theology claims that
    as the Jews rejected Jesus, God has now rejected them. The
    Jewish people have no destiny, no elective distinction and no
    calling. It is not proper to speak of Jews any more. Jews in
    Israel are Israelis, Jews in America are Americans, and so on.
    The only way that a Jewish person has any relevance is when
    he accepts Jesus as personal saviour and becomes a member
    of the church. Paul commences his discourse on Jews and sal-
    vation (Romans 9–11) by asking the question, "Did God
    reject his people?" His answer is, "By no means!" (Rom 11:1).

I am going to suggest that Replacement Theology that is intentionalist, that is to say not the result of distorted Bible teaching or
ignorance, is antisemitic, heretical and atheistic, for when we turn
to the Scriptures we find a very different picture. The burden of the
prophets is the return of the Jewish people to the land of Israel by
grace, there to be reconciled to God in the Messianic kingdom.
Passages such as Jeremiah 32:37–41 and Jeremiah 33:24–26 and
Ezekiel 36:16f. express the burden most lucidly.

    The charge that the notices of Isaiah 11:11–12, 43:4–8;
Jeremiah 23:3–8, 31:7–11, 32:37–42; Ezek 11:17–19, 20:41–42,
36:16f.; and Zephaniah 3:19–20 were fulfilled, following the return
from the Babylonian exile cannot be the case. The record clearly
states that only Benjamin and Yehuda returned, along with a
number of priests and Levites. The number of returnees is variously numbered from as low as 15,000 to a high figure of 55,000
(Nehemiah 7:8f., Ezekiel 8:1f.). The contention that the prophecies of return must have been fulfilled as the matter is not mentioned in the New Testament illustrates a lack of understanding
of the fact that the transmission of biblical literature was generally by speech. Any speaker, when addressing an audience,
addresses them within the parameters of their repertoire of appropriation. That is to say the orator does not explain every detail and
nuance. As all Jewish people of the New Testament period were
well aware of their destiny and the Scriptures concerning the

future, the speaker would not need to mention them unless they were subject to change or re-interpretation.

The title Israel

References to "Israel" in the New Testament, taken in context, all refer to physical Israel. The one reference which is controverted or opposed is in Romans 9:5 where Paul uses the expression "the Israel of God". In view of the clear fact that the word Israel never refers elsewhere in Scripture to the Christian church, it is far better to interpret this passage as referring to the body of Jews who believe in Jesus. For remember that a believing Jew is a member of two covenant peoples – the church and Israel.

Texts used in support of Replacement Theology include Romans 2:28–29, which is cited as affirming that the term "Jews" now applies to Gentile Christians. What Paul is saying is in continuity with his whole teaching: that in all matters of faith, authenticity is a matter of personal intention, not biological accident. The Jewishness that he is speaking of here refers to one who practises and fulfils Torah.

Paul hastens to remind his listeners that he agonises over his own people. He employs the unusual device of triple emphasis to confirm the centrality of what he is about to proclaim concerning the continuity of God's relationship with the Jewish people (Romans 9:1). He then reminds his Gentile audience that the people's defining relationship with the Lord remains intact:

> Theirs is the adoption as sons, theirs the divine glory, the covenants, the receiving of the law, the temple worship and the promises. Theirs are the patriarchs, and from them is traced the human ancestry of Christ, who is God over all, forever praised! Amen. (Romans 9:4–5)

Romans 9:6 – "For not all who are descended from Israel are Israel – is considered to illustrate the discontinuity of the Jewish people. It is stated that the true Israel should be understood in conjunction with Romans 4:13 where Paul says that the promise to

Abraham was through his righteousness that comes through faith. The problem here is that the Romans 9:6 passage belongs within a different context. This passage, in fact, is Paul pointing out that physical descent is not a guarantee of a place in God's family. The opening statement is simply a preamble to Paul giving a short teaching, using the example of Ishmael to illustrate the point he is trying to make, not that there is a new Israel being assembled but simply that lineage does not equal salvation.

Is it antisemitic to evangelise the Jews?

A second question that must arise and be considered is the much contested subject, "Is it antisemitic to evangelise the Jews?" Jacob Jocz places the question within the correct parameters when he suggests that:

> The Jewish position *vis à vis* the gospel is a complicated one. The Jewish people are not outside the covenant, Judaism is not without the knowledge of God. **The dialogue between the church and the synagogue is a domestic one**.

It seems to be a universally held opinion that Judaism and Christianity are discontinuous. They were continuous only for a short period. Opinions on the point of discontinuity vary from the death of Jesus to the end of the apostolic age. A further point of discontinuity held by both Christians and some Jews is when Paul insisted that Jesus was the Messiah and a divine being.

The question as to whether it is antisemitic to evangelise the Jews is a vexatious one. Is Jewish evangelism antisemitic? The question has become obfuscated by tendencies to ignore the priority of salvation for the Jews expressed in Romans 1:16, due to an overbearing guilt complex about the Holocaust, the move away from Scripture, emphasis on the experiential, Replacement Theology and difficulties relating to the State of Israel.

There are basically four views on the subject of Jewish evangelism:

1   A Jewish person needs to receive Yeshua as their personal saviour in the same way as all others do. We will not detain ourselves on this point as one hopes that the reader accepts this position.

2   The Jews are a renegade, reprobate people who are cursed by God. As such, any evangelism is a waste of time spent on an undeserving people. The latter opinion is of the vulgar, antisemitic type and once again need not detain us. There is, however, a second strain to the element that is based upon Romans 11:15 where Paul writes, "For if their rejection is the reconciliation of the world, what will their acceptance be but life from the dead?" It is usually conjectured that the passage implies a rejection by God of a people he no longer has any use for. This view ignores vv. 1–2 where Paul points out that by no means has God rejected his people and, when taken in the context of the passages it is seated within, it is clear that Paul is referring to Israel as a whole. The emphasis is on their rejection, not God's. Furthermore, such a position demeans the character of God who is faithful. As Paul asks, "Does their unfaithfulness cancel out God's faithfulness?"

3   Christianity and Judaism are separate faiths and both are legitimate. As such, evangelism is wrong because it disparages the integrity of the faith of the subject group. If it is felt that evangelism is a legitimate approach to someone of another religion then we also should be open to being approached ourselves by representatives of another faith. It is better, therefore, to maintain the diversity. This is of course ecumenicalism that views all faiths as a way to God.

4   A view that is held by several people involved with Jewish ministries known as dual covenant theory, which of the four may be regarded as the most dangerous. Sadly, it is often held by those who have a deep love for the Jewish people as well as those on a highly emotional or guilt-driven level. The theory postulates that there are two covenants, one for Jews and

another for Gentiles. As such, evangelism is not needed and, in effect, evangelism is nothing more than Christian antisemitism and neo-colonialism. Dual covenant theology is a manifestation of the spirit of antisemitism that operates through a spirit of deception, misplaced guilt or compromise. A second strand that is generally unarticulated is the notion that as the Jews are God's chosen people, they fall outside the normal parameters of the need for salvation by individual confession of faith in the Messiah.

Those who hold to an articulated theory of two covenants sometimes have bought the line that evangelism in the post-Holocaust period is singularly inappropriate to Jewish sensitivities. The oft-repeated statement: "You have robbed us of our Scriptures, and our lives. You can't get away with killing us physically so now you are trying to destroy the faith which is our defining character" has in some cases led to an evangelical paralysis.

Mitch Glaser points out that dual covenant theology is not a new idea and, in fact, reflects a Jewish idea raised to combat persecution and forced conversion (*Mishkan* 11). The tension still exists with works such as *What Christians Should Know About Jews and Judaism* by Rabbi Yechiel Eckstein (1984), following the earlier writings of Franz Rosenzweig (1886–1929) in *The Star of Redemption* (1921). Rabbi Eckstein expresses a heartfelt desire that Christians would accept Judaism as a legitimate and adequate faith for Jews. Rosenzweig's view can be encapsulated in a letter to Eugen Rostock alluding to John 14:6 which he saw as holding great truth [for the Gentiles]:

We are wholly agreed as to what Christ and his church mean to the world. No one can reach the Father except through him . . . But the situation is quite different for one who does not have to reach the Father because he is already with him. And this is true of the people of Israel [though not of individual Jews]. (Kai Kjaer Hansen in *Mishkan* 21)

Other Jewish scholars, particularly in recent times, reject the notion out of hand and feel that Judaism and Christianity are two separate and, therefore, distinct religions, and that any discussion regarding continuity is a meaningless exercise (Jacob Neusner, *Jews and Christians. The Myth of a Common Tradition,* London, 1991). Therefore, *ipso facto,* a Jewish Christian is an apostate who has converted to a completely different faith, rather than one who is in a position of continuity.

An argument advanced by some supporters of dual covenant theology is that when Paul took the gospel to the Gentiles, he did so in the assurance that Israel would be or [even] was saved as a divine act (Romans 11:25–27). Franz Müssner is representative of those who believe that this dynamic act of salvation will happen at the Parousia. There is a separate way of salvation for the Jews (*Traktat über die Juden,* München, 1979). Another view offered is that in Romans 10:17–11:36 the name of Jesus is not mentioned. Furthermore, the passage does not say that Israel will accept Jesus as Messiah when this act of salvation takes place. The two arguments above would seem inconsistent with the fact that Paul in his opening address to the audience in Rome emphasises that the gospel is to the Jew first (Romans 1:16). There is no legitimate application of the passage as being a historical reference in the past tense, or as a realised element. The theme is consistent with Paul's teaching in 1 Corinthians 1:18, 15:2 and Ephesians 1:13. In Romans 11:23 Paul speaks of the re-grafting into the olive tree which once again is consistent. Another salient fact overlooked in this area is that the first believers who made a decision to accept Jesus as Messiah recorded in the book of Acts were Jews. Is it logical that for a period Jewish people had to accept Jesus as Messiah to gain salvation, then at a certain unknown point in time it became unnecessary? The conjecture that salvation was through acceptance of Jesus as Messiah by the generation who had rejected him, but that for succeeding generations it was unnecessary, is naïve in the extreme.

A further suggestion is that the text does not call for Israel to turn to Jesus as Messiah as it does not deal with conversion by human endeavour, but dynamic salvation by God. An idea such as this is supported, for example, by Bernhard Meyer, and depends upon holding a heavily defined view of predestination.

Ellen Charry suggested at the 1988 General Convention of the Episcopal Church that there needed to be a "redefined Christian witness to Jews as dialogue: a sharing of one's faith convictions without the intention of proselytising". Whereas she did not contend for the validity of Judaism or propound a dual covenant theology it is, therefore, implicit that Jewish evangelism was proscribed to Episcopalians. Charry went on to suggest that this did not preclude sharing one's faith with a Jewish person if invited to do so. The position nevertheless precludes intentional evangelism and is therefore clearly at odds with the gospel.

An encouraging response to the above came from Dr George Carey, the former Archbishop of Canterbury, at the Inaugural Donald Coggan Lecture at the National Cathedral, Washington DC 24 April 2001. Quoting his predecessor, Dr Carey pointed out that in his complex dialectical wrestling in Romans 9–11, if Paul had simply meant that Moses was for Jews, and Jesus was for Gentiles, he could have said so far more straightforwardly. He quoted Tom Wright, Canon of Westminster Abbey, who noted that in "the late twentieth century, in order to avoid antisemitism the church in advocating the non-evangelisation of Jews has acted in a manner that Paul regards precisely as antisemitic".

In conclusion, the salvation of the Jewish people only takes place through their acceptance of Jesus as the Messiah, therefore the evangelical priority stands firm. We do not find one biblical example of the apostles or leaders forbidding Jewish evangelism. Not to evangelise is to deny the Jewish people the opportunity of salvation. There can be no positive reasons not to evangelise other than the antisemitic, no matter how reasoned or attractively presented they may be. Underlying some reasons that are not theologically based is a fear of rejection from Jewish people on the behalf of the parties involved. It is better to suffer rejection from a Jewish individual than risk many Jewish people's rejection by the Messiah.

CHAPTER EIGHT

CONCLUSIONS AND CONSIDERATIONS

The unpalatable truth is that antisemitism is
fundamental to Christianity. A sequence of instances
makes it clear that Christian charity is less reliable
than Christian malice.
Frederick Raphael

Frederick Raphael made the scathing comment above on the persecution of the Jews of Europe. Sadly, the comment, as we have illustrated, is based in truth. The objective of this book has not been to prove the point that antisemitism has a long history and that its seedbed was the Christian church. The purpose has been in a modest way more to address the "why" questions raised by the data examined and to attempt to help the reader to be cognisant with the signs and symptoms of the phenomenon. Eldon J. Epp propounded the view that, facing the facts as historical study reveals them, no matter how unpleasant the findings may be, will at least allow for a decent intellectual understanding of the past and possibly also of the present. (*Antisemitism and the Popularity of the Fourth Gospel in Christianity, ibid.*) The historical amnesia of the church will continue at its peril. We cannot escape from history: it must be confronted and redressed where possible.

One of the big questions that must arise is why did antisemitism develop within the very body that was supposed to love the Jewish people, share with them in the gospel and be partners with them in the restoration of Israel, waiting with them for the return of the Messiah and the consummation of the Kingdom of God? The answer is painfully obvious. The salvation of Israel is a prelude to the end of the age. The enemy is all too familiar with this and has attempted to destroy the vehicle that God intended to use to make Israel jealous (Romans 11:14), comfort his people (Isaiah 40:1) and be co-heirs in Messiah with. A Jew-hating church could not possibly win the Jews to their Messiah. When the church develops a passion for Jesus it should also develop a passion for God's representative people and, along with Paul, earnestly desire their salvation (Romans 9:1).

How then do we as Christians respond to the bitter legacy of antisemitism and the guilt and shame arising from it? Firstly, we should pay attention to the caution sounded by Elie Wiesel and Emile Fackenheim, not to be overly hasty, not to apply facile explanations, and be too ready to draw conclusions. Fackenheim summed up the situation well when he stated that:

> Rather than face Auschwitz, men everywhere seek refuge in generalities, comfortable precisely because they are generalities. And such is the extent to which reality is shunned that no cries of protest are heard even when in the world community's own forum obscene comparisons are made between Israeli soldiers and Nazi murderers. (Jewish Faith and the Holocaust, in *Commentary* vol. 46, August 1968)

Karl Barth reflecting on the matter in the closing days of the Holocaust declared that, "the question of the Jews is the question of Christ (*Verheissung und Verantwortung der Christlichen Gemeinde im heutigen Zeitgeschehen*, Zürich EV, 1944). Further, he contended that "Antisemitism is a sin against the Holy Ghost" (*The Church and the Political Problem of our Day*, New York, 1939), to which Franklin Littell adds, "Antisemitism is not just a particularly nasty form of race prejudice. Antisemitism is blasphemy" (*The Crucified Jew*, ibid.). The issues must be addressed in Littell's words ". . . not to save the church but for the love of Jesus of Nazareth and his people." We must realise that it is not a crisis of Christian faith that we are dealing with, but a case of Christian faithlessness. We can conclude that there are three kinds of antisemitism that have as their centre the spirit of Antichrist:

1. Christian antisemitism which is both heretical and apostate. Following Franklin Littell, we define heretical as that which claims to be a true representation of the Christian faith but has compromised and holds a view and eschews a practice or practices that are contrary to biblical standards. Dispensationalism, which holds that the Jews will return to the land and gain salvation after the so-called secret rapture and the return of the Lord, falls into this category. (See F. Wright, *The Death and Resurrection of Heaven and Earth, Recovering Eschatology*, due 2003.)

We define apostasy as that which has abandoned the Christian faith and loyalty to the community and its beliefs.

2. Post-Christian antisemitism arising from the abandonment of the Judeo-Christian ethic. Those who consider themselves to be humanists, and glory in the triumph of human achievement and have no belief in God, often fall victim to this type of antisemitism. The New Age movement has many similarities with the occult-pagan revival in Nazi Germany.

3. Non-Christian antisemitism. This is generally of a religious type and is most aptly typified by Islamic antisemitism. The claim by the Arab nations that they are not antisemitic, simply opposed to Israel, can clearly be illustrated as a fallacy. The worldwide attacks on synagogues and Jewish institutions that are not Zionist in intent or practice is the clearest illustration. In a two-week period during the 2000–2001 Intifada there were over two hundred such attacks with the highest percentage being in France (Simon Wiesenthal Centre Report, 2001).

The following is a suggested protocol offered for the combating and eradication of antisemitism:

1   The recognition that antisemitism is a spiritual force that can only be combated by spiritual means. This is the most important consideration, but cannot even be considered unless the protocols below are observed. The spiritual means are progressively outlined below.

2   Acknowledge that Jews and Christians worship the same God and that salvation comes through the life, death and resurrection of the Jew, Jesus.

3   The church is engrafted into the Covenant. It has not superseded the Jews as the sole beneficiary of the Scriptures, prophets and the work of the Messiah. God has not cancelled, re-called or abolished the covenants he made with the Jewish people.

4   Acknowledge that the Christian is not superior to the Jew. The Jews remain God's representative people.

5   The Christian church must accept its responsibility for the antisemitism it grew, nourished and promulgated. You cannot change history. It has already happened. The Austrian Christian philosopher Friedrich Heer (God's First Love, London, 1970) and David Tracey (*The Interpretation of Theological Texts*, Unpublished Lecture, Indiana University, 1984) both suggest that the passivity of the church and much of its impotence arise from what Tracey describes as the escape from history. Unless history is confronted, there can be no possibility of any forward movement. A groundbreaking document prepared by nine German Catholic theologians and presented by Pope John Paul II to The International Jewish Committee for Inter-Religious Consultations in Jerusalem suggested that the [Catholic] Church confess that she bears co-responsibility for the Shoah and has burdened herself with guilt.

6   Christians, despite a poor historical relationship with the Jews, should not be ashamed of the gospel. It remains the power of God unto salvation to the Jewish people first (Romans 1:16), a priority we ignore at our peril. The priority remains.

7   We should build bridges based on mutual respect and understanding. It is unhelpful to disseminate caricatures. Christians
should at least attempt to develop a working knowledge of the
main tenets of Judaism and the practice thereof.

8   Acknowledge our spiritual debt to the Jews and support them
materially where needed (Romans 15:27).

9   Acknowledge that the Scriptures arise from the Jews and that
both Jews and the emergent community of believers in Yeshua
shared the same Scriptures that we enjoy today.

10 Acknowledge that Jesus was an observant Jew who lived a
Jewish life in Judea before the destruction of the Temple in 70
CE.

11 Recognise the common origins of both Christianity and
Rabbinic Judaism.

12 Recognise that some early writings should not be properly
categorised as either Christian or Jewish. Many of the writings of the first and second century properly belong in a bridging period, when the definition was far looser than we have
generally supposed.

13 Recognise that the New Testament was addressed to a Jewish
audience. It should not be read from a point of discontinuity
or studied in isolation from Second Temple Judaisms.

14 Recognise that the "polemical" content of the New Testament
is not antisemitic but is a helpful sociological picture of the tensions of the time between competing Judaisms.

15 Recognise that the emergent community should properly be
understood as a sect within Judaism.

16 Recognise that the Gospel writers, Paul and the other New
Testament authors were all theocentric, used the Old
Testament as their source book, saw themselves in a line of
direct Jewish eschatological continuity and all desired to see
the Messianic age unfold. Be prepared to acknowledge that 80
per cent of the Christian Bible is quotations from, or allusions
to, the Old Testament and that ten per cent of the teaching of
Jesus is likewise.

17 Acknowledge that some Scriptures can only be applied to the Jewish people and have not become the property of the church, or cannot properly be applied to the church (c.f. the heading of Isaiah 40 in the Schofield Bible – "God comforts his church"). Paul reminds us in Romans 9:2 and following that theirs is "the adoption as sons, the divine glory, the covenants, the receiving of the law, the Temple worship, the covenants, the patriarchs and the human ancestry of Christ".

18 Acknowledge that both Jews and Christians are attestation to God's presence in the world.

19 Acknowledge that God's promise to the Jewish people concerning the land of Israel still holds and that there is a curse from God upon those who would divide the land (Joel 3:2). It is important to pray for national government on this issue, particularly as Britain has a bad record in these matters. At the time of writing, the undignified scramble by world leaders to find themselves a place in posterity as the deliverer of the Middle East Peace Process and gain a Nobel Prize endangers the wellbeing of the nation of which the politician is the head or represents.

20 The church must repudiate the teaching of contempt and establish new and appropriate ways of teaching that present the Jews in a faithful, biblical manner.

21 Restore the Jewishness of Jesus and re-establish the Jewish roots of the Christian faith. The commission is to make the Jewish people jealous (Romans 11:14). The opposite has generally been the case. Some Gentiles are extremely envious of the Jews and their faithfulness to their inheritance and continuity. The church must present an authentic expression of the Kingdom of God in its biblical context.

22 Recognise the privilege of being involved in the return of the Jewish people to Israel (Isaiah 49:22) and be aware of the ministry of bringing comfort, sometimes in practical ways, to the Jewish people worldwide (Isaiah 40:1f.).

23 Develop a biblical eschatology that considers the role of the Jewish people and the land of Israel.
24 Recognise that the Shoah is part of Christian history as well as Jewish history.
25 Avoid offensive terminology. The term "Jew" in common usage is often used as an abusive expression. Jewish people is to be preferred. Reference to the "Old Testament" is unhelpful; there is nothing old or redundant about it. "The Scriptures" or Tanakh is to be preferred. The expression "crusade" for evangelistic endeavours is most unhelpful. It simply fuels the notion that the endeavour is at least passively genocidal.
26 Keep alive the memory of offence as a safeguard for the future.

Protocol 26 may well be the key to building a bridge between Jewish people and Christians. It is important that the wreckage caused by the spirit of antisemitism and the place of the Shoah as the climactic event is not forgotten. In the words of the Baal Shem Tov: "Forgetfulness leads to exile whilst remembrance is the secret of redemption."

Long before the Spanish philosopher uttered his famous and oft-quoted dictum that "those who forget the past are condemned to relive it", the above words were spoken by R. Israel Ben Eliezar otherwise known as the Baal Shem Tov (Master of the Good Name, 1700–1760), the founder of Hassidism. Memory is both a precious and fragile thing. If understanding is impossible, knowing is imperative, because what happened could happen again. As Primo Levi poignantly remarked, commenting upon his poem *Shema* written shortly after his return from Auschwitz to his home in Turin, on 10th January 1946, "consciences can be seduced and obscured again".

The Holocaust and other pogroms against the Jewish people did not only destroy those who died, but continued to destroy those who survived. Many, such as the philosopher Julian Amery and possibly Primo Levi (1919–1987) committed suicide, because they were haunted by the spectre of their experience. It has been suggested that both committed suicide, as they could not live with the guilt of having survived. Friends with whom Levi had spoken in the weeks preceding his death related that he had become increasingly depressed by the growing obliviscence of the Western world, perceiving that it was anxious to forgive and forget. (In studies of memory, obliviscence is the opposite of reminiscence following P. Boswood Ballard *Obliviscence and Reminiscence*, Cambridge 1913.) In his last and possibly most significant book, *The Drowned and the Saved* (*I sommersi e i salvatori,* Turino, 1988) Levi entitled the first chapter, "The Memory of Offence". He pointed out that memory is the sum of our life's experiences. It is the crux of our personality, the crutch upon which our future rests. Memory is likened to a physical organ. With exercise it remains vigorous; without use it atrophies. The memory of offence has both individual and collective connotations.

Collective memory

Collective memory is an essential part of national identity and as such is a complex issue, particularly in the aftermath of national conflict and suffering. In the case of societies that have been the subject groups of genocide, as Peter Novick observes, there is almost a tacit subscription to a view that is very nearly Freudian in its application. There is a cycle of trauma and repression of memory. Trauma may be defined as incapacity to respond to events of such high intensity within the individual or society that the memory has to be repressed. The repressed data inevitably returns and may re-traumatise. The trauma-repression-return of the suppressed model has generally been accepted to account for the long delay in the production of Holocaust materials following the defeat of Nazi Germany.

The weakness of what we term the TRR model is that it ignores or inadequately explores the concepts of collective memory. The outstanding study on collective memory remains the pre-war studies of Maurice Halbwachs (*On Collective Memory*, ed. Lewis A. Cozer, Chicago, 1992). Halbwachs suggested that to dialogue with collective memory one needs to adopt a structured multiplex approach that accepts that there will be ambiguities. One will encounter moral ambiguities particularly when approaching motivational behaviour, as opposed to studies in historical conscience or factuality. Collective memory can be viewed as being both historical and, in a sense, anti-historical, as it is both reductive and does not accept ambiguities, generally wishing to present linear developments and an overarching standard of behaviour which may be compartmentalised. Similarly, memory has no time-consciousness and the "pastness" of the historical process becomes merged into the present consciousness. Halbwachs insisted that all memories, even those of intimate personal life, are social narratives which are the product of years of discussion and interlocution around the kitchen table, at the workplace, social settings in church, or wherever people congregate. Shared evaluations are transmitted and become a part of group collective history, identity and order of relations. Many stories that could be repeated are filtered out as inappropriate.

The latter brings us to the problem of what today is termed "useful" or "non-useful memory". Who is to decide what is useful and what is redundant in terms of memory? Society and social tensions are susceptible to irritation, change and disruptive events like wars, depressions, or political assassinations, all of which alter the stability of social life. As such, the non-useful memory of yesterday could be essential at a later time to deal with crisis, trauma or post-trauma. Rupture often can necessitate a change of view that requires a collateral response in the collective memory. If we change the way we think about the world, we automatically update memories to reflect our new understanding. Therefore, it can be said that both world-views and historical discourse affect collective memory (Edmund Blair Bolles, *Remembering and Forgetting: An Inquiry into the Nature of Memory*, New York, 1980).

Collective memory can be employed as a political device, which as Andy Markovits and Simon Reich remark, "is the lens through which the past is viewed". One purpose of collective memory is to help "both masses and élites interpret the present and decide on policy" (Andrei S. Markovits and Simon Reich, *The German Predicament: Memory and Power in the New Europe,* New York, 1997). Memory in Halbwachs' view is chosen rather than imposed but, as we have shown above, in "official histories" the State designs the collective memory by employing revisionism and manipulation, so in a sense collective memory is not so much "chosen" but "chosen for" the individual and the society.

The memory of the suffering of the Jewish people has been recorded by them and is an essential part of their group identity and psyche. During the Crusades, especially the First (1095–1099), the Jewish communities of the Rhine, Danube and any others that the Crusaders encountered, were mercilessly exterminated. The communities of Rhineland produced "Memorbücher", entries of which to the present time are recited on the anniversaries of the events. (*See The Cross Became a Sword, the Knights of Christ and the First Crusade*, London, 1995.) Likewise, when the immediate trauma of the Holocaust began to ease a little, memoirs of survivors began to appear. As most of the survivors are reaching the ends of their lives there has been a great initiative to collect oral history, both in written word, audio and film recording. The biggest enterprise has been undertaken by the director Steven Spielberg. The initiative has not been welcomed by Holocaust deniers, and some PMPZ writers such as Tom Segev and, particularly, Norman G. Finkelstein (Norman G. Finkelstein, *The Holocaust Industry,* London and New York, 2000) insist that the Holocaust has become nothing more than a cynical money-making industry and tool of Zionism. Others such as the German historian Franz Joseph Strauss view such undertakings as retrogressive and contend that they stagnate international relationships. At the 130th anniversary of the Catholic German Student Societies he insisted upon . . . "the right of the

Germans to normality . . .[as] no society can live with a criminal-ized past" (*Sudetendeutsche Zeitung*, 22 June 1987).

There are two dangers that are apparent, both of which, although not obvious, are elements of antisemitism. Firstly we should remember, and not forget. Although the statement might sound simplistic, if conflated to "we must establish and hold an authentic memory and not lose the lessons of the offence", then we will not fall prey to the dictum of George Santayana above.

Secondly we should not neutralise or trivialise the sufferings of the Jewish people. A danger that has appeared over the last fifteen or so years has been using the Holocaust as a backdrop for roman-tic fiction. Not all fiction based around the tragedy should be con-sidered as trivialisation. One only has to think of William Styron's *Sophie's Choice* as an example. It has never ceased to surprise me that in major book stores the biographical works of Primo Levi, including *Se questo e un uomo* (Turin 1947, various English edi-tions entitled, *If this a Man* or *Survival at Auschwitz*), *The Truce* and *The Drowned and the Saved* (London, 1986) along with Elie Wiesel's *Night* (London, 1981) in paperback, are to be found amongst the fictional works.

Dilution, or possibly better, devaluing of memory, may be noted in the 1988 work of Professor Arno Meyer of Princeton University, entitled, after a lament of Solomon Bar-Simpson during the Crusades, *Why did the Heavens not Darken? – The Final Solution in History* (London 1988). Mayer, at the outset of his study, contends that he desires the Holocaust to be rescued from the cult of memory, which was impeding historical understanding. He establishes his platform clearly with the statement that the voice of history should be polyphonic, as opposed to the voice of memory that is uniphonic. In a sense such a position devalues the worth of testimony. Mayer's view is a somewhat surprising response for one who was himself a refugee from Nazism.

A further level of trivialisation we might term the "dilution of memory" by generalising specific terms. Language in modern usage has a great tendency to either borrow or transplant terms.

This practice is often the result of "news-speak". It is a gross distortion to apply terms that are expressions of mass death and suffering in a blasé way. The late Primo Levi, in an interview with Ferdinando Camon (*Autoritratto di Primo Levi,* Padova, 1987) shortly before his death, expressed his dismay at such practices. Levi pointed out that slogans such as "school equals concentration camp", and the employment of this term to describe poor conditions in schools, factories and hospitals were a gross distortion. None of the above imprison people against their will, neither are human beings processed through gas chambers in a mechanised machinery of suffering and death. Nor are people's possessions and even body parts harvested. The term "Holocaust" is now almost a label for any kind of atrocity or social condition seen to cause suffering, real or perceived, or any kind of mass destruction. The term recently has been applied to the large-scale destruction of animals in the UK as a result of the foot and mouth epidemic. The prize for the most ludicrous, trivialising usage of the term, however belongs to the disgraced TV evangelist Jim Bakker who reassured television viewers that "If Jim and Tammy can survive their Holocaust of the last two years, then you can make it" (*Los Angeles Times*, 3 Jan. 1989).

One should however sound a caution not to over-react to misapplication as this action in itself may have a trivialising effect. To shout "antisemite" at everyone who disagrees with you or takes a position that is uninformed can cause more damage than help.

Neutralising memory

One should always be sensitive to the fact that the Nazi tragedy affected all of Europe and unleashed untold suffering upon all the nations involved. The sufferings, as we have shown, were far more severe on the Eastern Front and involved the Jewish people in particular. To use the title of Rachmiel Frydland's book, it was a time *When Being Jewish Was a Crime*. The world's Jewish people were under the sentence of death, either by execution or its surrogates.

Einsatzgruppen Operational Situation Report USSR 173, of 25 Feb 1941 illustrates the point clearly:

> In the course of a routine Security Police screening of an additional part of Leningrad, a further 140 had to be shot. The reasons were as follows, active communists, those carrying out seditious and provocative activities, partisans, those who have committed espionage, and **those belonging to the Jewish race.**

One can see from the report that the death sentence was carried out on purely racial grounds.

The Neutralisation of Memory has been particularly prosecuted in Poland. Polish losses were some of the highest percentage-wise in the hostilities, and numbered around 3,300,000 persons. It is also true that many others including up to 3.5 to 4 million Russians perished in the extermination camps. However, to remember one's ethnic national dead at the expense of the Jewish people, by either ignoring them or denying them a place in the national memory, is grossly antisemitic. The case of the Carmelite Convent of the Holy Blood is a prime example. The erection of crosses at the site of Auschwitz elicited a vigorous response from world Jewry. Those who went to protest at the site were manhandled and abused. Cardinal Joseph Glemp would not hear any criticism and added fuel to the fire with a series of aggressive responses. During the Communist period, the sites of the extermination camps were largely used for Soviet propaganda. We well remember in the early 1980s visiting Auschwitz. At the time, the sufferings of the nations had each a "pavilion" which was a two-storey building in the main camp. The Jewish people merited only one floor, an exhibit, whilst Albania merited the same, and other satellite countries merited whole buildings.

The denial of memory is a major tactic of Holocaust deniers who wish to contradict the memory of survivors and the testimony of those who perished. The leading exponents are Arthur Butz, Robert Faurrison, Ernst Zundel, Fred Leuchter and David Irving. The most influential work is produced by the Institute of

Historical Review whose website is a leading example of revisionism and misquotation. The Holocaust deniers' position can briefly
be outlined as:

1   The Jews were not killed in gas chambers, or at least not on
    any significant scale. The particular emphasis on gas chamber
    denial is pivotal to contending the points below, as the appa-
    ratus is the symbol of mechanised, or industrialised mass
    killing. Furthermore, Zyklon B gas was inappropriate for
    mass killing. Such contentions were given the *coup de grâce*
    by the publication of the French pharmacist Jean-Claude
    Pessac's findings in 1989 and subsequent studies.
2   There was no deliberate or authorised policy in Nazi
    Germany concerning the extermination of the Jews. Mass
    killings were actions that should be understood as ad hoc indi-
    vidual excess, committed without authorisation. On occa-
    sions, it is contended that Hitler was a weak leader who knew
    little of the matter (David Irving, *Hitler's War*, London,
    1977), and that the atrocities were carried out by local leaders
    in a surfeit of zeal. Within the camps, victims died at the
    hands of other inmates. Those who were executed were exe-
    cuted on legitimate grounds as they were criminals, subver-
    sives, spies or saboteurs.
3   The high number of Jewish victims is grossly exaggerated. The
    numbers were not in millions but were considerably lower. The
    numbers have been wildly over-inflated in a vulgar scheme to
    extract money out of misplaced guilt from the rest of the
    world. Further to this, Jewish people have used the lie to steal
    billions in reparations and succeeded where they had failed
    before in destroying Germany's good name and reputation.
    Capitalising upon misplaced international sympathy, they
    used the opportunity to displace another nation in order to
    establish their own state [of Israel].
4   The Holocaust is a myth that was devised after the war as anti-
    Nazi black propaganda. The myth is perpetuated in order to

maintain and fuel the Holocaust industry which is run by Jews and the State of Israel as a money-making machine. *The Diary of Anne Frank* is a forgery and an example of exploitation (the book has sold over 20 million copies). (After the death of Otto Frank in 1980 the diary was given to the Netherlands State Institute for War Documentation who undertook a massive investigation, which deemed the diary authentic.)

5   Emigration (or deportation), not extermination, was the Nazi plan for dealing with Germany's Jewish problem. If Germany had planned total extermination, no Jews would have survived, as Germany was a most efficient bureaucracy.

6   Jews who disappeared during the years of Second World War vanished into Soviet-held territories, not German. Many others were transferred secretly by the Zionists to the USA.

Holocaust denial commenced prior to the Allied victory. In April 1945 Himmler signed a handwritten official order (extant) that the camps would not be surrendered and that no prisoner should be allowed to fall into the hands of the enemies alive. He instructed his camp commandants to destroy records, crematoria and other signs of the mass destruction of human beings. The corpses of the victims of the Einsatzgruppen were disinterred by Jewish *Sonderkommando* and burned. The *Sonderkommando* were in turn executed and joined the pyre. Removal of the evidence of extermination camps was also attempted.

One of the first writers to publish what was to become one of the foundations of Holocaust denial was Paul Rassinier, a French Communist and partisan who was captured and interned as a "political" prisoner at Buchenwald. In 1945, Rassinier was elected as a Socialist member of the French National Assembly, resigning for health reasons after serving for two years. After reading reports of exterminations he responded, "I was there and there were no gas chambers." This is no surprise as he was confined to Buchenwald, located in Germany. Using his status as an ex-detainee, he began on a career of denying the existence of gas chambers and mass extermination at other camps. *Le Passage de la Ligne* (Crossing the Line, 1948) and The *Holocaust Story and the Lie of Ulysses* (1950) contain the two-fold thrust of his arguments:

1   Some atrocities were committed by the Germans but the reportage is grossly exaggerated.
2   The Germans were not the perpetrators of these atrocities, in fact they were more humane than other inmates were. The atrocities were carried out by the Capos and other prisoner officials.

The Drama of European Jewry (1964) attacked the genocide myth as a creation of the Zionists as part of a massive Jewish-Soviet-Allied conspiracy to "swindle" Germany out of billions of dollars in reparations.

Rassinier's work was soon picked up and deployed by anti-semitic, pro-Nazis in the United States, including W.D. Herrstrom, an extreme right-wing evangelist, national socialists such as George Lincoln Rockwell and revisionist historian of the First World War, Harry Elmer Barnes at Smith College.

The Irving v. Penguin Books and Deborah Lipstadt libel trial of January 2000 was one of the most significant events in the recent history of antisemitism. Although it was not obvious from the media reportage, in reality it was not Deborah Lipstadt who was on trial but the very existence of the Holocaust itself. The action began in 1996 when David Irving, a historical writer and apologist for Adolph Hitler, sued the American Jewish academic Deborah Lipstadt for libel. In her book, *Denying the Holocaust: The Growing Assault on Truth and Memory* (Penguin, 1994), in common with other academic writers on the Holocaust, she presented Irving as a Nazi apologist and rehabilitator of Nazism. She further accused him of bending the evidence until it conformed to his ideological leanings and political agenda, and of being an extremist and a liar, as well as being one of the most dangerous spokesmen for Holocaust denial. Irving had enjoyed a variegated career, moving from best-selling author to pariah status as it became ever increasingly obvious that he supported illegitimate positions.

Irving was not a stranger to litigation. Some 30 years previously he was the joint defendant along with his publishers for libelling the commander of Convoy PQ 17 which had been attacked by U-boats. It emerged that, during the writing of the book, Irving had deliberately libelled the Commander in the hope that a suit against him would increase sales for the book. Irving also appeared at the trial of Ernst Zundel in Canada when he was tried for Holocaust denial in 1984 and 1988, when to do so was a crime in Canada. It was during this time that Irving met the notorious Fred Leuchter, a designer of execution equipment, who was shortly later to produce *The Leuchter Report*, denying the existence of the gas chambers at Auschwitz, Birkenau and Majdanek. Irving was so impressed with Leuchter that he published the report in the UK under his own imprint and became convinced that the Holocaust was a hoax. In the forward to *Auschwitz, the End of the Line*, Irving contended that the whole gas chamber myth was an initiative of the British Psychological Warfare Executive in 1942 that promulgated the "news" that the Germans were employing gas chambers to kill millions of Jews and undesirables.

Irving played a smart card when he petitioned in London, where the onus in a libel trial is on the defendant to prove that they did not commit the libel, as opposed to the USA where the onus is the other way round and the plaintiff has to prove that the libel was damaging. In doing so, Irving had calculated that if the action took place in London then, rather than his having to prove that he had suffered from her accusations, Deborah Lipstadt would effectively have to prove the historicity of the Holocaust. A theme of Irving's defence was that he was the innocent victim of a Jewish plot to discredit his international good reputation as a historian and to silence him. Judge Gray, whilst maintaining that history was not on trial, used 378 paragraphs in his summing up to deal with historical matters. The judge conceded that the book did indeed represent an attack on Irving, mounted in order to discredit him as an historian, but ruled that Irving had failed to illustrate that this was undertaken from a position of personal hostility. After commending Irving as a competent military historian whose work on archives was superb, Judge Gray condemned him by stating that what mattered was his integrity as a writer. He stated that Irving's view of Hitler had an air of unreality and, concerning the gas chambers, which as noted above are central to Holocaust denial, the judge concluded that no fair-minded historian would have serious doubt that there were gas chambers at Auschwitz and that they were used to kill hundreds of thousands of Jews. More damningly, he stated that Irving was an antisemite and that his words were directed against Jews either individually or collectively. Further, the judge stated that the charge that Irving was a racist was established: "As a historian he has deliberately falsified and distorted evidence . . . [his] treatment of historical data is so perverse that it cannot be due to inadventure." (For a good account of the Irving Trial, see D. D. Guttenplan, *The Holocaust on Trial*, London, 2001.) Deborah Lipstadt makes the seminal comment that *"If Holocaust denial has demonstrated anything, it is the fragility of memory, truth, reason and history."*

Memory must be kept alive. As Stanley Munsat (*The Concept of Memory*, New York, 1967) points out, there is a difference between memory and remembering. Memory is a constant, perhaps just below the surface conscious state that is either present, or can be triggered involuntarily and often in spite of the person's will. Conversely, remembering indicates a sporadic retrieval, often by volition, an action that can be anything from an attempted retrieval at will, or be selective, or have a purposeful beginning and end. The memory of the Christian offence against the Jewish people seems to have been remembered by the Jews and discarded by Christians until recent years. The memory of the offence dealt with in a non-sentimental or maudlin way can be one of the enabling factors towards reconciliation.

Conclusion

Is there a possibility of healing nineteen hundred years of Jewish–Christian relations? Maybe it is wrong to speak of "relations" as, until the latter part of the last century, apart from a period of the Polish–Lithuanian Commonwealth and a few other exceptions, they did not exist. Maybe we should simply talk about Christian–Jewish animosity or Christian–Jewish conflict. The question then properly should be: "Is there a possibility for Jewish–Christian relationships?" If so, they will be contingent upon the above protocols that are offered only as a starting point, and by no means claim to be definitive. Relationships being formed from the Christian side will have to face concrete realities such as the Holocaust, the State of Israel and the role of Israel among the nations, if dialogue is going to be meaningful. Samuel Sandmel (*Antisemitism in the New Testament,* Philadelphia, 1978) commented that as the relational problems within Christianity concerning these matters were caused by Christians, then surely in the present age, Christians working for an intellectual understanding of the problem can shape and determine what Christianity is or can be. Once determined and defined, Christians should subsequently be enabled to relate meaningfully to Jewish people. To this end, some years earlier, Friedrich Heer (*God's First Love*, London, 1970) pointed out that a return to the Hebrew roots of the faith, coupled with the roots of Christ's own piety, which saw man in relationship to God, his fellow man and the creation, is the route to bringing healing to, and from, the church. Along with Heer's pleasing statement we must add that the church must be involved in a large-scale re-education programme of both clergy and laity, and not avoid any of the issues, no matter how contentious. Prayer initiatives must become an intrinsic part of the programme, which by its very nature will immediately find a high priority in spiritual opposition.

A pressing issue that needs to be confronted is the matter of Jewish believers. The tension is two-fold. The Gentile church needs to accept Jewish believers and not attempt to Gentilise them. The Jewish believer has suffered greatly through history. St Jerome (331–419) despised them as being neither something nor nothing. During the Inquisition, new believers, whether genuine or not, were always under suspicion, and it has often been the case that when a Jewish person comes to faith in Jesus as Messiah there is an insistence that he assimilate. A great fear of Jewish believers is losing their identity. Messianic fellowships are valuable but they stand as an illustration of the Gentile churches' failure to provide adequate resource and understanding for the needs of the Jewish believer. There can on the other hand be a tendency, because of history, for some Jewish people to accept Jesus and not the church and then they tend to struggle along without the benefit of fellowship.

There have been some encouraging statements from the churches regarding the Jewish people and the Shoah in recent years. One may mention *Nostrae Aetate*, 26 October 1965, the statement of the Lutheran Church in America of 18 April 1994, the joint statement of Hungarian bishops of November 1994, the meeting of the German bishops to re-examine relationships with the Jews, 23 January 1995, the statement of the Polish bishops of January 1995, the declaration of the French bishops on the site of the Drancy collection and deportation camp in September 1997, the Holy See's *We Remember: A Reflection on the Shoah* (March 1998), and the *Declaration of the Austrian Evangelical Churches of Austria* on 28 October 1998. Sadly there seems to have been little uptake or resonance in the churches as a whole.

Part 2

When Two Worlds Collide:
Anti-Judaism and Anti-Israelism

CHAPTER NINE

THE JEWS UNDER ISLAM

[A nation is]
a group of people united by a mistaken view about the
past and a hatred of their neighbours.
(Ernest Renan)

Our war against the Jews is an old struggle that began
with Muhammad and in which he achieved many
victories . . . It is our duty to fight the Jews for the sake
of Allah and religion, and it is our duty to end the war
that Muhammad began.
Al Aram, 26 Nov 1955

When dealing with Arab–Jewish relations, and in particular the animus against the Jewish people held by the Arab nations, it is inappropriate to use the term "antisemitism". The term "semite" has no meaning when applied to groups as heterogeneous as the Arabs or the Jews. Likewise, it is nonsense to attempt to apply the term to animosity or hatred against the Arab nations by third parties, as there is not a single occasion that the term has been used outside the context of hatred of the Jewish people. We, therefore, suggest that a three-staged approach to the matter be applied using three differing terms:

1   Islamic anti-Judaism
2   Pan-Arabism
3   Anti-Israelism

The terms will become self-evident as the sources below are examined. The reasons, although co-terminus, emanated from the three different positions. All three have the same spiritual dynamic, which is the spirit of antisemitism. In the section dealing with Jewish-Arab relations in the modern period we have deliberately used sources that pre-date the formation of the State of Israel, and majored on official documents of the Mandatory Powers to avoid subjectivity on either side of the coin.

Arab–Jewish relationships can be viewed as having undergone six phases:

- The beginnings of the Zionist settlements, as of 1882, whilst Palestine was under Ottoman rule;
- The period of the British mandate from 1918, during which time the Mufti inspired riots and anti-Jewish settlement became defined. This was also a time of large-scale illegal Arab immigration;
- The phase of conflict setting in with the founding of Israel in 1948;
- The phase following the defeat of the neighbouring Arab states in the Six-day War of 1967;
- The breakthrough of Islamification following the Iranian Revolution of 1979, which in turn thereby influenced radical movements like the Hamas, Hisbollah and Intifada;
- The failure of the peace process.

An overview of the Arabs

Traditionally Arabs are tribal, nomadic desert dwellers (Heb. "Arav" – one who lives in the desert). At risk of stating the obvious, it should be pointed out that not all Muslims are Arabs, and not all Arabs are Muslims. Today the term "Arab" has shifted from its original application, namely a nomadic desert dweller in the Arabian peninsula, to cover those nations that up until recent times would have been incensed to be categorised as "Arabs", namely Egyptians, [to a degree] the Lebanese, Iraqis and Iranians (Persians). In the latter case it was considered particularly offensive by a nation who had retained their national language, Farsi, after conversion to Islam.

The biblical account of the Arabs finds its first expression in the account of the mocking of Sarah by Hagar (an Egyptian) in Genesis 16:4, following the pregnancy that led to the birth of Ishmael, and Isaac's son Esau (Edom), both of whom are considered the founders of the race. The Genesis account of the births of the two progenitors carries severe warnings. In the case of Ishmael:

He will be a wild kicking donkey of a man; his hand will be against everyone and everyone's hand will be against him and he will live in hostility against all of his brothers. (Genesis 16:12)

The truth of the prophetic words can easily be demonstrated by the inability of the Arab nations to form a cohesive unity. The postwar history of the Arab nations is littered with over thirty wars and in excess of fifty assassinations or attempted assassinations.

The words spoken over the twins Jacob (Israel) and Esau (Edom) compound the matter: "Two nations are in your womb, and two peoples from within you will be separated." (Genesis 25:23 cf. Malachi 1:3 and Romans 9:13. The fulfilment of Edomite hostility may be seen in Numbers 20:14f. and Genesis 27:41–45.

A few examples of the ongoing antagonism can be found in Numbers 14:14–16; 24:20; Deuteronomy 25:17–19; Judges 3:13–14; 5:14; 6:3–10; 7:12–22; 10:6–14; 1 Samuel 14:48; 15:2f.; 27:1f.; 28:18–19; 30:1f.; Psalm 83:5–7. Haman the Agagite is reckoned to be a descendent of the Amalekites, Esther 3:1 cf. Numbers 24:7.

The Arabs play no significant role in Middle-Eastern history in the early period. The first time the Arabs appear as a distinct people group is in 2 Chronicles 17:11, where they are associated with the Philistines (see also 2 Chronicles 22:16 and 26:7). It seems, however, that the first inroads into the land were during the Babylonian exile and that the Arabs were a contrary force during the rebuilding undertaken by Nehemiah (Nehemiah 2:19; 4:7; 6:1–6).

The Islamic world

We need not be detained by a history of Islam *per se*, however one should understand the division in Islam between the Da'ar al-Islam (World of Islam) and Da'ar al-Arb (World of War). Jihad is to be waged against the Dar al-Arb in perpetuity until the world comes into submission. In the Dar al-Arb there are two categories: people of the book and pagans.

The outstanding characteristic of the picture of the Jewish people as presented in the theology, philosophy, literature and art of the classical Islamic world is one of singular unimportance. There is nothing of the invective, polemic or teachings of contempt, demonopathy or refutation of Judaism as exampled in the Christian writings of the Early Church Fathers, Petrus Venerabilis, Ramon Lull, John of Capistrano and Bernardino of Sienna as well as a multitude of less well-known polemicists. The prevailing views of Jews are found in the Qu'ran of which a sample is offered below.

The Qu'ran on the treatment of The People of the Book

There are two classical stereotypes of Islam and its relationships with others. The first perpetrated by Edward Gibbon in *The Decline and Fall of the Roman Em*pire, is that of the horseman wielding the Qu'ran in one hand and a sword in the other. This stereotype views Islam as offering its opponents the choice of conversion or death (J. Bury edition, London, 1909–1914, vol. 5 p. 332). The other picture, frequently employed today by Muslim apologists, is one of a golden age of tolerance where those of other races and religions live together in a utopia of harmony and co-operation. As Bernard Lewis points out, both stereotypes are fictions of comparatively recent origin and arose in the West. One should understand that the concepts of religious tolerance and racial harmony are of recent origin and both historical and present-day amnesia have pervaded many studies. Until the twentieth century and possibly even the post-war period, there was a general absence of, or ambivalence towards, toleration and racial harmony, not only in the Middle East but also in Western Europe.

To be a full member of society in the Islamic world there were three pre-requisites: to be a [Islamic] believer, to be male, and to be free. Of the essential categories of inferiors, the woman and the slave were not considered to be responsible for their status. In the matter of the unbeliever, the matter was of an entirely different order as it was considered to be a matter of choice. The woman and the slave were perceived to have some intrinsic value, but the value of an unbeliever was questionable. Within the ranks of the unbelievers there were two basic categories: those who had received the truth in some measure; Jews, Christians and the ambiguous "Sabians". The second category were the pagans who were considered as hardly worth anything at all. On the grounds of *al-kafru millatum wāhida* (all unbelief is but one religion), the Muslims did not make any real attempts at subdividing the categories of pagans.

The following passages from the Qu'ran give an overview of how Jewish people and Christians were first perceived. The suras below basically cover the beliefs that the Jews were unworthy recipients of the Scriptures, essentially evil, and that not accepting Islam was not an error: it was deliberate. The suras state that the Jews are in a wretched and reduced state because of their disobedience; they pervert words from their meanings and are slanderers of the true religion; and they are a cursed people who murdered the prophets of old.

> Fight against those to whom the Scriptures were given, who believe not in Allah, nor in the Last Day, who forbid not what Allah and His apostle have forbidden, and follow not the true faith, until they pay the tribute out of hand and are humbled. (Sura 9:29)

> O you who believe! Take not the Jews and the Christians as friends. They are friends to one another. Whoever of you befriends them is one of them. Allah does not guide the people who do evil. (Sura 5:51)

There is to be no compulsion in religion. Rectitude has been clearly distinguished from error. So whoever disbelieves in idols and believes in Allah has taken hold of the firmest handle. It cannot split. Allah is All-hearing and All-knowing. (Sura 2:256)

Wretchedness and baseness (humiliation) were stamped upon them (that is, the Jews), and they were visited with wrath from Allah. That was because they disbelieved in Allah's revelations and slew the prophets wrongfully. That was for their disobedience and transgression. (Sura 2:61)

Have you not seen those who have received a portion of the Scripture? They purchase error, and they want you to go astray from the path. But Allah knows best who your enemies are, and it is sufficient to have Allah as a friend. It is sufficient to have Allah as a helper.

Some of the Jews pervert words from their meanings, and say, "We hear and we disobey," and "Hear without hearing," and "Heed us!" twisting with their tongues and slandering religion. If they had said, "We have heard and obey," or "Hear and observe us," it would have been better for them and more upright. But Allah had cursed them for their disbelief, so they believe not, except for a few. (Sura 4:44–46)

And for the evildoing of the Jews, We have forbidden them some good things that were previously permitted them, and because of their barring many from Allah's way, And for their taking usury which was prohibited for them, and because of their consuming people's wealth under false pretence. We have prepared for the unbelievers among them a painful punishment. (Sura 4:160–61)

The Jews say, "Ezra is the son of Allah," and the Christians say, "The Messiah is the son of Allah." Those are the words of their mouths, conforming to the words of the unbelievers before them. Allah attack them! How perverse they are!

They have taken their rabbis and their monks as lords besides Allah, and so too the Messiah son of Mary, though they were commanded to serve but one God. There is no God but He. Allah is exalted above that which they deify beside Him. (Sura 9:30–31)

The Jews say, "Allah's hands are fettered." Their hands are fettered, and they are cursed for what they have said! On the contrary, His hands are spread open. He bestows as He wills. That which has been revealed to you from your Lord will surely increase the arrogance and unbelief of many among them. We have cast enmity and hatred among them until the Day of Resurrection. Every time they light the fire of war, Allah extinguishes it. They hasten to spread corruption through-out the earth, but Allah does not love corrupters! (Sura 5:64)

Indeed, you will surely find that the most vehement of men in enmity to those who believe are the Jews and the polytheists. But you will also surely find that the closest of them in love to those who believe are those who say, "We are Christians." That is because there are among them priests and monks, and because they are not arrogant. (Sura 5:86)

An irony in the relationship between Islam and the land of Israel, which of course includes Jerusalem, is that the Qu'ran recognises the Jewish right to the land. The taking of the land is referred to in positive terms. Note the harmony with the Hebrew Scriptures:

And [remember] when Moses said to his people: "O my people, call in remembrance the favour of God unto you, when he produced proph-ets among you, made you kings, and gave to you what He had not given to any other among the peoples. O my people, enter the Holy Land which God has assigned unto you, and turn not back ignomin-iously, for then will ye be overthrown, to your own ruin." (Sura 5:20–21)

Even more striking, there is a passage that implies that in the last days when the people of Israel are relocated from the Diaspora to the land of Israel the Muslims should help:

To Moses We [Allah] gave nine clear signs. Ask the Israelites how he [Moses] first appeared amongst them. Pharaoh said to him: "Moses, I can see that you are bewitched." "You know full well," he [Moses] replied, "That none but the Lord of the heavens and the earth has revealed these visible signs. Pharaoh, you are doomed."

Pharaoh sought to scare them [the Israelites] out of the land [of Israel]: but We [Allah] drowned him [Pharaoh] together with all who were with him. Then We [Allah] said to the Israelites: "Dwell in this land [the Land of Israel]. When the promise of the hereafter [End of Days] comes to be fulfilled, We [Allah] shall assemble you [the Israelites] all together [in the Land of Israel]. We [Allah] have revealed the Qu'ran with the truth, and with the truth it has come down. We have sent you [Muhammad] forth only to proclaim good news and to give warning." (*Night Journey*, Sura 17:100–104)

And thereafter We [Allah] said to the Children of Israel: "Dwell securely in the Promised Land. And when the last warning will come to pass, we will gather you together in a mingled crowd." (Sura 17:104)

(Qu'ranic texts drawn from M. Marmaduke Pickthall *The Meaning of The Glorious Qu'ran* (Beirut, 1973); A Yusuf 'Ali, *The Holy Qu'ran – Text, Translation and Commentary* (Maryland, 1983); A. Maududi *The Holy Qu'ran – Text, Translation and Brief* (Lahore edition. Verses may vary between editions.)

Ibn Ishaq states:

. . .[that] at that time the Rabbis of the Jews began to manifest their hostility toward Muhammad. He claims that their motivation was that of jealousy, envy, and malice because Allah had conferred distinction upon the Arabs by choosing him as his messenger from amongst them. Some men from the Aws and Khazraj who had remained in their paganism joined them. Those who adopted Islam accepted it only to protect themselves from being killed, while remaining hypocrites in secret. They felt inclined toward the Jews because they belied the prophet, because they strove against Islam. The Rabbis of the Jews would question the Apostle of Allah and harass him. They brought to him abstruse questions in order to confuse the truth with falsehood. (Ibn Hisham, *al-Sira al Nahawiyya*, vol. 1 (Cairo, 1955)

Islamic Jewish stereotypes

The view of the Jewish opposition to the prophet in both the Qu'ran and the Sacred Biography is not centred upon their opposition, but rather on their defeat and humiliation (Sura 2:61). The expressions "humble", "humility" and "humiliation" (*dhull* or *dhilla*) are used widely in the Qu'ran (Sura 2:61) to describe the state of the Jews, as they are in Islamic poetry and folklore. The perpetual state of humiliation of the Jews is viewed by Qu'ranic authorities as the just ongoing punishment for their refusal to accept the prophet. Until the twentieth century they were regarded as a nonentity, caught between the two great powers of Islam and Christianity. When individual Jews reached positions of influence or power, particularly in Egypt, it was considered by some to be a religious duty to bring them down. The poll tax (*jizyah*) levied on the Dhimma was considered by the Qu'ranic commentator Mahmūd ibn Umar al-Zamakhsharī (1075–1144) to be a sign of their humiliation (Zamakhhsharī, *Al kashshāf*, II Cairo, 1353, Cairo edition, 1954, pp. 147). The one paying the *jizyah* was to be ritually humiliated in public whilst making the payment by being shaken or slapped as he appeared with bowed head and bent back. Other Islamic authorities speak against severe treatment in providing the humiliation (Abu 'Ubayd *Kitāb Al Amwā* (770–838), Cairo, 1954).

Under the Dhimma, Jews were not allowed to bear arms or to ride a horse. In a martial society such as Islam, those who are not militarily proficient are considered to be cowardly. The stereotype of humility was, therefore, accompanied by the stereotype of cowardice. A vivid example may be drawn from the latter years of the Ottoman Empire where, out of absolute contingency, Jews were admitted into military service. A humorous story was circulated that a number of patriotic Jews had formed a volunteer militia to defend the Turkish homeland. The militia was fully equipped and undertook training. On the completion of their preparations prior to their departure for the front lines, they requested a police escort in case they were attacked by bandits.

The same real-world view persists today, as illustrated by an example taken from current Palestinian Islam. Sheikh Muhammad Ibrahim Al-Madhi, of the PA, in a sermon preached broadcast live on PA TV, on 6 June 2000, from the Sheikh Ijlin Mosque in Gaza, called for Jihad education for children and for Jews and Christians to be given the status of Al-Dhimma [protected second-rate citizens] under Muslim rule. He declared that:

We welcome, as we did in the past, any Jew who wants to live in this land as a Dhimmi, just as the Jews have lived in our countries, as Dhimmis, and have earned appreciation, and some of them have even reached the positions of counsellor or minister here and there. We welcome the Jews to live as Dhimmis, but the rule in this land and in all the Muslim countries must be the rule of Allah. . . . Those from amongst the Jews and from amongst those who are not Jews who came to this land as plunderers, must return humiliated and disrespected to their countries.

On the other hand, those Jews who are local and who have lived with the Palestinian people and with the locals from amongst the Christians – there is nothing bad with their living [amongst us] in harmony and peace. This is the kind of peace we understand. The Arabs and Muslims must speak, because our choice is the Jihad for the sake of Allah. (MEMRI Special Dispatch No 240 PA, 11 July 2001)

It is erroneous to view the above as misplaced medievalism. Today, under Sharia law, those wishing to profess or promulgate any other faith are faced with the choice to desist or death. In Kashmir, women attempting to pursue modernism by not covering their faces are threatened with acid being thrown in their faces, and public mutilations for even petty crimes are common in the Islamic world.

In the Islamic foundation narratives, the Qu'ran, the Sacred Biography, the Commentaries and later religious writings, the Jew is presented, as he is in Christian narratives, as an evil malevolent force. Wretchedness and baseness are stamped upon them (Sura 2:61). Here, however, the similarity ends and a point of divergence arises. In Islamic thought, the Jew is not to be feared, but is regarded as impotent, defeated, disempowered and humiliated, without the power to exercise any evil. An exception is found in the writings of Ibn Ishaq, who states that from among the Jews of Banu Zurayq, there was one Labid b. Asam. It was he who cast a spell upon the Apostle of Allah (Muhammad) so that he was unable to have sexual relations with his wives (Ibn Hisham, *al-Sira al Nahawiyya*, vol. 1, Cairo, 1955).

The origins of the Jewish people in the area around Medina formally known as Yathrib are generally considered to predate the Arab presence. The dates and circumstances of their arrival are shrouded in mystery but, by the time of the birth of Muhammad in 571, there were considerable numbers of Jews in Arabia. The Jewish people were well integrated into the life and culture of the peninsula, spoke Arabic and had assimilated many of the values of desert society. They were organised into clans and tribes, as can be seen by reference to the poetic works of the pre-Islamic Jewish poet al-Samaw'al b Adiya (Eng. trans. A. J. Arberry, *Arabic Poetry: A Primer for Students*, Cambridge, 1965).

Holocaust denial is a regular motif in the Arab press, as well as admiration for Hitler. An article in the Egyptian government daily *Al-Akhbar* provides a good example:

> With regard to the fraud of the Holocaust... Many French studies have proven that this is no more than a fabrication, a lie, and a fraud!! That is, it is a "scenario", the plot of which was carefully tailored, using several faked photos completely unconnected to the truth. Yes, it is a film, no more and no less. Hitler himself, whom they accuse of Nazism, is in my eyes no more than a modest "pupil" in the world of murder and bloodshed. He is completely innocent of the charge of frying them in the hell of his false Holocaust!!
>
> The entire matter, as many French and British scientists and researchers have proven, is nothing more than a huge Israeli plot aimed at extorting the German government in particular and the European countries in general. But I, personally and in light of this imaginary tale, complain to Hitler, even saying to him from the bottom

of my heart, "If only you had done it, brother, if only it had really happened, so that the world could sigh in relief [without] their evil and sin."

The extermination of The Banu Qurayza

Mohammed's relationships with the Jewish tribes are well documented. There were three main tribes living in the Medina area. They were resistant to the message of the prophet. The steps taken by Muhammad were typical of the severity that would be a pattern to follow. The Banu Qainoqua had its assets seized and confiscated on the charge of conspiring with the Meccans against the prophet. The tribes were further warned to depart with all speed to Syria lest they be destroyed. The Banu Nadhir were driven from Medina and settled at the oasis of Khaybar, roughly 95 miles from Medina. In 629 they once again were faced with Mohammed's forces. Following around six weeks' hostilities they surrendered. Under the terms of the treaty they were allowed to remain at the oasis and follow an agricultural life with one half of the produce payable as tribute. The treaty with the Banu Nadhir became a standard for Islamic terms with unbelievers. The Banu Nadhir were expelled from Khaybar during the caliphate of Umar (634–44).

According to Ibn Hisham, as related to him by al-Zuhri, the angel Gabriel appeared to Muhammad during noonday prayers and asked him if he had put aside his arms, to which he replied in the affirmative. Gabriel replied, "The angels have not yet put aside their weapons, and I have just returned from seeking the enemy. Allah commands you, Mohammed, to march against the Banu Qurayza."

Muhammad summoned a muezzin to call out the people and command them that afternoon prayer should not be celebrated until the territory of the Banu Qurayza was taken. An army led by Ali marched to the fortifications where he reported he heard them speaking about Muhammad in a disrespectful manner, upon which he returned and reported the matter to him. The account records conversation between Muslim leaders and Kab b. Asad on behalf of those defending the walls, which probably is fictional. The Jews were offered stark choices. Either they followed Muhammad, or kill the women and children and then fight the army, or thirdly, as it was a Sabbath eve, it might be opportune to make a surprise attack against the army. In the event the Jews were overwhelmed and Muhammad commanded that every male that had attained puberty should be executed. The property of the Banu Qurayza along with the wives and remaining children were divided amongst the army of which Mohammad retained one fifth for himself. From amongst the women he took Rayhana b Amr b Khunafa as his personal possession who he reportedly offered to marry after she accepted Islam. She refused and died as his chattel. (Ibn Hisham, *al-Sira al-Nabawiyya*, vol. 2 Cairo, 1955) pp. 233–45.

Although living under the Dhimma, Islamic massacres of Jewish communities featured throughout the Islamic world. A few examples are Cairo 1012, Fez (Morocco) 1032, Marrakesh 1146, Baghdad 1333, Fez 1640, Basra 1776, Algiers 1801, Damascus (following a blood libel) 1840, Djerba 1864, Tunis 1869, Fez 1912, Constantine 1934, Damascus 1936, Baghdad 1941 and Tripoli 1945.

Blood libels reached new heights in the nineteenth century and, although the Damascus Affair, as it is known (1840), caught the attention of the international community, other blood libels, usually attended by outbreaks of violence, occurred in Aleppo (1810, 1850, 1875), Antioch (1862), Damascus (1840, 1848, 1890), Tripoli (1834), Beirut (1862, 1874), Dayar al-Qamar (1870), Jerusalem (1847), Cairo (1844, 1890, 1901, 1902), Alexandria (1870, 1882, 1901–1902), Port Said (1903, 1908), Mansura (1877), Damanhur (1871, 1873, 1877, 1892), Istanbul (1870, 1874), Büyüdere (1864), Kuzguncuk (1866), Eyub (1868), Edirne (1872), Ismir (1872, 1874), Urmia (1854), and Shiraz (1910). There was also an increased incidence within the Greek and Balkan states under Islam. The following points concerning Islamic blood libels should be considered:

- They invariably occurred where there was a Christian community.
- The libels generally originated within the said community.
- The libels were generally promulgated in Christian publications.
- The libels were supported, or even on occasion instigated by diplomats from Western [Christian] countries.

In Islamic lands, however, the Jewish communities under threat could usually call on the Ottoman authorities to intervene on their behalf. Following the Damascus Affair, and the establishment of the British consulates, appeals could be made for assistance.

The blood libel persists. The Israeli Foreign Ministry submitted a serious complaint to the United Nations against Abu Dhabi in November 2001 for broadcasting a TV programme of a skit in which Prime Minister Sharon is portrayed drinking Palestinian blood. An article timed to coincide with Purim appeared in the Saudi daily *Al-Riyadh* recycling the classic elements of the blood libel:

> For this holiday [Purim], the victim must be a mature adolescent who is, of course, a non-Jew – that is, a Christian or a Muslim. His blood is taken and dried into granules. The cleric blends these granules into the pastry dough; they can also be saved for the next holiday. . . the blood of Christian and Muslim children under the age of 10 must be used, and the cleric can mix the blood [into the dough] before or after dehydration.

The apparatus employed is described as a needle-studded barrel about the size of the human body, with extremely sharp needles set in it on all sides. The needles pierce the victim's body and the victim's blood drips from him very slowly:

> . . . the victim suffers dreadful torment that affords the Jewish vampires great delight as they carefully monitor every detail of the bloodshedding with pleasure and love that are difficult to comprehend. (*Al-Riyadh*, March 13, 2002, Dr. Umayma Ahmad Al-Jalahma of King Faysal University in Al-Dammam, tr. MEMRI)

Although there was a discernible shift towards modernisation in Turkey and some other parts of the Ottoman Empire in its latter days, the situation in Persia (Iran) remained reactionary towards the Jewish people. The main elements are described below:

Persia (Iran)

The Jews were obliged to live in a part of the town separated from the other inhabitants as they were considered unclean, and contact with them brought defilement. If they entered a street inhabited by Muslims they were pelted by boys and mobs with stones and dirt. Similar phenomena, or worse, may be observed today if a Jew accidentally enters an Islamic area in Israel. The uncleanness of the Jews was thought to wash off in the rain and contaminate the very ground.

They had no rights to carry on trade in stuff goods nor were they allowed to keep any open shop, even in their own quarter. Trade restrictions only allowed them to trade in spices and drugs, or carry on the trade of a jeweller. A Jew entering a shop was forbidden to inspect the goods and was required to stand at a respectful distance and enquire politely as to the price. If he should inadvertently touch the goods, he was obliged to take them at any price the seller chose to ask for them.

Jewish civil rights were virtually non-existent. If a Jew was recognised in the streets, he was subjected to the greatest insults. The passers-by spat in his face, and sometimes beat him unmercifully. Children reaching their teens would strike a Jewish person they encountered on the street, attempting to fell him with a single blow. If a Persian killed a Jew, and the family of the deceased produced two Muslims as witnesses to the fact, the murderer was fined 12 tumauns (600 piastres); but if two such witnesses were incapable of being produced, the crime remained unpunished. Jewish homes were vulnerable to attack for the purposes of theft and intimidation. If the individual sought to defend himself physically he put his life in danger either at the hand of the assailant or the judiciary. In civil disputes heard before the Achund [religious authority], if the plaintiff could produce two witnesses, the Jew was condemned to pay a heavy fine. Failure to pay resulted in public humiliation and punishment by being stripped to the waist, bound to a stake and receiving forty blows with a stick. If the sufferer uttered a sound, let alone a cry of pain, the preceding blows were not counted and the punishment recommenced. Similar punishments were the sentence for any behaviour considered insulting to Islam or its adherents. Children were not spared similar measures.

In addition to the poll tax, any Jews who had occasion to travel were required to pay a special tax in every inn and every caravanserai he entered (J. J. Benjamin, *Eight Years in Africa and Asia from 1846–1855*, Hanover, 1859, Ephraim Neimark, *Masa 'be-eretz ha Kedem, ed. a ya'ari*, Jerusalem, 1946). Lord Robert Curzon (1810–1873) described outbreaks of anti-Jewish violence in both Shiraz and Isfahan, largely instigated by the Muslim cleric Sheikh Agha Nejefi, which led to the use of the bastinado on one culprit guilty of murder, whilst the Zil-es-Sultan, in response to the attacks, imposed renewed archaic disabilities upon the Jewish populations (R. Curzon, *Persia and the Persian Question*, London, 1892).

Antisemitic literature of a general nature first made its appearance in the late nineteenth century but increased rapidly from the turn of the twentieth century with the importation of the protocols of the learned elders of Zion. The protocols remain a favourite tool of the Arab nations and are widely distributed.

CHAPTER TEN

THE BRITISH MANDATE

We too are in agreement with the cultural antisemites,
insofar as we believe that Germans of the Mosaic faith
are an undesirable, demoralising, phenomena.
Arthur James Balfour

The British Mandate was part of a system created by the League of Nations whereby, "peoples not yet able to stand by themselves", would be administered by "advanced nations". In the course of time, the said nations would transfer authority to the local population. The British Mandate of Palestine refers to the period 1920–1948, with its borders excluding Trans-Jordan from 1922 forward. The British conquered Palestine and the surrounding areas, and established a military administration known as Occupied Enemy Territory Administration (O.E.T.A.) which, despite the Balfour Declaration of November 1917, they continued to administer by way of the Ottoman Law. The outcome of the Paris Peace Conference (1919), and the San Remo Conference (1920) paved the way for the exercise of Mandated power. The San Remo Conference decreed that Britain was to be responsible for implementing the Balfour Declaration through negotiations with "an appropriate Jewish Agency . . . by facilitating Jewish immigration . . . and encouraging close settlement on the land". The terms were ratified in 1922.

The British Mandate was a time when institutionalised antisemitism played a disastrous role in the fortunes of the Jewish people. Ironically, Britain had been the home of some of the leading Philo-Semites: the Clapham Sect and George Eliot in particular held the view that Britain's God-appointed task was to return the Jewish people to their ancient homeland (c.f. *The Orient*, 27 June 1840, *Westminster Review*, LXV, Jan. 1856, *The Leader*, 12 Jan. 1856 *Fortnightly Review*, 15 May 1865). The background to the Balfour Declaration is well enough known not to be repeated here. However, the reasons behind it and Balfour's own perceptions are generally not well known. In a similar manner to Martin Niemoeller, a certain myth has arisen around the character of Arthur James Balfour (1848–1930) as may be noted in the superscription to the current chapter.

The name "Palestine" appears to have been brought into general Roman usage to designate the territories of the former Jewish principality of Judea following the defeat of the Bar Kochba revolt (135 CE) when the country was renamed Syria Palestina. In the early twentieth century the name "Palestine" came into general usage in the land by Christians and by westernised Muslims. **The name was not used officially, and had no precise territorial definition until it was adopted by the British to designate the area which they acquired by conquest at the end of the First World War which became known as the British Mandate.**

Zionist tensions

At the conclusion of the nineteenth century there were several tensions facing the Zionist movement. For the Eastern Jews the primary concern was to sustain their communities and their cultural identity in the face of the Russian and Polish nationalist oppression, pogroms, the unrest and agitation from revolutionary movements and the effects of collapsing empires. (See Salo Baron, "Early Approaches to Jewish Emancipation", *Diogenes*, Vol. XXIX, 1960.)

Western Jews, seeking to achieve emancipation, undertook vigorous assimilationist measures and attempted to remove any last vestiges of Judaism and to integrate themselves into what the Young Hegelians called the "civil society" (Udi Adiv, *Return* No. 5, December 1990, London). Assimilated Jews clung to the hope that the progressive forces at work in Western society would dissipate the antisemitic impulse, making way for a complete emancipation.

To Orthodox Jews, emancipation undermined the traditional Jewish way of life. They viewed the combined tensions of materialism, individualism, rationalism and secularism as threats to the essential foundation of Jewish life (Salo Baron, *ibid*).

Some of the leading Hassidic dynastic leaders were opposed to Zionism in general as they felt that it was in conflict with the understanding of their role in the Diaspora and the concordat with the host countries. Further, it precipitated the work of Messiah in returning the exiles to Israel.

Meanwhile, antisemites continued to hold the ancient animus in either its vulgar, sophisticated, or scientific form. In the eyes of the antisemite, Jews were, and would remain, Jews. A single, simple solution to the Jewish problem by placing them in a single geographical entity, whatever that meant in real terms, was not an unattractive proposition.

All of the above took place in an atmosphere of change. The Austro-Hungarian, Ottoman and Russian Empires were all in decline and the notion of the nation state was finding a firm footing in the Western world.

Prelude to the British Mandate

Although the Ottoman Empire was in decline, it was not in the general interests of the Western powers to move towards dissolution. If it had not been for Western influence, the Empire would have collapsed during the nineteenth century.

The mid- to late nineteenth century saw not only the rising of nationalist aspirations but also expansionist desires. Mohammed Ali, the governor of Egypt, saw a window of opportunity to establish an empire. The intervention of Western powers saw his dreams turn to dust. Nationalist movements arose in Greece, Bulgaria, Serbia, and Bosnia-Herzegovina, and if the Western powers had not worked to keep the Empire from collapsing, the political map might have changed. The concern of the Western powers to keep a bloc, even in reduced form, was expressed in an Interdepartmental Committee in 1915, even though Turkey had sided with Germany in the war. The reasons are generally considered to be that the Young Turks aspired to regain Egypt and additional territory in the Russian-held Balkans. It is important to state at this juncture that the Young Turks' aspirations were to create a multinational empire – not a homogeneous Turkey.

The question of the founding of Arab nationalism

It is considered that at this stage the notion of Arab nationalism moved from a conceptual to a dynamic framework. As the conflict unfolded, the Hashemites postured as nationalists to cover their desire to create an empire. When Sharif Husayn, ever the opportunist, realised that the Turks were losing the war, he revolted against the Ottomans. Although his action was at the least premature, the British felt constrained to support him.

The question of Arab nationalism is not straightforward. It would be misleading to call this an Arab revolt for two reasons. The revolt of Sharif Husayn and his followers was not in a pan-Arabist conceptual framework, with a programme of Arab liberation – it was simply to build an empire and establish a dynasty. As Ephraim Karsh points out, many Arabs viewed themselves as subjects of the Sultan and regarded any revolt against his authority as blasphemy. It is a telling point that, whereas the Jewish people in the Diaspora yearned for a national homeland, as illustrated by the Zionist Congress of 1897 held in Basle, attended by hundreds of representatives and in receipt of letters from 50,000 people, an Arab Congress held in Paris in 1913 attracted only thirteen people. The data illustrates in a clear way that Arab nationalism, in particular concerning Israel, is a modern, not a historical or moral phenomenon.

The Balfour Declaration and the San Remo Conference

As shown above, the Balfour Declaration, rather than being something new or innovative in its conception, merely recognised the long-standing moral, ethical and historical right of the Jewish people to a national homeland in their ancient land. The Balfour Declaration and the San Remo Agreement were not simply two twentieth-century documents. As is well known, various suggestions had been put to the Zionist organisation concerning a national homeland for the Jewish people, all of which were unacceptable. James Parkes suggested that there are five roots concerning the legitimacy of the claim of the Jewish people to the land that are embedded in the experience of the Jewish people:

- Judaism as the religion of the Community;
- The Messianic hope;
- Jewish history, and the long experience of dispersion and inequality;
- The continuity of Jewish life in Palestine;
- The unique relationship between the Jewry of Palestine and the whole Jewish people. (James Parkes, *Whose Land?*, London, 1970)

As Parkes correctly points out, Zionist propaganda has performed a disservice to itself on many occasions by disregarding the above considerations. They were not simply bridging a two-thousand-year hiatus. They were augmenting a population which had never ceased to exist in the country. A whole chain of successive Islamic rulers had recognised their right to exist there.

In 1939 the British Government implemented White Paper recommendations limiting Jewish immigration and restricting land sales to Jews. It was anticipated by Britain and the Arab leaders that this would lead to the establishment of a new Palestinian state with an Arab majority and a permanent Jewish minority.

Arab rioting, against both the British and the Jewish people, commenced with the establishment of the Mandate. Following the Arab rioting of May 1922, the Haycraft Commission of Inquiry was established. The Commission found the Arabs responsible for the violence, claiming that the cause could be traced to Arab anxiety at what they considered to be Britain's pro-Zionist commitments.

The Haycraft Commission led to the Churchill White Paper of 1922, which has since been regarded as a reneging upon the Balfour Declaration and the intents of the San Remo Conference. The paper stated that government did not wish to see Palestine become "as Jewish as England is English", but rather "the establishment of a centre in which Jewish people as a whole may take, on grounds of religion and race, an interest and a pride". The paper was in effect a product of Sir Herbert Samuel and, whereas the White Paper confirmed the right of Jewish immigration, it carried the condition that this should not exceed the economic absorptive capacity of the country. The notion of "absorptive capacity" was destined to be dealt with by alarming double standards (see chapter 11).

Various reports and papers by the British Government show that there seemed little or no will to honour the Balfour Declaration or the San Remo Conference and they always seemed anxious to placate the Arabs.

The Peel Commission was established in August 1936 to examine problems of Arab revolt. The findings published in July 1937, following over 130 testimonies from interested parties of all sides, recommended the partition of Palestine into a Jewish State comprising part of the coastal plain, the Jezreel valley and most of the Galilee. An Arab State would absorb most of the remaining territory along with Transjordan. A British-controlled corridor would operate between Jerusalem and Jaffa. A striking idea of the Peel Report was that of population transfer. Although King Abdullah was not opposed to the ideas contained within the Report, the Arabs rejected the plan and the Zionists were divided in their responses.

The Woodhead Commission established in 1938 was charged to investigate the recommendations of the Peel Commission. It would appear that the Commission was more a diplomatic attempt to appease the Arabs than a body with any teeth. The Commission's conclusion was that partition was not practical.

The next step was to call the sides together and hope to salvage some credibility in the eyes of the major powers. In London during February 1939, a conference was called at St James Palace by the Colonial Secretary, Ramsay MacDonald. The vain hope of the conference was to find a resolution to problems between the Arabs and the Jews in the light of the failure of the idea of partition, which was now viewed as a last resort. The futility of the conference was clearly illustrated by the intransigent attitude of the Arab delegation, representing the Arabs of the land and five other countries, who steadfastly refused to sit down with the Jewish, Zionist delegation led by Chaim Weizmann.

The differing agendas were obvious from the start. The Jewish representation were pressing for greater immigration, more settlements and the right to raise a defence force. The Arabs rejected all such notions and demanded the prohibition of Jewish immigration and land purchases by the Jews, rejecting the Balfour Declaration outright.

The St James Conference is considered by some to have been nothing more than a cynical piece of politicking by the British Government, who hoped to gain international approval for their plan not to pursue partition as they had realised that it was an unworkable option whilst appeasing the Arabs. MacDonald's final comment was that he desired to cease the Mandate and establish a state aligned to Britain.

As the war came to an end, once again the question of Mandated Palestine came to the fore. Clement Attlee, the British

Prime Minister, was keen to spread the burden and invited the USA to become involved in the new initiative. As the result of a Committee of Enquiry 1945–6, the USA proposed the immediate immigration of 100,000 Jewish persons, the cessation of restrictions on land transfer and that until the question of the Mandate be resolved, the land be considered to be under a Trust. Britain rejected the recommendations.

In April 1947, Britain referred the matter to the United Nations which appointed an eleven-member committee to investigate. It was known as The United Nations Special Committee on Palestine (UNSCOP). In the event, the committee could not agree and published two reports known as the majority and minority reports. The former recommended partition, creating two new states, one Jewish and the other Arab. On the question of Jerusalem, the recommendation was that it should become an international city. The matter was brought before the UN on 29 November 1947 and was adopted as resolution 181. Thirty-three countries supported the plan, thirteen opposed it, and ten abstained including Britain. Thus began the end of the British Mandate.

The reason for Britain earnestly desiring the end of the Mandate is still open to speculation. It is considered by some that it was part of the post-war de-colonialisation programme that included India. Others felt that the perpetual conflict and the growing empowerment of the Jewish people had resulted in armed groups such as the Irgun, led by Menachem Begin. The bombing of the King David Hotel in July 1946 and the hanging of two British sergeants in July 1947 in retaliation for the executions of members of their organisation were symptomatic. The Stern Gang were gaining notoriety and the Haganah were running an illegal immigration scheme. Out the annual budget of £24 million, around £8 million was spent on security.

The Mandate was one of Britain's least successful administrations and was stained by partiality and an underlying antisemitism, the consequences of which are still felt today.

CHAPTER ELEVEN

THE MUFTI OF JERUSALEM

Kill the Jews wherever you find them. This pleases God,
history and religion.
Haj Amin Husseini

Towards the sunset of the Ottoman Empire, Islam, which had been severely challenged by the advances of the West and to some extent in various Islamic countries, began to soften. Things were to change when there was a resurgence of Islam and the traditional line became re-focused. It is considered by some Islamic writers that things changed with the rise of Haj Amin Effendi el-Husseini, Mufti of Jerusalem, and President of the Supreme Muslim Council (1893–1974) who was the dominant figure in Palestine during the inter-war years. It is surprising that outside of Joseph B. Schechtman's work, little in-depth research has appeared in the English language. The Husseinis and the Nashashibis were the dominant families amongst the Arabs in the land. Although he had no valid claim to the distinction, el-Husseini constantly insisted that he was a direct descendant of the prophet, a claim considered to be spurious, particularly as those recognised as descendants of the prophet carried no titles to distinguish them from ordinary Muslims. The family were al-Aswads (Blacks), whose origins were in the Yemen via Egypt. They rose to prominence by a series of successful marriages, particularly to the family of Sheikh Abugosh, a wealthy landowner in the Jerusalem area. Another marriage was into the El Husseini clan who claimed direct descent from Caliph Ali and Fatima the only daughter of the prophet. From this point in time, contrary to custom, the groom adopted his wife's name and the family were known as el-Husseini.

Amin was born in 1893. At the age of 19 he studied Islamic philosophy at the Azhar University in Cairo, a course he never completed. After the first year he made a pilgrimage to Mecca and Medina enabling him to use the title "Haj", which in the Islamic world was considered better than a degree. After serving as an officer in the Turkish army during the First World War, he served as a clerk to the Arab advisor to the military government of Jerusalem. At this time, with his blue eyes and reddish hair, physically resembling the young Alec Guinness, he is described as being very much the "man about town". He was perfumed, bejewelled and overdressed, belying his fanatical nationalism. After a few minor civil service posts in Damascus he was discharged and returned to Jerusalem. He gained a teaching position in the Rashidieh School, a Muslim teachers' seminary. He busied himself addressing gatherings of Arab nationalists and writing for *Suriyah al-Janubiyah* (Southern Syria). From the beginning of 1920, Amin led anti-Jewish polemics that resulted in a pogrom against the Jews in Jerusalem on 4 April 1920. This included a large number of visiting pilgrims. The Arab police either joined in, or stood back and watched appreciatively. If it had not been for the intervention of Vladimir Jabotinsky's Jewish Self-Defence League, the toll of five Jewish dead, four Arab dead, 211 Jews and 21 Arabs wounded and two Jewish girls raped would have been much higher. The military eventually intervened and both Amin and Jabotinsky were brought before a military tribunal. Amin skipped bail and fled to trans-Jordan. Jabotinsky was sentenced to fifteen years' imprisonment. The following year on 7 July 1921 Sir Herbert Samuel (Jewish), became the first British High Commissioner for Palestine. He declared a full amnesty for all prisoners sentenced by military courts with the exception of Amin. Seven weeks later he changed his mind and extended the pardon to Amin.

Herbert Samuel was very proud of his impartiality and, when Kamal el-Husseini (Amin's half brother) the Mufti of Jerusalem died, Nashashibi, who was Mayor of Jerusalem, felt it right to appoint Amin as his successor. The position of Mufti was one of the most powerful in the country as he was the supreme legal advisor in questions of religious canon law, and his opinions were considered to be authoritative by judges, courts, legal representatives and private individuals. The Husseini family immediately launched a large-scale propaganda programme in glad support of this suggested nomination. The appointment was in the hands of an electoral college consisting of Ulama (scholars), Imams (readers of prayer), Hatibs (preachers of the major mosques of Jerusalem), Muslim members of the *Baladiah* (municipal council), and the *Idarah* (local government). The college had to select three appropriate candidates whose details were to be given to the *Wali* (provincial governor), who would then make a report on the candidates to the Sheikh al Islam in Istanbul, who in turn would make the final decision.

According to a letter in the *New York Times*, the six candidates included two members of the Religious Court, the Supervisor of the Omar Mosque and the Judge of Jerusalem (Prof. A. S. Yahuda, NY School of Social Research, *New York Times,* 2 Jan 1944). The electoral college opposed Amin's candidature on the grounds that he was not qualified, having failed to complete his course or take the examination. British officials, disregarding the issue, insisted that he be added to the list. In the event, he came fourth out of the six candidates. As such he should have been dropped. However, as all three candidates to be put forward were Nashashibi sponsored, Sir Herbert Samuel persuaded the candidate with the highest number of votes to stand down.

As Turkish rule was to all intents and purposes finished, the decision was not made by the Sheikh el-Islam but by Sir Ronald Storrs, who appointed Amin to the position of Mufti without further ado.

It is interesting to note that the Palestine Royal Commission

Report of 1937 includes a note that implies that, although unopposed, Amin's appointment was not confirmed by a letter or ever gazetted (*Palestine Royal Commission Report, Cmd* 5479, London, 1937). The same report comments that his even more powerful appointment at the hand of Samuel a few months later as leader of the Supreme Muslim Council with authority over all *Waqf* (religious endowments) and *Sharia* (Moslem courts) was similarly not by election but by a remnant of secondary electors left over from the former Turkish government. Effectively, the report says that he was "unelected". The report expresses concern that as the functions, status and precedence had not been determined, there were no legal limitations on his power.

In his new offices, the Mufti enjoyed control over considerable sums of money. *Waqf* funds amounted to £67,000 per year and the Orphans' Fund to £50,000 per year. From the time of his appointment to his flight to Lebanon in 1937, Amin was on many occasions pressed to publish the expenditures of these funds, but he persistently refused to do so. It emerges that extremely minimal amounts went to the designated beneficiaries of the funds and that the monies were expended on weapons and the recruitment of militant, violent nationalists. As an order for the publication of expenditure could only be made through a court of law, over which the Mufti had all jurisdiction, the possibilities of realising the publication were nil while he was in tenure. Some commentators have argued that his relative, Yasser Arafat, has practised the same disregard for designated funds for the relief of poverty and suffering by expending them on the apparatus of terrorism and an affluent lifestyle.

As the appointer and dismisser of clerics, Amin took the opportunity to fill the mosques with nationalist activists who could preach their message of hatred of the Jews and the British at every level and at every opportunity. The preachers to the *fallahin* (peasants) took every opportunity to instil into their congregants' minds that the murder of a Jew was a virtuous act. Within a few weeks of his appointment as Mufti, the second pogrom took place in Jaffa in the wake of a large-scale distribution of the *Protocols of the Learned Elders of Zion*. Widespread anti-Jewish violence peaked with the murder of thirteen Jews at the Jewish Immigration Centre. The rioting led to the declaration of martial law. Almost immediately, the Mufti's network busied itself circulating false rumours that the Jews were attacking peaceful Arabs. An immediate Arab response was attacks on Kfar Saba and Ain Hai. On 5 May a column numbering several thousand Arabs, armed and marching in military formation, attacked Petah Tikvah. The following day they turned their attentions to Hedera and Rehovot. A British investigation led by Sir Thomas Haycraft, whilst affirming that the Arabs were the aggressors, blamed Zionist aspirations for the whole affair, strengthening the Mufti's position. On 14 May, Samuel suspended future Jewish immigration, a measure that was to last until July when he recommended a more stringent policy. Meanwhile illegal Arab immigration continued apace.

Baron Plummer, who had been Governor of Malta, replaced Samuels in 1925. He took a harder line with the Mufti and, during his tenure until 1928, the Mufti did not take much direct action. In 1928 Sir John Chancellor replaced Plummer and the Mufti decided it was time to up the stakes. The opportunity arose in 1929 during Yom Kippur when the Jews set up a portable partition to divide men from women at the Kotel. Accounts vary as to whether the Mufti observed this immediately or whether British officials put the idea into his mind (Conor Cruise O'Brien, *The Siege*, London, 1988). Either way, he protested loudly that the Jews had violated the sanctity and practice of Islamic property. The Kotel is sacred to Jewish people as being a remnant of the last Temple of the Jewish nation. The revisionist Qu'ranic understanding posits that the Wall is where Muhammad tethered his miraculous horse Buraq, at the Haram esh Sharif, following his flight from Mecca to Jerusalem and before his ascent to heaven. The site is known as al-Buraq in honour of the horse. The Chief of Police, Douglas V. Duff, and his officers, on orders of the District

Commissioner Edward Keith-Roach, descended upon those at prayer and removed the screen.

The Mufti's first action was to send a memorandum to the British administration, implying that the erection of this partition was the first step of a Jewish action to mount an invasion of the Haram esh Sharif (Temple Mount). The initiative was accompanied by a vicious propaganda campaign in the press. The British dismissed his accusation out of hand. Not put off from exploiting the incident, he presented evidence of the Jewish plot to the Shaw Commission, accompanied by supposed pictorial evidence, which was little more than a picture of the Dome on the Rock with Hebrew lettering on the walls. The Shaw Commission dismissed his accusation in scathing terms (*Cmd, 3530*, 1930, p. 73).

In August 1929 the matter exploded. A Jewish boy kicked a ball into an Arab garden. In the fracas that followed the boy was stabbed to death. The scenes that followed resemble many incidents the reader will be familiar with on current television news. The Mufti preached an inflammatory sermon in the Mosque of Al-Aqsa, while Zionists demonstrated at the Wall. On 23 August large crowds of Arabs descended on Jerusalem armed with clubs and knives. Douglas Duff, being aware that he could not repulse them as there were insufficient numbers of Arab policemen, approached the Mufti. The Mufti met him with charm and protested innocently that this was a response to the recent events, which had made them afraid of the Jews. The Chief of Police departed reassured! Later that morning, the Mufti addressed a mass meeting and, although the British seemed to think that there was nothing included that could be called incitement, at the end of the meeting the crowd rushed into the street and attacked every Jew in sight, killing several.

The violence lasted for several days and spread through the country, the worst slaughter occurring at Hebron. By the time police and military reinforcements arrived, as the authorities had refused the request of the Zionist authorities to use the Jewish police or even arm a number of Jews, 133 Jews had been killed by Arabs, and 339 wounded. Whilst defending themselves near Tel-Aviv, the Jews launched a counter attack in which six Arabs were killed. The armed police reinforcements, in an attempt to bring an end to the matter, killed 110 Arabs and wounded 232. Although the British authorities were responsible for the Arab deaths, the Mufti and his supporters put the blame squarely on the Jews.

It is generally considered that the 1929 pogrom marked the end of any hopes for peaceful co-existence. The Arabs hardened their position and concluded that, as the Jews had been saved by the British, the simple answer to the fulfilment of their nationalist hope was to eliminate the British and, in the process, the Jews would also be eliminated. The Shaw Commission concluded that although the attacks on Jews were "unpremeditated", and that the Mufti was not responsible, he had not done enough to stop the riots. As a measure to prevent such future occurrences, the Jewish immigration schedule of 3,300 labour certificates was suspended.

The Mufti bided his time and for the next five years expended a great deal of energy and finance in disseminating propaganda and organising weapons and resources for the right moment. The moment he chose came in 1936 when on 19 April he inspired rumours that Jews were murdering Arabs. An assault against Jews in Jaffa led to three visiting Jews being murdered. At this time the Mufti had assumed power over the ten-member Higher Arab Committee. He publicly announced support for the general strike in Nablus that demanded the end to Jewish immigration. On 5 May he was approached to persuade the High Committee to speak out against illegal acts. The Mufti, feeling that the balance of power was within his grasp, ignored the request and within 72 hours had called a nationwide congress that unanimously adopted a motion for civil disobedience, initially by non-payment of taxes, due on the 15th of the month. The British authorities, instead of a rapid response, followed a "softly, softly" line which in the Arab mind was simply a sign of weakness. Thus encouraged, the Mufti "upped the ante" by encouraging attacks on Jewish settlements.

Sniping and banditry became the rule of the day on the roads. As a result of an emergency powers' enactment, action was undertaken by the authorities, which resulted in 60 arrests on 22 May, followed by the arrest of a few senior figures the following month. The Mufti, as usual, was left out of the proceedings. The British somehow held the opinion that he was assisting them (*New York Times*, 23 June 1936). A measure of the Mufti's guile and influence can be illustrated by the fact that 90 per cent of Arab terrorists detained and imprisoned belonged to the Nashashibi faction. The remaining 10 per cent belonged to various other factions.

From this point on, the Mufti felt emboldened to organise a real national army, which he financed by means of violence, banditry and blackmail. Unwilling donors were given short shrift (M. F. Watters, *Mufti Over the Middle East*, London, 1942, pp.14–15). The organisation was rewarded with fairly rapid results and by mid–1937 there were two defined groups, one operating in Samaria and one in the Galilee, as well as two terrorist groups, one covering the south, operating from Jerusalem and one covering the north, operating from Damascus. By the end of 1938, numbers had reached over 1,500 men under arms. The strike, which was beginning to lose its energy, was called off in October 1936 at the request of the sovereigns of Iraq, Yemen and Trans-Jordan, giving the Mufti an opportunity to advance the stakes even higher, as he perceived that the British would not be inclined to mount an action to clear the land of rebel units. One month after the general strike ended, a Royal Commission, known as the "Peel Commission" laid the responsibility for the disturbances firmly at the feet of the Mufti. The government seemed content to be inactive whilst the violence and murder were directed against Jews and Arabs.

Things were to take a dramatic turn on 26 September 1937 when the District Commissioner for the Galilee, L. Y. Andrews, and his police escort were murdered at Nazareth (GB, CO, *Palestine Report*, 1937, Colonial No 146). The response was brisk and on 30 September, under the provisions of a Defence Order in Council of

March that year that allowed the deportation of political detainees to any part of the British Empire, action was taken. An announcement was made that the Mufti was to be removed from office and the Arab Higher Committee was proscribed (*The Palestine Gazette*, Extraordinary, No 723, 30 September, 1937). The following day witnessed the arrest of six members of the committee, of whom five were deported to the Seychelles on October 21. The other detainee, Jamal el-Husseini, escaped to Syria. A further four members who were out of the country at the time were informed that they were prohibited from returning to Palestine indefinitely or until further notice.

The Mufti followed his usual practice of ignoring the Government's orders, in this instance his dismissal from the presidency of the Muslim Council and chairmanship of the *Waqf*. He contended that, as both posts were part of Islamic institutions, the British Government had no right of interference, let alone dismissal. In order to avoid anticipated deportation along with his Sudanese bodyguards, he sequestered himself in the Mosque area of the Temple Mount, believing that the British would not attempt to remove him from an Islamic holy place. He remained there until 15 October, when he boarded a ship to Ras el Nakoura on the Lebanese border, from where he subsequently proceeded to Damascus via Beirut (*New York Post*, 18 October 1937). Between late 1937 and 1938, whilst residing in Lebanon, he conducted terrorist activities in Palestine, where 297 Jews were killed and 427 wounded by his associates (*New Judaea*, London, May-June 1940). In a similar manner, Arab opponents of the Mufti came under increasing attack, his opponents being eliminated (*New York Times*, 15 October 1938).

The Mufti was an early admirer of Hitler's Nazi Germany and Mussolini's Fascist Italy. Arab students began to study in Germany and he began to receive financial assistance from both powers. As early as 31 July 1937 the Mufti had paid a visit to the German Consul in Jerusalem to enquire about the extent to which Nazi Germany would support the Arab cause against the Jews

(*Documents on German Foreign Policy, 1918–1945,* series D 1937–1945, vol. V; June 1937–March 1939, Washington DC, 1953, Doc. 566). In the event, the German Consul in Jerusalem was advised to discourage the Mufti from sending an agent to Berlin, as it was felt that such a movement might prejudice Anglo-German relations (Doc. 570 and 571). It appears, however, that his embassy was received, as Doctor Franz Reichert and Reinhard Heydrich assigned Carl Adolph Eichmann and Herbert Hagen, both of the SS, to make a study trip to Palestine. One of the objectives of the trip was to make contact with the Mufti (Response by Eichmann to a question by Judge Gideon Hausner, as reported in *The Jewish Chronicle*, 14 June 1961). They failed to meet the Mufti as the British only gave them 48-hour visas and the Mufti had by then departed. Leading up to the outbreak of hostilities, arms supplies, in particular rifles and portable machine guns, were supplied to the Mufti's rebels by Suhl and Erfuter Gewehrfabrik of Germany (*Marianne,* Autumn 1938). Every week the Arab journal *Falastin* and *Al Difa'a* published articles containing Nazi racial dogma and large portraits of leading Nazis.

The Mufti was not the only admirer of the Axis powers. Many Arab nations looked toward them as allies, protectors or even liberators. Hitler encouraged this view in a speech during 1938 at Nuremberg where he referred to "defenceless Arabs in Palestine". Arab Nazi organisations grew in the Arab world, with centres operating in Damascus, Aleppo and Beirut.

The Mufti arrived in Iraq via Lebanon in October 1939. Along with Rashid Ali al–Gaylīni, on the strength of assurances from the Axis powers, he mounted a successful *coup* in April 1941. From their new power base they attempted to carry out anti-British pro-German activities throughout the Arab nations, with particular attention directed towards Syria, which they viewed as a potential ally as it was under the rule of Vichy France. Their attempts met resistance from the "Society to Help Iraq", which later was to become the Ba'athist Party. German help was not forthcoming, and a small British-Jordanian force augmented by some auxiliary troops quickly overthrew the new government. The Mufti, Rashid Ali and a few supporters fled to Iran.

On 8 October 1941, after hiding in the Japanese and Italian Legations, the Mufti left for Italy, clean-shaven, hair dyed and in possession of an Italian service passport. He immediately contacted the Servizio Informazioni Militari, and within two weeks he had met Mussolini. Claiming to be the leader of a pan-Arabic organisation, he offered to join forces with the Axis against Britain. The condition for this alliance was that the Axis would recognise in principle "the unity, independence, and sovereignty of an Arab state of a Fascist nature, including Iraq, Syria, Palestine and Trans-Jordan" (D. Carpi, "The Mufti of Jerusalem", in *Studies in Zionism* 7, Spring 1983 – Carpi examined Italian documents in this leading study). The Mufti also expressed his willingness to discuss matters of particular interest in both religious and strategic matters, notably the holy places in the first instance and the Suez Canal in the second. The Mufti was given one million lire (40,000 USD) at that time to aid his efforts. According to the Mufti's own account of his meeting with Mussolini, the Duce expressed his antisemitism and anti-Zionism clearly, describing the Jews as British spies, agents and propagandists. He also supposedly expressed his view that the Jews had no historical, racial or other reason to make a claim to the land (B. Lewis, *Semites and Antisemites, an Inquiry into Conflict and Prejudice*, London, 1977). On 28 November 1941, the Mufti met Adolph Hitler who treated his offer cautiously. Whilst affirming his anti-Jewish position, he was for political reasons unable to "go public" in the way the Mufti desired.

His next tactic was to request that the Axis powers issue two statements, the first to Rashid Ali recognising the independence of Iraq. The second, which underlines the Mufti's greater ambitions, was to be addressed to both Rashid Ali and himself, declaring that the Axis powers would ensure the independence and unity of the Arab nations of the Fertile Crescent. The assurances were forthcoming in the first instance on 31 March and in the latter case on

28 April 1942. The assurances also contained support for the elimination of the National Jewish homeland in Palestine. Analysis of
the documents shows that the constructions were riddled with
escape clauses and that, in reality, the only concrete element was
the promise to liquidate the Jewish homeland (Lukasz Hirzowicz,
The Third Reich and the Arab East, London, 1966).

It was during his stay in Germany that he changed his title from
Mufti of Jerusalem to the more grandiose Grand Mufti of
Palestine. It is worth relating that previously there had not been
such a title as "Grand Mufti" (*Grossmufti*) and that Jerusalem was
now expanded to all Palestine. The new title clearly demonstrated
his ambitions.

Haj Amin's centre of operations was in a special office, firstly in
Berlin and subsequently in Obyin, known as the Büro des
Grossmufti with sub-Büros in other locations in Germany,
Switzerland, Italy, Egypt and Turkey. The Büro was responsible
for the broadcasting and dissemination of propaganda, espionage
and the recruitment of fifth columnists, the organisation of
Moslem military units in North Africa and Russia. He successfully organised a Bosnian SS Mountain Unit. The establishment
of Arab Legions and Brigades was another responsibility. He
organised an *Arabisches Freiheitskorps* in Germany and a German
Arab Legion in Greece. In Germany, the corps comprised Arab
students, prisoners and émigrés who wore the German uniform
with "Free Arabia" shoulder patches. The corps, instead of
fighting to free Arabia, were despatched to the Russian front,
where they were virtually eliminated. (*Daily Sketch*, 12 Feb. 1944).
Amin's various branch works were major providers of intelligence
on British troop movements. Below are some examples of his
radio broadcasts on the six so-called freedom networks (Berlin,
Zeissen, Bari, Rome, Tokyo and Athens).

... Today the Axis peoples are fighting for the liberation of the Arab
peoples. If England and America win the war, the Jews will dominate
the world. If, on the other hand, the victory is carried off by the Axis,

the Arab world will be freed. The Axis is befriending us. Fight for its victory. . . .

No one ever thought that 140,000,000 Americans would become tools in Jewish hands. . . How would the Americans dare to Judaise Palestine while the Arabs are still alive? . . . The wicked American intentions toward the Arabs are now clear, and there remain no doubts that they are endeavouring to establish a Jewish empire in the Arab world. More than 400,000,000 Arabs [?] oppose this criminal American movement. . . . Arabs! Rise as one and fight for your sacred rights. Kill the Jews wherever you find them. This pleases God, history, and religion. This saves your honour. God is with you. (Radio Berlin, 1 March 1944)

In June 1944, Dieter Wisliceny, Eichmann's deputy, told Dr. Rudolf Kastner, representative of the Budapest rescue council, that he was convinced that the Mufti had "played a role in the decision to exterminate the European Jews . . . repeatedly suggesting to various key players, and in particular, Hitler, Ribbentrop and Himmler, the extermination of European Jewry". Despite Eichmann's denials, Wisliceny contends that they were close friends, and that the Mufti had constantly incited him to accelerate the extermination measures. He was particularly opposed to any measure to exchange Hungarian Jews for fuel, trucks or munitions in the closing stages of the war. (IMT Nuremberg Affidavit of Engineer Endre Steiner, dated 5 May 1946, read over and approved for accuracy by Dieter Wisliceny. (See Maurice Pearlman, *Mufti of Jerusalem, the Story of Haj Amin el Husseni*, London, 1947.)

Simon Wiesenthal relates that Haj Amin visited not only Auschwitz but also Maidjanek. In both death camps he paid close attention to the efficiency of the crematoria, spoke to the leading personnel and was generous in his praise for those who were reported as particularly conscientious in their work. He was on friendly terms with such notorious practitioners of the "final solution" as Rudolph Hoess, the overlord of Auschwitz, Franz Ziereis of Mauthausen, Dr. Seidl of Theresienstadt, and Kramer, the butcher of Belsen (*Grossmufti – Grossagent der Achse*, Salzburg, 1947).

At the time of the Allied landing in Normandy on 6 June 1944, the Mufti was attached to the staff of Admiral Donitz. On 5 April 1945, a month before VE day, when the war was all but over, the following financial agreement was concluded between the Mufti and the Nazi authorities in readiness for the Mufti's return to the Middle East:

AGREEMENT

Between the Government of the Greater German Reich and the Grand Mufti of Palestine, Haj Amin el Husseini.
The Government, through its Foreign Office, concludes the following agreement with the Mufti:

1.   The Government puts at the disposal of the Mufti funds required to fight for liberation against the common enemy.
2.   An account is being opened for the Mufti with the Reich treasurer. The Mufti can draw against this until further notice 50,000 Reich marks a month. The account will be charged with expenses of the Foreign Office and other headquarters of the Reich organisation incurred for the Mufti or the movement conducted by him. These expenses – commencing April 1, 1945 – shall not exceed 12,000 Reich marks a month.

1.   The Mufti agrees to pay back the credit advanced. Amortisation and interest payments will be later agreed on.
2.   This is effective retroactively, as of April 1

Signed, in Berlin, April 4, 1945.

For the Foreign Office
                    S/Steengracht
                    (Gustav Adolph von Moyland Steengracht,
                    Secretary of State)

The Grand Mufti of Palestine
                    Amin el Husseini

(The full text appeared in an article by Drew Pearson in the *New York Daily Mirror*, 15 Sept 1947.)

As the war ground to an end, the Mufti, contrary to the general expectation that he would flee to Mecca, boarded a reserved aircraft on 7 May 1945 and departed for Berne, Switzerland. The Swiss authorities had made a pledge not to offer sanctuary to Axis war criminals and he was promptly handed over to the French border authorities. From the point of his arrest he was confined in a villa at Rambouillet, near Paris. The general expectation was that he would be handed over to the British. The activities in the House of Commons regarding moves for his extradition, to say the least, are somewhat confusing. Repeated questions from a number of sources over several months between 30 May 1945 and 5 April 1946 seem to illustrate a singular lack of enthusiasm about instituting any extradition procedure on the part of the Foreign Office, which was led by Ernest Bevin, a well-known pro-Arabist. Questions asked in the House generally were deflected by declaring "that it was a matter for the French". In January 1946, when the Mufti's role in the extermination of the Jewish people came to light following revelations of the IMT (International Military Tribunal), the question came into sharper relief. When asked by Mr Hoy, on 26 February, what was being done in regard to these revelations, Hector McNeil, the Under Secretary of State for Foreign Affairs, replied that "a special enquiry was being undertaken to obtain accurate records and there was nothing to add to previous statements as the one of 24th October where Bevin had stated that representations [to the French] had been made". On 5 April Mr Bevin told the House of Commons that the French had not so far agreed to the government request to hand over the Mufti (Parliamentary Debates, 5 April 1946).

Meanwhile, the Yugoslav Government showed more mettle than the British Government and, in July 1945, placed Haj Amin el-Husseni on the UN war criminals' list on a charge of raising SS Moslem divisions in Bosnia and Herzegovina which had been responsible for the murder of Serbs and Croats who opposed the

Nazis (*New York Post*, 19 July 1945). However, mysteriously, the charges were soon withdrawn, probably because of pressure from the Arab League.

The French responded with a front-page semi-official leader in *Le Monde* on 7 April which plainly stated that the Quai d'Orsay denied that Britain had made a request for extradition. A spokesman of the Quai d'Orsay informed the Paris correspondent of the *New York Post* that Mr Bevin had never legally applied for extradition, a straightforward procedure, to be enacted (*New York Post*, 9 April 9 1946). The French response caused a flurry of questions in the House, particularly by Labour MPs. Eventually, on 15th April Hector McNeil made the following somewhat surprising statement:

> The Mufti is not a war criminal in the technical sense of the term, since he is not an enemy national, and not a person who served in enemy forces.

McNeil then went on further to state that he was not a person who owed allegiance to the Crown, therefore he had not committed an offence against his own national law (*Parliamentary Debates*, 15 April 1946). The matter then seemed to subside with the exception of a challenge to the Government in the *Manchester Guardian* on April 29. Although the Government's false position on the matter prior to McNeil's statement was still being promulgated, the *New York Times* on 9 May reported that an authorised French source revealed that Bevin had merely requested that the French Foreign Office prevent the former Mufti from departing from the country and making his way to the Middle East. The French Foreign minister Georges Bidault had marked the request as being "acceptable". It seems that the Mufti was living a pleasant existence in a Paris suburb attended by a personal secretary, a chauffeur and two bodyguards whilst he conducted a wide-ranging correspondence with his associates.

The ambivalence to the situation illustrated by the Americans,

French and British may be best explained in continuity with other matters relating to war crimes in general, and to the Middle East contour specifically. Winston Churchill, who had in the early years been a vigorous advocate of prosecuting war criminals along with other international statesmen, felt that the matter of war crimes needed to be speedily concluded in order that the emerging Soviet threat could be dealt with. The unstable situation in the Middle East was also viewed as a potential theatre regarding Communist ambitions. This view was echoed in a speech made by Churchill in Zürich in October 1946 when he called for a speedy end to retribution and a turning from the horrors of the past to concentrate on the future (*Official Report*, House of Lords, 15 October 1946, Col 257, HMSO, London).

On 29 May 1946 the Mufti, clean-shaven and in European dress, boarded a TWA flight to Cairo, using a Syrian passport, an event only discovered by the French some ten days later. When in June his presence was revealed to the Arab world it met with rapturous acclaim. The Mufti played a role in the unrest and wars at the time of the partition of Palestine. On 1 October 1948, the Mufti of Jerusalem, Haj Amin Husseini, stood before the Palestine National Council in Gaza and declared the existence of an All-Palestine Government. In theory, this state already ruled Gaza and would soon control all of Palestine. Accordingly, it was born with a full complement of ministers to lofty proclamations of Palestine's free, democratic, and sovereign nature. But the whole thing was a sham. Gaza was run by the Egyptian Government, the ministers had nothing to oversee and the All-Palestine Government never expanded anywhere. Instead, this façade quickly withered away (Daniel Pipes, *Jerusalem Post*, 13 Sept. 2000). In 1949, when it was proposed to create Pakistan as the centre of the Moslem world, there was a move to make Amin Islam's leading figure, a hope he cherished as part of the Pan-Arabic-Pan-Islamic dream. Amin believed that becoming the leader of around 400 million Muslims, would be the key to the conquest of the Holy Land and the rise of Pan-Arabic identity with himself as the head. During the Karachi Conferences he continued to call for a co-ordinated Islamic move against Israel, Britain and America, warning that unless the Western Powers withdrew from the Middle East, World War Three was imminent (*Times Herald*, Washington DC, 3 March 1952). The initiative petered out by 1952 and Amin felt constrained to seek other roles of influence.

In conclusion, the Mufti represents the link connecting the two attempts to destroy the Jews, that of the Nazis and that of the Arabs. It is thus not surprising that the Mufti has a lofty place in the PLO's pantheon. Arafat saw the Mufti as an educator and leader, declaring in 1985 that he deemed it an honour to walk in his footsteps. Arafat stressed that the PLO continued to "march in the path carved out by the Mufti" ("Arie Stav, Arabs and Nazism" in *Outpost*, January 1996).

Arab population changes due to Jewish settlement

The Jewish development brought with it many benefits unheard of in the surrounding nations for the peasant and ordinary person. Schools, hospitals, primary health care, improved water supplies and sewerage were but a few innovations. Rapid advancements in agriculture were made by the chalutzim who introduced motorised pumps in place of the blinded camel or mule used to provide power. Stagnant pools were cleansed by planting eucalyptus trees, and primary irrigation introduced.

Statistics published in the *Palestine Royal Commission Report* (p.279) indicated a remarkable phenomenon. Palestine, traditionally a country of Arab emigration, became after the First World War, a country of Arab immigration (see table – appendix 5). A government inquiry into supposed land shortages caused by Jewish development came to the following conclusions:

> The shortage of land is, we consider, due **less to the amount of land acquired by Jews than to the increase in the Arab population**. (p.242)

We are also of the opinion that up till now **the Arab cultivator has benefited**, on the whole, both from the work of the British administration and **from the presence of Jews in the country**. Wages have gone up; the standard of living has improved; work on roads and buildings has been plentiful. In the Maritime Plains some Arabs have adopted improved methods of cultivation. (p.241)

Jewish development in both urban and rural areas drew large-scale immigration from Lebanon, Egypt, Syria and other neighbouring countries, as well as internal Arab movements where there was a large Jewish settlement. In the three major Jewish cities, the Arab populations shot up during this period, far beyond the rate of natural increase: Jerusalem – from 28,571 in 1922 to 56,400 (97 per cent); Jaffa – from 27,437 to 62,600 (134 per cent); Haifa – from 18,404 to 58,200 (216 per cent); Nazareth 89,600 in 1922 to some 151,000 in 1938 (by about 4.5 per cent per annum, compared with a natural increase rate of 2.5–3 per cent). In 1937 a government report concluded that as the rate of illegal immigration had been so high since the census of 1931, it was not possible to make an accurate estimate of the volume until another census was undertaken. (*Report by His Majesty's Government on Palestine and Trans-Jordan*, London, 1937 p. 221). In the event the census was not undertaken.

The League of Nations Mandate

When the League of Nations conferred the Mandate for Palestine upon Great Britain in 1922, it expressly stipulated that:

The Administration of Palestine . . . shall encourage, in co-operation with the Jewish Agency . . . close settlement by Jews on the land, including State lands and waste lands not acquired for public purposes (Article 6) . . . and that it shall introduce a land system appropriate to the needs of the country, having regard amongst other things to the desirability of promoting close settlement and intensive cultivation of the land (Article 11).

British policy, however, favoured strident extremist Arab opposition to the above provision of the Mandate. Of some 750,000 dunams of cultivable state lands, 350,000 (or nearly half) had been allotted by 1949 to Arabs and only 17,000 dunams to Jews, in clear violation of the terms of the Mandate. The Arab peasants who were supposed to be the beneficiaries of the distribution gained little or nothing. Prime examples are those concerning the Beisan (Beit Shan) lands and the Huleh Concession. The former case concerned 225,000 dunams of fertile land, eminently suited for development, that were supposed to be distributed in parcels of between 50 and 60 dunams per family, which was considered to be appropriate to support such a family over a year. In the event, six families, two of whom did not even live in the land but were domiciled in Syria, received 7,000 dunams, four families living in Egypt received 3,496 dunams, another family received 3,450 dunams and yet another received 1,350. The new large-scale landowners who had neither the expertise, equipment or desire to tend the land immediately involved themselves in selling off tracts of land at speculative prices. (*Palestine, Report on Immigration, Land Settlement and Development,* Sir John Hope-Simpson, Command Paper No. 3686, His Majesty's Stationery Office, 1930.)

The Hope-Simpson Report said that the British practice of ignoring the uncontrolled illegal Arab immigration from Egypt, Transjordan and Syria had the effect of displacing the prospective Jewish immigrants. He is quoted as saying, "They [Jews] paid high prices for the land, and in addition they paid to certain of the occupants of those lands a considerable amount of money which they were not legally bound to pay."

The case of Huleh area concerned 57,000 dunams of swampy but potentially high-grade land in the north. The land was placed in Arab hands firstly by the Turks and subsequently by the British on most attractive terms. The lands were to be drained and made ready for development. In the end, no work was undertaken and the lands were sold at a windfall profit to the Palestine Land Development Company. The Government insisted that a provi-

sion of the sale was that when the land had been drained and prepared, a certain amount was to be handed over to Arab tenant
farmers in the area without the benefit of compensation for the
work. The Palestine Royal Commission report of 1937 reveals that
in a four-year period Jewish settlers paid more than $20 million to
Arab landowners. Any Arab tenant farmers that were displaced by
the transactions under the provisions of the 1922 Protection of
Cultivators Ordinance were entitled to one year's notice. That the
treatment of the disposed was fair can be noted in that Jewish
organisations regularly paid more than the statutory minimum
compensation and that, of 688 instances recorded between 1920
and 1932, 526 remained in agriculture, of whom 400 found other
land. (*Palestine Royal Commission Report* 1937 Colonia No. 133,
p. 37.)

In 1931 Lewis French, the British Director of Development for
Palestine, charged with enquiring into the accusations that as a
result of Jewish land purchases there were a large number of landless, dispossessed Arab farmers in the land, conducted a survey of
landlessness. The Memoranda of the Government of Palestine
reported that 3,271 registrations to be recognised as "landless
Arabs" were processed. Of these, 2,607 were rejected outright as
they did not come within the category of being landless. A total of
664 cases were recognised, of whom 347 accepted the offer of
Government-sponsored resettlement. The remaining 317 declined
as they had either found new land or did not wish to be involved
in agriculture that involved irrigation, or did not want to leave
where they were due to climatic considerations (*Report on
Agricultural Development and Land Settlement in Palestine* by
Lewis French, December 1931, Supplementary Report, April
1932, and material submitted to the Palestine Royal Commission.
See also *Peel Report*, Chapter 9, para. 60).

The rate for land in Palestine in an arid area was around 1,000
USD per acre ($250 per dunam) in 1944, as opposed to fertile land
in the USA (i.e. Iowa) that sold at 100 USD per acre (US
Department of Agriculture Report, 1944).

Land ownership distribution on 14 May 1948

In May 1948 the State of Israel came into being but only in part of the area allotted by the original League of Nations Mandate. At this time the division of land ownership was:

- 8.6% owned by Jews;
- 3.3% by Israeli Arabs;
- 16.9% abandoned by Arabs who followed the call of the surrounding nations to get out of the way of the invading Arab armies who were *en route* to destroy the Jewish presence;
- 70% had been vested in the Mandatory Power, and accordingly reverted to the State of Israel as its legal heir (Government of Palestine, *Survey of Palestine*, p. 257).

The 70 per cent comprising this last area was mostly uninhabited, arid or semi-arid land. The Mandatory Government inherited the said territory from Turkey and it was known as "Crown" or "State" land. At no time under the British Mandate or the preceding régime had it ever been owned by Arab farmers. Revisionist accounts abound regarding land ownership, much of it expanding into the realms of pure fantasy. The case of Gilo, Jerusalem, offers a clear example.

It is a fallacy that Gilo was built on captured Arab lands. In fact, the majority of Gilo is built on land legally purchased by Jews prior to 1948. It is an "open secret" in Beit Jala that Jabra Hamis, former mayor of Beit Jala, sold Israelis the land on which parts of Gilo are built. In the 1948 war, Jewish lands in Gilo were captured and confiscated by the Jordanian Government. From 1948–67, Jewish landowners did not relinquish ownership of their land in Gilo, and when Israel recaptured the land in 1967, Gilo was built not because of war victories, but because of longstanding legal land purchases.

Beit Jala was a peaceful **Christian** town but the Tanzim, who are affiliated with Yasser Arafat, now control it. The Tanzim are not residents of Beit Jala, but have taken control of the town and, in a similar manner to PLO activates that led to their expulsion from Jordan and Lebanon, have taken complete control. In Beit Jala they have intimidated Christian residents into allowing their homes to be used as sites for armed offensives against Israelis. Earlier this year (2002), the tombstones in Beit Jala's Christian cemetery were destroyed. Damage to homes in Beit Jala by IDF forces are the result of defensive, not aggressive actions. **Outsiders will invariably view the amount of retaliation used in a subjective manner.**

The Palestinian refugee problem

The Palestinian refugees must rate as some of the most unfortunate people in the modern world. Since the beginning of the problem with the declaration of the UN Partition Resolution on 29 November 1947, they have moved into a second generation who have a fabricated revised history. The day following the resolution, rioting and attacks were launched upon Jewish communities by Arabs, not only from within the land but from supplementary guerrilla forces from the surrounding nations. A few weeks later on 25 January of the following year, the auxiliaries, militias and rioters were formed into a formal organisation known as the "Army of Liberation" under the command of the Syrian, Fawzi el Kawkji. Attacks were launched against Jewish communities wherever they were to be found, and the Jewish community in Jerusalem found itself under siege and cut off from the outside world. The Jewish community of the Old City was dispossessed when the Jordanian Arab Legion annexed the Old City under the command of "Pasha" Glubb, (Sir John Glubb, the British-born commander of the Legion). There was no major evacuation from Jewish settlements with the exception of four settlements that fell to Arab troops in the Etzion region. The Arab response was altogether different. The Arab population in 1947 was around 1.2 million. The more affluent of them left (30,000), often going to stay with relatives in the surrounding lands, as they believed it would be a short-lived action and they soon would be able to return to their homes. Another 200,000 left their homes due to the insistence of the Arab leaders that they would be in the way as the victorious army carved a swathe of destruction against the Jewish communities, notably Jaffa and Haifa. Still others, some 300,000, left as this action spread throughout the land and affected the areas they lived in. The totals are a matter for debate, but the best figure is probably 530,000. The Palestine Arab High Commission put the number at 300,000 after the second phase.

CHAPTER TWELVE

ANTI-ISRAELISM

*Today's brand of anti-Israelism risks becoming a new
socialism of fools – blaming the Jewish state for the
Islamic world's troubles, rather than the vast, structural
malaise afflicting that region.*
Jonathan Freedland, *The Guardian*, Wednesday 17
October, 2001

It was once put to the writer, "Is the Palestinian claim to Israel
about the land, or is it essentially over Jerusalem?" The answer is
not either or, but, in a sense, both. The claim is political on the one
hand and religio-political on the other.

Jerusalem is indeed a cup of reeling to the nations (Zechariah
12:7). The Palestinians claim that Al-Quds is their rightful capital;
the Israelis claim it as their eternal capital; the Vatican claims it
should be an international city; Muslims claim it is one of their
three holy cities. Some nations see nothing wrong with it being
divided; others remain indifferent.

The Jewish claim to Jerusalem

In traditional Jewish thought, Jerusalem, and the Temple Mount
in particular, was considered to be directly beneath the throne of
God (Rabbi D. Rosen. See Psalm 9:11; Psalm 20:1–3). The
esteemed scholar Maimonides declared that Jerusalem is
sanctified by the emanation of sanctity from the divine presence.

213

Maimonides further stated that Jerusalem is eternal, despite military conquests, as the Presence can never be banished or destroyed. Jerusalem in the medieval period was considered to be the centre of the world, as contemporary maps illustrate. The city is deeply entrenched in Jewish thought as is shown in the conclusion of every Yom Kippur fast and every Passover Seder by the recitation of the words, "Next Year in Jerusalem!" The Temple Mount is the site of biblical Mount Moriah where Abraham took his son Isaac to become a sacrifice in obedience to the Lord (Genesis 22:2f.), referred to as the *akedah*. Abraham was offering not only his son but also the promises of God and his entire future. Jerusalem is known as the city of life after this incident.

The liturgy for the bar Mitzvah contains prayers that "God may have mercy upon Zion, for it is the hope of our life", that "he may save her who is broken in spirit speedily even in our days", and that he would "gladden us, O Lord our God, with Elijah thy servant, and with the Kingdom of the House of David thy anointed. Soon may he come and rejoice our hearts. Suffer not a stranger to neither sit upon his throne nor let others inherit his glory." *The Talmud* reflects the centrality of the land and of Jerusalem in particular:

God said to Moses, "The Land is dear to me and Israel is dear to me. I will bring Israel who is dear to me to the Land that is dear to me."

Whosoever walks four cubits in Palestine is assured of the world to come.

It is better to dwell in a Palestine desert than to live in a land of plenty abroad.

To live in the land of Israel outweighs all the commands of the Torah.

The air of Palestine makes men wise.

Even the chatter of Palestine is worthy of study.

Palestine is the microcosm of the world.

Rabbi Abah used to kiss the rocks of Palestine.

Rabbi Chazah used to roll in the dust of Palestine.

Biblically, the most important texts refer to Jerusalem as the place that the Lord chose for his presence to rest (Deuteronomy 12:5–7, 11–14; 16:2; 26:2 cf. Psalm 48:3, Psalm 74:7). The concept of the resting place had a high profile in Jewish thought as the Lord's Presence had been with Israel throughout their desert wanderings. As the people of Israel became settled in the land it was important that the Lord's Presence found a place to rest. In the reign of King David the ark was brought there and initially kept in a tent until Solomon built the Temple. The Psalms known as the "Songs of Ascents" (Psalm 120–134) are pilgrim songs, probably sung by worshippers as they followed the Ark of the Covenant during religious festivals in the city. Sacrificial Psalms, such as Psalm 30, used at the dedication of the Temple, are examples of liturgical usage that centre on the Temple.

Jerusalem was the centre of worship because:

- the Temple was situated there and the priests and Levites dwelled there (1 Chronicles 9:34), including the high priest (John 18:15);
- the prescribed annual Feasts were held there (Ezekiel 36:38 with Deuteronomy 16:16 and Psalm 122:3–5);
- the prayers of the Israelites were directed there (1 Kings 8:38, Daniel 6:10);
- oaths were taken in its name (Matt 5:35).

Other titles accorded to Jerusalem include:

- the City of the Great King (Psalm 48:2);
- the Joy of the Whole Earth (Lamentations 2:15);
- the City of Truth (Zechariah 8:3);
- the Holy City (Nehemiah 11:1, 8);
- the Holy Mountain (Daniel 9:16, 20);
- the Throne of the Lord (Jeremiah 3:17);
- beloved (Psalm 122:6, 137:1–7);
- the location where the Messiah will return (Zechariah 14:4).

Jerusalem was the capital city of the Jewish people from the time of King David until its destruction by the Romans in 70 CE.

Following its destruction, Jerusalem remained the spiritual centre of the Jewish people with the exception of the schismatic temples of Elephantine (Yeb – Post-Exilic Period) and Leontopolis (IT Period). There has never been any other central place of worship (see F. Wright, *Two Schismatic Temples*, PARDES Occasional Paper 1, 1998).

There has been a continuous Jewish presence in and around the city, with the exception of a short period immediately after the Roman destruction and a few years during the time of the Crusades.

During the rule of the Ottoman Turks, the Jews were given certain powers of protection in the city. The British opened a vice-consulate in the city in 1839. The Consul was mandated to extend protection to all Jews who were subjects of any European Power. In 1845 there were 7,000 Jews, 5,000 Muslims and 3,400 Christians. In 1872 the Jewish population of Jerusalem was 10,600 Jews, 5,300 Christians and 5,000 Muslims.

In May 1948 there were 100,000 Jews in Jerusalem, out of the total population of 165,000. In May of that year the Jordanian Arab Legion invaded large areas of the UN proposed Arab-Palestinian State and parts of the intended Jewish State. The Legion entered Jerusalem and the Jewish community of the Old City surrendered. As a result, all Jews were expelled from East Jerusalem and the Old City. The Jordanian invasion was in conflict with UN proposals. The ancient synagogues and buildings were intentionally desecrated and destroyed. The years 1999–2000 witnessed the large-scale removal and destruction of Jewish archaeological artefacts from the Temple Mount which is under the Waqf jurisdiction of Jordan (lectures by Dan Bahat, Archaeologist of Jerusalem).

The Palestinian claim to Jerusalem

One is immediately faced with a crucial question. Is the Palestinian claim to Jerusalem co-terminus with the overall Islamic claim to Jerusalem as a Holy and, therefore, exclusive city. The immediate problem is to determine what is meant by "the history of Palestine". As Moshe Sharon points out, it is extremely difficult, if not completely impossible, to talk about a political history of Palestine after the destruction of the Jewish State in 70 CE and the suppression of the Bar Kochba revolt in AD 135. One may, however, construct a history of the Jews in Palestine until the eve of the Arab conquest (M. Avi-Jonah, *B'yme Romi u-Byzantion*).

Following the defeat of the revolt, the geographical entity became a minor, unimportant province within the Roman Empire. Following the Roman Empire, the land was successively under the rule of the Persians (614–629), the Umayyad Caliphate until the middle of the eighth century, the Abbasid Caliphate until the middle of the ninth century, the Egyptian Tulumid and Ikhshids until the second half of the tenth century, and the Fatimid Caliphate until the end of the eleventh century (although during the time of the Fatimids prior to the Crusaders taking Jerusalem in 1099, the Seljuq Turks had conquered large parts of the land). Up to 1187 the land was under the control of the Latin Kingdoms of the Crusaders until their defeat by Saladin, a Kurd (Kurds were the Medes of the Old Testament). The political seat of the Islamic rule was either Damascus or Cairo, until the middle of the thirteenth century. For the next 266 years the Mamelukes governed from Egypt.

The Ottoman Empire took power at the beginning of the sixteenth century and until the fall of the Empire in the early part of the twentieth century, the land was ruled from Istanbul via the Governor of Syria in Damascus. The land was governed as several sub-districts. It is of note that Palestine cannot possibly have had any importance or national aspirations over a period of thirteen hundred years as it is hardly ever mentioned in any Arab sources outside of scanty information contained in travel literature. The first historical work where it is mentioned appears at the close of the fifteenth century.

The effects of Islamic rule and the lack of importance may be illustrated further in the wasting of the land. Following Roman rule the land had largely been left to fall into disrepair but with the conversion of Constantine (306–367) in the early fourth century and the visit by his mother, Helena, the city of Jerusalem took on new significance. Following the building of Constantinople, Palestine was strengthened in administration, and fortifications were erected against the persistent banditry from nomadic groups that had become endemic. As a result of the pilgrim trade, the sedentary population grew and a thriving commercial and agricultural industry developed. Byzantine sources show that during the period prior to the Islamic incursion, Palestine reached its highest level of recorded prosperity and that the population peaked at between 3.5 and 4 million people. When the Islamic invaders arrived in 633 they inherited a prosperous, thriving, verdant country. The Ottoman census of the mid–sixteenth century showed an entirely different picture of 300,000 people living in a generally decayed, destroyed and abandoned land.

The process can briefly be described in the following manner. As a geographical entity of little importance, defence and internal security was given a low profile and the lands became subject to banditry by nomads. Cultivated land gave way to desertification as the sedentary populace departed. Military defences and fortifications were built in Egypt and Syria, and Palestine became something of a no man's land bounded by the sea on the western aspect. One should note that the Arabs had a deep-seated fear and loathing of the sea and had no desire to develop a naval defence force. The sea is referred to in Arab tradition as Hell, the pit, or a fire. Rather, they took an action similar to a scorched-earth policy and demolished coastal fortifications as a preventative measure against potential invaders establishing a land base prior to an attack either to the north or the south.

The only city established throughout Islamic rule was Ramlah, which was not a fortress, or defence but simply a commercial centre midway between trade routes. It served almost by default as the administrative capital of Palestine.

Throughout the thousand years, Palestine had not been the focus of theological importance or mercantile interest. Neither had it been the focus of expansionist or colonial aspirations. The Islamic interests were simply expedient. The Umayyad dynasty ruling in Damascus was faced with increasing opposition centred in the holy cities of Arabia and Iraq. The rulers in Damascus, therefore, needed a holy site within their immediate domain. It is important to emphasise that at this time the holy sites in the Holy Land were all considered to be either Christian or Jewish. The holy sites of Islam remained as they do this day, Mecca and Medina. Therefore it became necessary to develop a revisionist theory of the sanctity of holy site(s) in Palestine, particularly as there is no evidence that Muhammad ever visited Palestine, let alone accorded Jerusalem any real significance. Neither has Jerusalem been considered to be a place of *Haj* (pilgrimage), only a place of *ziara* (visit). The end was achieved by falsification, invention and supposition. The obvious first steps were to use traditions concerning Abraham and Ishmael.

The key text in the Qu'ran used to sanctify Jerusalem is contained in "Night Journey" (Qu'ran, Sura 17) concerning Mohammed's night journey from the "nearer" to the "further mosque". The Sura is also known as "al-Mi'raj", the Ascension of the Prophet Muhammad to heaven. In some editions of the Qu'ran the chapter is intriguingly entitled "The Children of Israel". The Ascension began at the Rock, usually identified by Muslim scholars as the foundation stone of the Jewish Temple. The Sura relates that, mounted on his magical horse Buraq, with a woman's head and a peacock's tail, he flew to the "further mosque", al-Aqsa. Upon arriving on the Western Wall of the Temple Mount (an existing part of the Herodian structure) he was attended by Gabriel who stood on the rock of sacrifice, also known as Abraham's Rock, where Abraham, Moses and Jesus, along with other ancient prophets, were gathered. After praying with this august gathering he climbed a ladder of light passing through the seven heavens into the very presence of Allah, who taught him about prayer. Within the first five centuries there was no definite site for al-Aqsa and it was suggested that it might even be in heaven (i.e. Taberi). In the early medieval period it was considered by some commentators to be an allegorical or apocalyptic motif. It is important to note that **the time of al-Mi'raj was when Jerusalem was under the rule of the Byzantines, prior to the Islamic expansion**.

The Qu'ran recognises the centrality of Jerusalem for Jewish people in the same way that Mecca is for Muslims.

The commentary of Qadn Baydawn reiterates the point:

> Verily, in their prayers Jews orientate themselves toward the Rock (sakhrah), while Christians orientate themselves eastwards...(M. Shaykh Zadeh Hashiyaah 'ali Tafsir al-Qadn al-Baydawn, Istanbul, 1979, vol. 1, p. 456).

We read:

> ... They would not follow thy direction of [Muslim] prayer (qiblah), nor art thou to follow their [Jewish] direction of prayer; nor indeed will they follow each other's direction of prayer (Sura 2:145).

The Caliphate came to the Holy Land in 637 and besieged Jerusalem for around four months. Fearing a repeat of the bloody massacre at the hands of the Persians less than twenty-five years previously, the Patriarch, Sophronius, pleaded for terms of surrender directly to the Caliph, Omar, requesting that he come to Jerusalem to accept the surrender personally. In the event Omar accepted, and came to the city by camel dressed as a poor man. He accepted the surrender and dealt generously with Sophronius whom he met on the Mount of Olives. The Patriarch requested that under the new rule Jews should be banned from the Holy City.

The Caliph agreed to the request but it appears he did not act upon it. He allowed the Christians to remain in the city and retain the holy sites with complete freedom of religious practice. The taxes and finances that had previously been paid to the Byzantines were now to be paid to the Caliphate. Once the surrender terms had been sealed, Omar proceeded to visit the Temple Mount to see the site of Mohammed's miraculous visit. The caliph was disgusted to see that the site was nothing more than a garbage heap. This may have been a deliberate action on behalf of Christians in the city to express contempt for the Jews.

The Dome of the Rock, which is basically a shrine, not a mosque, housing the sacred rock, was built during the reign of Caliph Abd al-Malik (685–705) ruling from Damascus at a time of rival caliphates. The edifice was built, according to legend, to outshine any religious structure in the area and attract pilgrims away from Medina and Mecca, which were under the rule of his rivals. Al-Walid, the son of Abd al-Malik, embarked upon a programme of reconstructing and improving the al-Aqsa mosque, using the columns generally thought to have been taken from the Church of St Mary that was constructed during the reign of the Emperor Justinian. A feature of the Dome is the band of friezes running around the walls that contain anti-Christian sayings.

The Arabic name for Jerusalem is al Quds, deriving from the root q-d-s, meaning "holiness". It is a shortened form of Bayt al-maqdis, "the Sanctified House". The name originally referred only to the Temple Mount, and was afterward extended to the city as a whole. This extension of meaning became common among Arabs from the tenth century CE onwards, some three hundred years after Islam's inception.

As rivalries and competing factions sought to gain power in the Islamic world in the mid-eighth century, the defences of Jerusalem were once again levelled (744–46), this time by Marwan II. The condition of the city deteriorated. An Islamic backlash to Christian developments broke out in 935 when a mosque was erected within the environs of the Church of the Holy Sepulchre, generally considered to be the most holy of the Christian sites. As the tenth century reached its end, Muslim antipathy towards Christians and Jews increased, the Holy Sepulchre being put to the torch by Muslim extremists. The Patriarch lost his life in the inferno and an urgent request was sent to the Byzantines for help. It was not forthcoming because of the death of the Emperor.

Worse was to follow. Caliph al-Hakim Abu Ali al-Mansur (996–1021) of the Fatimid dynasty ruled from Cairo and was known as a cruel and eccentric man whose sanity was in question. In the period previous to the reign of al-Hakim, Christian pilgrims had been tolerated in the Holy Land, some of the local inhabitants developing a thriving trade from them. In the early eleventh century, pilgrimages to the Holy Land attracted increasing numbers. In 1009 al-Hakim suffered increasing insanity. He forbade women to leave their houses and, to enhance this legislation, he imposed penalties upon those involved in the finishing of the production of women's shoes. Further measures included the forbidding of intoxicants, the prohibition of banquets and chess. His mental state drove him to destroy the Church of the Holy Sepulchre and launch a general persecution of both Christians and Jews. He gave orders that Christians and Jews should distinguish themselves by wearing distinctive coloured sashes (*zunnar*). Al-Maqrizi, a fifteenth-century scholar, described Al-Hakim's behaviour:

> The Christians were ordered to dress in black and to hang [large] wooden crosses from their necks. Churches were destroyed and their contents pillaged as also were their tenement houses . . . in the year 1013 the Jews were compelled to wear bells around their necks when they entered the public baths.

From the time the Turks took Jerusalem from the Crusaders for the last time there was a long period of relative inactivity. During this time, known as the Mameluke Era, Christian pilgrimages began to increase, local inhabitants making a living from the pilgrim trade. It was also a time of increased activity in the building of mosques and the development of Islamic culture. In the mid-fourteenth century a more tolerant attitude to the Jews developed and the Jewish community began to re-establish itself in the city. Under the Ottoman Turks, the Jews living in Jerusalem were given protection for the first time. It was reported that the Church of the Holy Sepulchre had a multitude of priests from different sects who did little other than engage in acts of violence against each other. The situation was so bad that, during the Easter period, Turkish guards had to be posted to keep the peace. The British established a Vice-Consulate in the city in 1839 with the express order that he was to extend his powers of protection to all Jews of European origin. From this point, encouraged by the new facility of protection, the Jewish population began to increase, and by 1845 the Jews comprised the largest community in the city, numbering 7,000 persons as opposed to around 5,000 Muslims and 3,400 Christians. Twenty-seven years later in 1872, as a result of the first *aliyah* (wave of return), the Jews living in Jerusalem numbered 10,600, outnumbering the combined Muslim and Christian communities. At the time of independence in 1948, the Jewish population numbered 100,000 out of 165,000.

On 9 December 1917, some five weeks after the historic Balfour Declaration, British forces took Jerusalem from the Turks. After a shambolic attempt at surrender by the Turks, General Allenby made his official entry into Jerusalem two days later. He chose to enter the city through the Jaffa Gate on foot in a respectful manner, as opposed to the Kaiser who some nineteen years earlier had entered the city astride a beautiful white horse with all personal splendour to mark the German–Turkish alliance.

The current Islamic theology of martyrdom

The concept of the Shahid (martyr) in modern Islamic thought, particularly that of the suicide bomber, a common event in Israel, shocked the world on 11 September 2001, with the joint attacks on the World Trade Center, the Pentagon and the abortive "fourth aircraft". The desire to become a Shahid even amongst children in Palestine and the Middle East received heightened publicity in the summer of 2001 with several articles appearing in the British press. The subject was also featured on BBC's *Panorama*. It has almost become a common sight to see the families of suicide bombers rejoicing in the death of their son and his victims. A TV news interview showed a mother declaring her son's death in an attack against the Israelis as "the happiest day of my life". Following the attacks, two distinct views were promulgated – one that Islam is a religion of peace and co-existence, which a simple read through the Qu'ran will bring into question:

> Let those fight in the way of Allah who sell the life of this world for the other. Whoso fighteth in the way of Allah, be he slain or be he victorious, on him We shall bestow a vast reward. (Sura 4:74)

> Those who believe do battle for the cause of Allah; and those who disbelieve do battle for the cause of idols. So fight the minions of the devil. Lo! the devil's strategy is ever weak. (Sura 4:76)

> The punishment of those who wage war against Allah and His apostle and strive to make mischief in the land is only this, that they should be murdered or crucified or their hands and their feet should be cut off on opposite sides or they should be imprisoned; this shall be as a disgrace for them in this world, and in the hereafter they shall have a grievous chastisement. (Sura 5:33)

The second view is that Islam by its nature is aggressive and seeks the submission of all the nations.

The real question of the differences between orthodoxy and orthopraxis was not highlighted. In a similar way to, say, Mormonism, where the Bible is only a part of the overall picture, similarly, the Q'uran is only part of the picture. There is also a difference between the views of commentators and jurists. In addition to the Qu'ran, the Hadith or sayings of the prophet, and the writings of the authorities play a prominent part. It is here that the more aggressive programmes may be found, along with the writings from the schism between the Sunnites and the Shi'ites.

A recent poll conducted by the Palestinian Centre for Public Opinion found that seventy-six percent of Palestinian respondents approved of suicide bombings that targeted Israelis. And Palestinian religious leaders have for some time been praising the virtues of suicide in the service of their cause. The attacks have also won support in the wider Arab world (Jeffrey Goldberg, The Martyr Strategy, *New Yorker*, 9th July 2001). Following the suicide bombing on 9 August in Jerusalem, Fahmi Huweidi described his feeling of happiness in an Egyptian Government sponsored daily newspaper:

> It would not be an exaggeration to say that the heroic and Fidaai [martyrdom] warriors are the only light in dark skies, they are the sole remaining sign of life in the Arab nation.... If we can still lift our heads with pride, it is only because we still have as models those young men who chose to die so that our lives would have hope and meaning and so that our long night will see a dawn with a message of hope (*Al-Ahram*, 14 August, 2001).

In May, Amru Nasif in the Egyptian newspaper *Al-Usbu* (disseminated by the Middle East Media Research Institute, in Washington, DC) called for mass suicide attacks against Israelis, and volunteered himself for a suicide mission. Mathematical calculations, he declared "illustrated [that] two hundred and fifty Palestinians have signed up for martyrdom operations, and it is not impossible to raise this number to a thousand throughout the Arab world. The average harvest of each act of martyrdom is ten dead and fifty wounded. Thus a thousand acts of martyrdom would leave the Zionists with at least ten thousand dead and fifty thousand wounded." Nasif also included a plea to Allah to let him become a shahid and grant him the honour of reaping as great a harvest as possible of Israeli lives.

The encouragement of the virtues and rewards of martyrdom are promulgated by the religious leaders of the Palestinian

Authority. The following was preached by Sheikh Isma'il Aal Ghadwan, broadcast live on Palestinian TV from the Sheikh Ijlin mosque in Gaza. Commenting upon the words of the Prophet to Jaber bin Abdallah who was sad after the battle of Uhud in which his father was killed, he clearly marked out the position:

Allah said to him: ". . . Do not consider those who have died for the sake of Allah as dead, but as alive, and as being provided for by their Lord."

This good news . . . has passed down to our people who still make great sacrifices, defending the honour of the Islamic nation. The sacrifice of convoys of martyrs [will continue] until Allah grants us victory very soon. The willingness for sacrifice and for death we see amongst those who were cast by Allah into a war with the Jews should not come at all as a surprise.

Oh believing brothers, we do not feel a loss . . . The martyr, if he meets Allah, is forgiven with the first drop of blood; he is saved from the torments of the grave; he sees his place in Paradise; he is saved from the Great Horror [of the Day of Judgement]; he is given 72 black-eyed women; he vouches for 70 of his family to be accepted to Paradise; he is crowned with the Crown of Glory, whose precious stone is better than all of this world and what is in it." (Friday 17 August 2001, MEMRI Special Despatch No 261, 23rd August 2001)

The suicide bomber and his role as martyr had become firmly established in the months leading up to 11 September, the trail being blazed by the Palestinians. The Sheikh of Al-Azhar, Muhammad Sayyed Tantawi, the highest religious authority in Egypt, ruled that "the Palestinian youth who bomb themselves amongst people who fight against them are considered martyrs (Shuhada). On the other hand, if they bomb themselves amongst babies, women, and elderly, they are not considered martyrs." (Ruz Al-Yussuf [Egypt], 18 May 2001) A similar ruling was made by the Saudi Mufti.

The above luminaries were attacked almost at once by distinguished journalists and jurists. Dr. Mustafa Ghalush, a lecturer at the Al-Azhar University, stated, "He who incites and he who carries out are the same, according to Islam" (*Al-Liwa Al-Islami*

[Egypt], 14 June 2001, tr. MEMRI *Inquiry & Analysis* No. 65, 26 July, 2001, henceforth MEMRI 65).

Dr. Muhammad Kamal Al-Din Al-Imam, a lecturer on Islamic law at the Alexandria Law Faculty, proposed that there was no such entity as an Israeli civilian:

> The [Israeli] society as a whole are a military force raised from various countries in order to occupy someone else's land. Muslim warriors by no means commit suicide. Each part in their bodies speaks [the language] of Martyrdom for the sake of Allah.

Al-Imam further added that the religious authorities have allowed the killing of a Muslim, if the heretic enemy is using him as a shield and there is no other way of killing this heretic, but to kill the Muslim along with him. He explained, "It follows, therefore, that if it is permissible to kill a Muslim, it is surely permissible to kill civilian enemies" (Al-Liwa Al-Islami [Egypt], 14 June 2001, MEMRI 65).

A further motif declares that had the Muslim knights possessed explosives at the time, they would have used them . . . "Therefore, what the Palestinian (Martyr) does to the Zionist enemy with his belt of explosives is the highest form of Martyrdom . . ." (*Al-Haqiqa*, Egypt, 12 May 2001, MEMRI 65). A similar line was taken by the PA Mufti, Ikrima Sabri, who also criticised the Saudi Mufti in a Friday sermon at the Al-Aqsa Mosque that was aired live by the PA radio, on the basis of early Islamic deeds in battle (*The Voice of Palestine Radio* (PA), 25 May 2001).

Dr. Mustafa Al-Shka', of the Al-Azhar Islamic (Egypt) Studies Centre, reminded readers, "We were commanded to fight against the enemies using all means." To encourage potential suicide bombers he stated:

> My blood is required for the sake of Allah, but the form of its [sacrifice] was not determined. The important thing is that I kill as many enemies as possible and turn into a Martyr (Shahid). He who fights with a sword, kills one heretic; on the other hand, he who bombs

himself kills many of the enemies of Allah, and therefore this is a higher level of Martyrdom. (*Al-Liwa Al-Islami* [Egypt], 14 June, 2001, tr. MEMRI 65)

Dr. Ali 'Aqleh 'Ursan, the Head of the Syrian Arab Writers' Union described:

the march of liberation, that will take place only by the use of force, through Jihad, and through Martyrdom . . . It is the blood of Sayyed Al-Shamuti recalling the battles of Badr and Al-Qadisiya, where Muslim horsemen had battled large that writes history, and the black ink cannot soil the golden pages written in the blood of the Shahidim, on their way to liberate Palestine, the Golan, and South Lebanon . . . Al-Usb'u Al-Adabi [Syria], 9 June 2001, tr. MEMRI 66)

Following The Tel-Aviv Disco Bombing by Said Al-Hotari, the bomber's will was published in the HAMAS paper *Al Risla*. Expressing his anticipation of meeting the Prophet Muhammad and the "leader of Martyrs, the Engineer, Yahya 'Ayyash" (assassinated by the Israelis) he spoke of his intention:

I will turn my body into bombs that will hunt the sons of Zion, bomb them, and burn their remains... There is nothing greater than being martyred on the soil of Palestine for the sake of Allah. (*Al-Risala* HAMAS (PA), 7 June 2001, tr. MMRI 66)

That suicide bombing is esteemed not only by Palestinians, but also by the Islamic world is amply illustrated by the three-day telethon held in Riyadh to support families of Palestinian suicide bombers. Saudi citizens donated £70 million, expensive cars including a Rolls Royce donated by one of the royal princesses, and gold jewellery. Similar televised appeals gained £34 million in Abu Dhabi, £7 million in Bahrain, £24 million in Dubai and £4 million in Qatar. It is thought that the total amount of such appeals will exceed £150 million in total. King Fahd restated his support for the suicide bombers with a personal donation of 10 million riyals (£2 million approx). Prince Alwaleed bin Tala, considered to be one of the world's richest men, donated £18.5 million. The Prince was in the news following the September 11th tragedy when Mayor Giuliani of New York returned his $10 million donation to the relief fund after the Prince took it upon himself to criticise US policy on the Palestinian question.

A nauseating element of the telethon was the appearance of children carrying plastic guns and wearing replicas of the shahid's explosive belt giving donations of fake semtex (*The Times*, London, 13 April 2002).

Latterly teenage girls have begun to take on the role of the Shahid. It has almost become a mantra that "the Palestinian people love suicide more than Israelis love to live". There seems little chance of peace until, to paraphrase Golda Meir's resigned statement, "the Arabs love their children more than they hate us" [the Israelis].

Part 3

Responding to the Holocaust and Developing the Theology of Catastrophe

CHAPTER THIRTEEN

CAN THEOLOGY SURVIVE AFTER AUSCHWITZ?

*There is multiple importance to the perspective of the
believer who cried out within the abyss of the
catastrophe itself for the mercy of heaven. Did he hear
God's voice? Did he see lights flicker through the thick
curtains? Or was he surrounded by darkness, emptiness
and destruction? And if he saw sparks of light and
heard the Bat Kol, how did he justify the judgement?*
Mendel Piekaz

The task of constructing or maintaining theology after Auschwitz
is a labyrinthine endeavour. The question we have asked obviously
poses the challenge: is any theology viable following the
Holocaust in an age of mass, and often mechanised, killing? As
post-Auschwitz Christians, we are faced with the challenge of
authentic response. The tension was expressed clearly by the
Catholic theologian, Harry James Cargas:

> Eleven million people were murdered by the Nazis. Six million of
> them were Jews. One million of the Jews were children. They were
> murdered in the heartland of Christian Europe. Those who harried
> the Jews and most of the guards and those who administered the
> policy of death were baptised Christians. Even Hitler, a baptised
> Catholic, was never excommunicated. (Harry J. Cargas, *Shadows of
> Auschwitz*, A Christian Response to the Holocaust, Crossroads, New
> York, 1990)

Although it is widely recognised that foundational Nazism was anti-Christian, it is clear that anti-Judaism was enabled in Germany because of centuries of Christian anti-Jewish teaching.

A satisfactory post-Auschwitz theology must include the following elements:

- the need to return to history;
- an acknowledgement that the Holocaust was a concrete reality;
- an acknowledgement that the Holocaust is part of both Jewish and Christian history;
- an acknowledgement of Christian responsibility whilst developing a hermeneutic that illustrates that the New Testament is not in itself an antisemitic document – likewise Christology *contra* R. R. Reuther et al;
- a renegotiation of the parameters of theodicy, including a theology of disaster;
- a development of a proper theological understanding of the State of Israel;
- a moving from the specific to the inclusive whilst maintaining the uniqueness of the Holocaust;
- a development of an understanding of Jesus that at no point extrudes him from the context of the Jewish environment that produced him;
- a resistance to the paralysis of guilt.

Models of responses to the Holocaust

Following the Holocaust there have been nine models offered as responses:

1   The Holocaust is like all other tragedies and merely raises again the question of theodicy. It does not significantly alter the problem or contribute anything new to it.

2   The classical Jewish theological doctrine of *mi-penei hata 'einu*, (because of our sins we were punished) which was evolved in the face of earlier national calamities can also be applied to the Holocaust. According to this account, Israel was sinful and Auschwitz is her just retribution.

3   The Holocaust is the ultimate in vicarious atonement. Israel is the "Suffering Servant" of Isaiah (ch.53f.). She suffers and atones for the sins of others. Some die so that others might be cleansed and live.

4   The Holocaust is a modern *Akedah* (sacrifice of Isaac). It is a test of our faith (Eliezer Berkowitz).

5   The Holocaust is an instance of the temporary "Eclipse of God". There are times when God is inexplicably absent from history or unaccountably chooses to turn His face away (Martin Buber).

6   The Holocaust is proof that "God is dead. If there were a God He would surely have prevented Auschwitz; if He did not then He does not exist" (Richard L. Rubenstein).

7   The Holocaust is the maximisation of human evil, the price mankind has to pay for human freedom. The Nazis were men, not gods. Auschwitz reflects ignominiously on man. It does not touch God's existence or perfection.

8   The Holocaust is revelation. It issues a call for Jewish affirmation. From Auschwitz comes the command: Jews survive! (Emil Fakenheim).

9   The Holocaust is an inscrutable mystery. Like all of God's ways it transcends human understanding and demands faith.

Of the nine suggestions above the ones that have found the greatest response appear below along with some more contemporary thought.

Mi-penei hata'einu

Mi-penei hata'einu, or the idea that the Holocaust was God's punishment for sin, is seen in terms of Divine action and Divine providence, and Divine justice and Divine punishment. An argument along these lines was vigorously promulgated by the late Satmar rebbe, Joel Teitelbaum, who saw the Third Reich as God's instrument, punishing the Jewish people for their sin. The great sin in Teitelbaum's estimation was Zionism, which was a premature attempt by Diaspora Jewry to bring about the end of the Galut. Zionism was an insurrection against God and should be viewed as rebellion. To make things worse it was a secularly driven movement in which politics and empowerment replaced Divine providence. An evidence of its insidious nature was that its programme had beguiled even religious Jews – it clearly was a work of Satan. Such a rebellion was worthy of punishment. In his own words:

> No one seems to be aware that, because of these sects who appealed to the hearts of the nation and violated the oath prohibiting hastening the end by assuming power and freedom before the designated time, six million Jews were unfortunately killed . . . anyone who observes the Zionist idea, their actions and their devious behaviour, from beginning to end, will have no doubt that all of the misfortunes and sufferings which were inflicted on us were because of them. Teitelbaum, Y. "Ma'amar Shalosh Sh'vuot" in *Va-Yoel Moshe*, New York, 1959 section 110, see also *Al ha-ge'ulah,* New York, 1967)

The view that Zionism was responsible for the Holocaust also found resonance in the work of Rabbi Yitzhak Hutner who, whilst recognizing the role of the Mufti in the Holocaust, feels that Zionism was the cause of the first joint Christian–Muslim initiative against the Jewish people (see Lawrence Kaplan Rabbi Isaac Hutner's "Daat Torah Perspective on the Holocaust", *Tradition*, 18, Fall 1980).

A rather different dimension of *Mi-penei hata'einu* which is shared by some Christian Zionists was propounded by Menachem Immanuel Hartom in 1962, at a time where the post-trauma of the Holocaust was easing enough for questions to be asked. Hartom pondered upon what could be such a great sin that it warranted the meting out of such a terrible punishment.

Reviewing the traditional teachings concerning the Galut, he points out that the Galut in itself is the worst measure of punishment that could befall the nation. Throughout the exile, following the destruction of the Temple and the Bar-Kochbah Revolt, the yearning had been in the Jewish heart for a return to the ancient homeland, and that the hope for the future was contained in a return to the homeland. The measures of emancipation in the Western European countries and the movement towards assimilation led to blindness that had rendered the hope of the return a non-issue. Those enjoying measures of emancipation had in their hearts abandoned the hope of return. Rather than Zionism being a new phenomenon, the Jewish people for the first time since their post-Second Temple exile had ceased to be Zionist, looking upon the return as an apocalyptic or metaphysical category. The punishment for abandoning the hope for a return to the land caused them to be visited with the appropriate judgment and punishment. Having desired to abandon their homeland and identity and become part of other nations they were clearly and precisely shown that these lands were not their home. It is no coincidence that Germany, which Jews had venerated as the epitome of culture, sophistication, erudition and advancement should become the instrument of their destruction (Menarchem Immanuel Hartom, "Hirhurimal ha-Shoah", *deot*, 18, winter 1961). Hartom's dictum that the abandonment of the hope of the return to the land was the causation of the Holocaust has the strength of scriptural precedent in Ezekiel 20:33–37. The cry of the people that they want to be like the other nations elicits a sharp response from the Lord, who proclaims that it will never happen and that he will rule with wrath poured out and judge them in the wilderness of the peoples. The latter expression denotes that the nations where the Jews have felt they were flourishing will be as wilderness in the days of judgment and wrath.

Franklin Sherman, one time Professor of Christian Ethics at the Lutheran School of Theology in Chicago, points out that the notion of the Holocaust as God's judgment on the Jews is repellent, yet Christians must recognise that for centuries the church promoted such a theory to explain the fall of Jerusalem, and viewed the Roman armies as God's divine instrument of punishment for their rejection of Jesus as Messiah (Sherman, Franklin, *Speaking of God after Auschwitz*, in Paul D. Opsahl and Mark H. Tanenbaum (eds.), Philadelphia, 1974).

Hester Panim (the silence of God lit hiddenness, or the turning of the face)

> I believe in the sun even when it is not shining
> I believe in love even when not feeling it
> I believe in God even when he is silent

The anonymous inscription above, found on the wall of a cellar in Cologne where Jewish people had been hiding from the Nazis, is a poignant introduction to the concept of Hester Panim.

Hester Panim has received widespread usage, particularly amongst the Orthodox, in attempting to find a theological response to the Holocaust. Hester Panim is explained in the Bible as being due to sin (Deuteronomy 31:8) and as a mysterious, inexplicable happening (Psalm 44, Psalm 13, Isaiah 8:17, and Isaiah 45:5). Hester Panim is not a purposeful act on the part of God. As God is not subject to human freedom of choice, it is better understood as God withdrawing his hand because of the sins of the nation of Israel. God hid his face, as assimilation and modern secularism had broken off all contact between Israel and God. The severance became reciprocal, God hiding his face as a consequence of the severance, not as a punishment.

Eliezer Berkowitz contends that,

> Not for a single moment shall we entertain the idea that what happened to European Jewry was divine punishment for any sins committed by them. It was injustice absolute. It was injustice countenanced by God.

Hester Panim may be regarded as judgement or as apparent divine indifference toward the plight of man. A leading text to help the reader understand Hester Panim is Isaiah 45:15. The text supports the idea that God's self-concealment is an attribute of the divine nature. Although he may be sought, he may neither be found nor dialogued with. Generally speaking, God cannot as a rule intervene whenever man abuses freedom or displeases him. If he interrupts evil-doing, the possibility for good could also potentially be prejudiced. There would be no possibility for mankind to be involved in ethical or moral decision-making, which is an essential part of freedom and responsibility, even if he chooses the wrong alternative. As he does so, there will inevitably be suffering for the innocent.

If man is to exist as a free-will being, God must co-exist alongside him, and suffer the pain and sorrow of one waiting for the sinner to repent and come into right relation with him. It is the tragic paradox of faith that God's direct concern for the wrong-doer means that God himself must enter long-suffering with him. A contingency of God's infinite patience and suffering with the sinner causes him to abandon the victim to an undeserved fate. If man is to be a responsible, moral creature, God must absent himself from the historical process, although he must remain present in history so that history's end will not be a triumph for evil. God is powerful, not through intervention but through self-restraint.

The question immediately comes to mind: how, and where do we witness God in history, given the paradox? Berkovits' reply is that he reveals his presence through the survival of Israel. Not through his deeds, but through his children. The return to the land and the State of Israel in the face of despair revealed God's presence not only to Israel but also to the world. When all seemed lost and when the fate of the Jewish people seemed to be extinction he worked a miracle (Eliezer Berkowitz, *Faith After the Holocaust*, New York, 1973).

The Detachment of God

Arthur Cohen developed the Detachment of God motif as a response to Hester Panim (*Tremendum, A Theological Interpretation of the Holocaust*, New York, 1981). He has suggested that the traditional notion of the Divine is mistaken, based upon an erroneous desire for a non-existent, interruptive God. If such a deity existed and in fact possessed the ability to interfere in history, then mankind and creation would no longer be an independent domain which is an expression of God's creative love. Mankind in this scheme of things would be mere automatons. God is self-limiting. No matter how depraved mankind becomes, God cannot intervene. As God has no concrete role in the historical process, *ipso facto* he cannot be held responsible for the Holocaust. Cohen's model renders God functionally irrelevant and is self-contradictory in viewing a future involvement of a God who was alarmingly absent in the past.

Divine Providence

Bernard Maza expanded the notion of *Mi-penei hata'einu*, and the Ezekiel 20 passage above, considering that the outpouring of God's wrath was in order to revitalise the Torah (Maza, Bernard, *With Fury Poured Out*, KTAV, New York, 1986). The Holocaust is seen as a work of Divine Providence intended to drive back to the Torah the communities who had either become weakened in their observance or departed from it, because of assimilation, emancipation and Zionism. The Holocaust was the vehicle that drove those who survived, or lived outside the theatre of the Nazi operations, to the study of the Torah.

Ignaz Maybaum uses the crucifixion of Jesus as a model for the Holocaust (Ignaz Maybaum, *The Face of God After Auschwitz*, Amsterdam, 1965). He said that, "The Golgotha of modern mankind is Auschwitz, the cross; the Roman gallows is the gas chamber." The millions of victims who lost their lives were chosen by God to die for the sins of mankind as suffering servants in the Isaiah 53 sense. Further to this, the Holocaust brought attention to God's plans for the future in a way that might be understood and fulfilled. It should be understood in terms of the *akedah* (Genesis 22). In Auschwitz, the Jews suffered vicariously for the sins of mankind. The Akeda paradigm likens the victims to Isaac, innocent victims who are sacrificed (unlike the biblical Isaac) as a test of faithfulness. The Suffering Servant model, drawing primarily on Isaiah 53, lays no blame on the victims, seeing their suffering rather as a vicarious, if mysterious, event.

Maybaum also appeals to Old Testament passages where the enemies of Israel are seen as the instruments of Divine Providence (e.g. Jeremiah 27:6). The Holocaust is the final "day of awe" laid upon God's people by God in preparation for the advent of a messianic age.

There is a differential between *Churban* (destruction) and *gezarah* (evil decree). Churban cannot be averted and is progressive. The Holocaust is the third *Churban* and as such helps in human advancement and spiritual development. Maybaum considers that the sacrifice of the victims was in order to bring life to those remaining alive.

The above views are difficult for both Jews and Christians to understand in terms of what they know of God and the traditions of the respective faiths. In Christian theology it is God who suffers on the cross, in Maybaum God remains in heaven and inflicts indescribable suffering upon millions of helpless people. There is always an inherent difficulty when borrowing categories from differing faith concepts. Maybaum suggests that Christians do not appropriate the true significance of the crucifixion, as they do not understand the higher principle of the *akedah*. Christians would conversely contend that Maybaum does not understand the dynamic centrality of the crucifixion.

The Death of God

Richard L. Rubenstein pronounced God dead in his daring work, *After Auschwitz: Radical Theology and Contemporary Judaism.* He pointedly raised the question that would remain to this day the single greatest challenge to the monotheistic faith. He contends that the Holocaust decisively disproves the existence of God and proves the bankruptcy of Jewish theology. Not only Jewish bodies went up in smoke at Auschwitz, but the Covenant as well: "the Covenant died there" (R. Rubenstein, "Auschwitz and Covenant Theology" *Christian Century*, 21 May 1969, in reply to Leroy T Howe, "Theology and the Death Camps", *Christian Century* 19 Feb. 1969. As the universe itself is absurd, it is hardly surprising that disfigurements in human history, as exampled by the Holocaust, occur. The fitting response is for Jewish people to depart from their ancient theology and move toward a more naturalistic system of values. Rubenstein's theory of the death of God is not that of the cynical humanists of the Enlightenment, but rather posits the death of God in society. At no time has he advocated that God does not exist, and charges that he advocates atheism are not founded. Rather, Rubenstein contends that we are living in "the time of the death of God" which is best summed up in his own words:

No man can really say that God is dead. How can we know that? Nevertheless, I am compelled to say that we live in the time of the "death of God"... When I say we live in a time of the death of God, I mean that the thread uniting God and man, heaven and earth has been broken. We stand in a cold, silent, unfeeling cosmos, unaided by any purposeful power beyond our own resources. After Auschwitz, what else can a Jew say about God?

I believe the greatest single challenge to modern Judaism arises out of the question of God and the death camps. I am amazed at the silence of contemporary Jewish theologians on this most crucial and agonising of all Jewish issues. How can Jews believe in an omnipotent, beneficent God after Auschwitz? Traditional Jewish theology maintains that God is the ultimate, omnipotent actor in the historical drama. It has interpreted every major catastrophe in Jewish history as God's punishment of a sinful Israel. I fail to see how this position can be maintained without regarding Hitler and the SS as instruments of God's will. The agony of European Jewry cannot be likened to the testing of Job. To see any purpose in the death camps, the traditional believer is forced to regard the most demonic, anti-human explosion in all history as a meaningful expression of God's purposes. The idea is simply too obscene for me to accept. (R Rubenstein, "The State of Jewish Belief" in *Commentary 42*, August 1966)

In some ways Rubenstein's notion has similarity to Nietzsche's madman running around the market place with a lantern looking for God, with the cry "God is dead and we have killed him!" God has no effective role in the norms, morals and ethics of society; it is as if he does not exist. The tension arising from Rubenstein's position is that it renders God powerless and, as such, a victim of his creation.

Rubenstein, however, did not abandon religion altogether and posited a religion without God. The position has something in common with Julian Huxley's *Religion Without Revelation* (1957), Mordecai Kaplan's *Judaism without Supernaturalism* (1958), and R Jack Cohen's *Case for religious Naturalism* (1958) and majors on the idea of agnosticism, with a central focus upon the Jewish people.

The Theology of Survival

Emil Fackenheim sees no salvific import in Auschwitz but only a challenge to survive. The Holocaust should not be understood in terms of the character of God but the character of man. The challenge of the Holocaust is not in what happened but rather in appropriating the implications of the event. The voices of the six million call for Jewish survival. As such, Jewish people are under a sacred obligation to survive. Jews are "forbidden to despair of the God of Israel, lest Judaism perish" (*Judaism* 16, Summer 1967, and the more developed *The Jewish Return into History: Reflections in the Age of Auschwitz and a New Jerusalem*, New York, 1978, and *To Mend a Broken World*, New York, 1982). Traditionally there were 613 commandments in Judaism. Out of the dust and ashes of Auschwitz God has now issued a 614th commandment, that of survival. The Jewish people are forbidden to grant Hitler a posthumous victory.

The Theology of Protest or The Abandonment of God

Paul Marcus and Alan Rosenberg contend that God abandoned his people in their hour of need. The abandonment has led to rage, despair and disappointment, leading some to give up their faith altogether ("Survivors' Faith" *in Holocaust and Genocide Studies*, vol. 3 no. 4, 1988). In continuity with the Jewish understanding of relationship with the deity one must protest, or to use their term, rage at God. To argue with God is a biblical practice as can be illustrated in Jeremiah 4:10; Habakkuk 1:1–4,5,13; Jeremiah 12:1, Psalm 44 (see F. Wright "Chutzpah K'Lapei Shamayim: An absent dimension in Christian devotion" in *The Journal for Biblical and Hebraic Studies* vol. 4:3, 1999).

Elie Wiesel

Wiesel's thought is probably best expressed in *Der Prozess von Schamgorod* (*The Trial of God*, Paris, 1979). The action takes place in the year 1649 in the aftermath of the Khmelnitsky massacres in the Ukraine. Wandering players who have lost their way are constrained to perform their Purimspiel in Shamgorod. The subject demanded is that God be put on trial on charges of being indifferent, cruel, hostile and harbouring a dislike for his chosen people. There follows an immediate crisis as, not surprisingly, no one can be found who is willing to take the role of God and proffer his defence. That this should be the case should come as no surprise. Who can be blamed? He has allowed all of his defenders to be killed. A stranger appears who most willingly and eloquently undertakes the task of the defence. His oration is listened to with close attention by all assembled. Suddenly, throwing aside his mask, the stranger reveals himself as Satan and, as he takes his departure, he both mocks and reviles his listeners for being such simpletons as to listen to him. The punchline comes with the declaration of Berich, the innkeeper, who brought forth the charges that, whilst remaining a Jew, he would increase his vigour in shouting ever louder his accusations.

A similar element is found in *Beggar in Jerusalem* (Avon, New York, 1971). A broken Ukrainian Tzaddik cries out that God no longer deserves the love and passion of his people: survivors are massacred and their deaths held up as objects of ridicule. God should know that before dying he will cry and shout. Wiesel's views overall can be contradictory at times as in *Anni Ma' anim* where he expresses a yearning for an interventionist, beneficent God.

The problem with the theology of protest is that it can lead to abandonment of faith. Many who hold to this position are obfuscated by disappointment, hurt and anger that are at times contradictory.

The Theology of Liberation

Jurgen Moltmann, as one of the very few Christian writers who have had the courage to respond to the Holocaust, stated that God is not dead – he is present, but inactive. He is fully involved. Death is in God, God suffers by us, and suffering is in God.

Moltmann quotes from Elie Wiesel's book *Night* where the SS hanged two Jewish men and a youth in front of the whole camp. The men died quickly but the death throes of the youth lasted for half an hour:

> "Where is God, where is he?" someone asked behind me. As the youth still hung in torment in the noose after a long time, I heard the man call again, "Where is God now?" And I heard a voice in myself answer, "Where is he? He is hanging there on the gallows."

Moltmann points out elsewhere that any other answer would be blasphemy. There cannot be any other Christian answer to this torment. To speak here of a God that did not suffer would effectually make God a demon.

Marc Ellis applies the ideas of the Latin American Liberationist writers such as Gutierrez, Sobrino, Boff and J-B Metz, to devise a post-Holocaust response. God is interventionist, and attention should be paid to the prophetic dimension and models built to provide the prophetic contour within which the State of Israel is consequential. The Jewish people need to move away from focusing on themselves alone and develop a solidarity with others who are suffering and, in turn, they will rediscover their own humanity. Although a pioneering work in its own right, *Towards a Jewish Theology of Liberation* focuses more on the condition of post-Holocaust Jewry than on tensions that led to the events.

The inadequacy of Theodicy

Theodicy is the theological category that attempts to show that it is possible to affirm the justice of God, the omnipotence of God, the love of God, and the reality of evil, without contradiction. The term is generally attributed to Gottfried Wilhelm Leibnitz in his treatise *Theodicy: Essays on the Goodness of God, The Freedom of Man and the Origin of Evil* (1710). The term is derived from a compound of two Greek words *theos* (God) and *dike* (justice). The problem is one that has perplexed scholars through the ages which, as Nachmanides pointed out, underlies for many the "who" questions of faith and apostasy (*Perush le-sefer Kohelet* in *Kitevi Rabbenu Moshe ben Nahman*, C. Chavel, ed. New York, 1953). Epicurus neatly addresses the tension. Is God willing to prevent evil but unable? Then he is impotent. Is he able but not willing? Then he is malevolent. Is he both able and willing? Whence is evil? (q David Hume, *Dialogues Concerning Natural Religion*, New York edition, 1966).

When developing a Theology of Catastrophe the first proposition is that the category of theodicy is inadequate. The problem of evil and suffering in its primary form holds five tensions which may be expressed as five propositions:

1   God is good and therefore cannot be the source of evil (Mid Ps 5:7 ed. Buber, 1891, Gen Rab 3:6, 51:3; BT Ber 60b);
2   God is omnipotent;

3   God is omnipresent;
4   Evil exists;
5   God is interventionist.

Along with the five propositions above, if the following conditional clauses are added to provide workable models, it becomes obvious that the enterprise is doomed from the start.

1   God is either intelligible or not intelligible; it almost goes without saying that the propositions require a god that is intelligible. If God is not intelligible, then the whole issue of theodicy becomes somewhat irrelevant. One might be bold enough to suggest that theodicy is the locus classicus in the modern age of the differentiation between Hebraic and Greek thought. In Hebraic thought the emphasis is on what you do [in relationship to God] as opposed to the Hellenistic ideology where the stress is on what you think!

2   Dualism must be avoided. At this point the role of the satan needs to be considered. There is little material in the canonical literature to build a dualistic model, but when applying a Greek mindset to the question, as in the instance of the Trinity, one is almost irrefragably constrained to produce a dualistic appropriation (for a Hebraic understanding see S. Hawthorne, 'Three in the One God of Israel', *Roots and Branches*, London, 1998). When we turn to the canonical writings, however, we find a strikingly different picture. In the Book of Job, the satan appears in his role as the accuser and it is made clear that he is only allowed to operate by divine consent. When Job's troubles increase, then Satan receives no further notices. As such it is clear that the satan is not an independent power or even a "manifest darker side of God". The essential monotheism of Israelite consciousness is thus maintained.

3   Theodicy strips away the eschatological contour of biblical thought, hence giving at the best a one-dimensional monochrome picture.

4   Theodicy is affected by socio-economic distancing in the West. As such it cannot hope to engage with a subject group. In the modern age, vicarious involvement in world crises by media coverage has removed a defining contour of the question of pain and suffering. Vicarious involvement in a suffering world is provided by news coverage and occasional opportunities to contribute financially to any victim group.

5   Although using historical data, theodicy escapes from history by failing to attempt to draw empathetic models. Liberation theologies may in one sense be considered as reactions against Christian passivity in the face of a suffering world, be they, for example, Jewish, Latin American, black, feminist or Korean.

If the first proposition holds that God is benevolent, it must be sustained throughout. If the second proposition holds, God is all-powerful and able to operate the fifth proposition that he will, because of the first proposition, intervene on behalf of his people. The third proposition demands that God is aware of the sufferings of his people. As the fourth proposition may easily be illustrated to hold, we are then constrained to seek to authenticate the first second, third and fifth propositions.

The question of theodicy attempts to build models in which the primary tension, proposition number one, can be held. The whole question of theodicy begs another question, almost before it comes into the arena, namely, "Is theodicy a legitimate subject, given its primary postulations which owe little or nothing to Hebraic thought, but find resonance in Stoicism and neo-Platonism?"

The following are considerations, which are generally held when examining the phenomena of pain and suffering:

- Suffering is punishment for sinful behaviour either individually or collectively.
- Mankind and the animal world are vulnerable to accident, disease, and other destructive assaults upon our existence because of their design.

- Free moral beings have the ability to misuse their freedom and cause harm to others or ourselves.
- Suffering is designed as a means of enabling spiritual growth.
- Destructive interactions are contingencies of beings who live in society.
- The world is under the domination of the Evil One. Pain and suffering are collateral with the cosmic conflict.
- Pain and suffering are purposeful in preservation and development.

All of the above considerations have yielded little in the way of consolation or hope. The biggest challenge is to the character of God himself, and they leave us in danger of adopting Stendhal's gloomy response that the only excuse for God is that he does not exist.

Avoiding the theological detour – the thought of wartime Jewish leaders

Gershon Greenberg, a research fellow at the Institute for Holocaust Research, Bar-Ilan University, and Professor of Philosophy and Religion at the American University, Washington, DC, recently pointed out in a review essay of Eliezer Schweid's *Ben Hurban Le'yeshua* for John Hopkins University, that twentieth-century Jewish religious thought generally has circumvented the Holocaust. Pre-war Jewish thought (Hermann Cohen, Rav Kook, Martin Buber, Franz Rosenzweig) almost seamlessly co-enjoins with the non-Holocaust writings of Kaplan, Heschel and Soloveichik, as well as post–1967 Holocaust theological literature (Rubenstein, Berkowitz, Fackenheim, Arthur Cohen and Irving Greenberg). Things began to change in the mid-1980s with the publication of Nehemiah Polen's, *Divine Weeping*, Rabbi Kalonymous Shapiro's "Theology of Catastrophe in the Warsaw Ghetto", *Modern Judaism*, vol. 7, October 1987, and works by Mendel Piekaz (*Hatecuda Ha'hasidit*

Ha'sifrutit Ha'ahronacal Admat Polin, Jerusalem, 1979), Pessah Schindler, Efraim Shmueli and Eliezer Schweid (*Ma'avak^cad Shahar* Tel Aviv, 1990), and Greenberg himself (*Confronting the Holocaust: A Listing of Articles and Books Reflecting the Jewish Religious Responses to the Holocaust in Its Immediate Aftermath (1944–1949)* [Yiddish and Hebrew] Ramat Gan, 1994). Schweid in particular insisted that such an approach led to an erroneous perception, and that the thought of Jewish leaders and thinkers who lived through the times was central to an authentic response. In common with all historical constructions, primary sources are always to be preferred to secondary ones and *responsa* developed *in situ* should play a valuable role in retrospective theological development.

The leaders of the Jewish communities found themselves in a situation that, although predicated in a continuum of antisemitic hatred, had never faced a world-reaching offensive against them. Whereas pogroms had claimed lives in the thousands, the mere concept of universal destruction and mass killing in tens of thousands raised the need for a vital theological response if faith was to be meaningful and there was to be any hope of faith for the future. One must bear in mind that in this time of absolute crisis the writers were entering into an unknown arena, and their word, that was considered binding upon the communities that they led, now took on an extra dimension. One can hardly begin to imagine the weight of responsibility felt by the leader, cut off from contact with other leaders, devoid of discussion with others facing similar tensions. In times such as these the merest glimmer of hope was seized upon, and the escape, survival or rescue of even a solitary person, was greeted enthusiastically and regarded as a miracle wrought by an interventionist deity. The movement towards identifying those who were destroyed as martyrs also began to take on an identity. Those put to death were considered to have died *ha Kiddush ha Shem* (sanctifying God's Holy Name) and as such were players in an eternal plan of redemption.

The work of Schweid

Schweid examines the thought of seven principal characters from the wartime period, including the leaders of the Lubavich and Belz Hassidic dynasties who sought to console their followers and maintain their confession through the terrible and tragic years. The characters examined are Elhanan Wasserman, Yosef Yitshak Schneersohn, Aharon Rokeah, Issakhar Teykhtahl, Kalonymous Kalman Shapira, Eliyahu Dessler and Yehuda Ashlag. A brief comment upon responses of Yosef Yitshak Schneersohn and Aharon Rokeah follow, with a longer section on the thought of Kalonymous Kalman Shapira, from whose writing the concept of developing the Theology of Catastrophe arose. The written resources deployed were in the form of literature created to be disseminated to the appropriate parties and, as such, have the strength of reflective thought, as opposed to the recording of data or personal, individual thoughts, such as those of diarists or those attempting to create proto-histories. The greatest value of the works is the challenge of change, as following the Holocaust it became ever-increasingly obvious that things were never going to return to the way they had been before. The consequences of the flight of the Lubavich to America and the leader of Belz Hasidim to Eretz Israel were to have a profound effect in the post-war period.

Yoseph Yitzak Schneersohn

The Lubavich Habad movement started in the Smolensk Oblast which was located in the Mogilev province of Belarus. Lubavich became the acknowledged centre of Habad Chassidism after their founder, Shneur Zalman, moved there in 1813. Between the two world wars, they transferred their centre first to Latvia, then to Poland, and finally to the United States. During the Holocaust, the leader of the movement was Yoseph Yitzak Schneersohn. Joseph Yitzak Schneersohn responded to the challenge facing the Habad in America whilst Jews were suffering in Europe. He looked to two major events in Judaism, Purim and Hanukkah, positing that they bequeathed a legacy of Teshuva (penitent return). In Schneersohn understanding, Teshuva could not only reverse sin: if there was a universal Teshuva, the presence of Divine will that had been cut away by sin, would enhance the redemptive process.

A key to understanding Schneersohn's thought is his delineation of the models of relationship between God, Israel, the Jewish people and the nations. Israel related to the nations, and God to nature, as soul to body. In turn, God related to earthly experience through Israel, as the national soul. Israel's internal destiny was determined by her tie to God in terms of Torah, Mitsvot, and worship. But Israel sinned, undermining both her own destiny and the earth's access to divine will. As a result of Israel's sin the Hester Panim took place. The lower powers of the natural world and the sitra achra recognised this and became powerful. Haman and his subsequent surrogates and successors understood this dynamic and, realising that Israel's sins made her vulnerable, rose up against them. As in the days of Esther, Teshuva brought redemption and could do so again. There was an historical precedent. Three Purims into his residence in the USA a greater sense of urgency can be noted in his writing. He went as far as to say that the arrival of the Messiah was to be soon but, as there was still a general absence of Teshuva, the Messiah's arrival probably would be too late. (For Schneersohn's wartime writings see *Ha'keriya Veha'kedusha*, a wartime periodical of Mahane Israel.)

Aharon Rokeah

The Hasidic Belz dynasty, which takes its name from Beltz in Galicia, was founded by Shalom Roke'ah (1779–1855), and became one of the most important and influential of the Hasidic groups. During the Holocaust, the Belz leader was Rav Aharon Rokeah (1880–1957). As the Nazi war machine reached Belz, Aharon escaped to Sokol and then to Przemysl where 33 members of his family were murdered. After being captured, he was sent to the ghettos of Vizhnitsa, Cracow and Bochnia. Subsequently, in 1942, he was sent to Kaschau (Hungary) and then to Budapest. In 1944, along with his brother Mordecai, he succeeded in fleeing from Budapest to Eretz Israel. His escape was regarded as *Siyata de'shemaya* (by divine assistance). His presence in the land brought about a bonding of cabalistic motifs with himself and the land, and opened a new door of hope. For those unfamiliar with Hasidic thought, the differing dynasties have different theological appropriations of the role of the Tzaddik (see F. Wright, *Within the Pale op cit.* for an overview of the development of Hasidism). As in Belz Hasidism, the stress is on the individual as opposed to collectivity: the mere presence of the Rebbe in Eretz Israel caused the movement to place aliyah as a theological necessity. The yearning to join the brothers Rokeah in the land where the redemptive process was being enhanced by their presence offered hope to those stranded in Budapest. Therefore, the Hester Panim, as they understood it, was simply a manifestation of the tragedy. Aharon Rokeah contended that there is an interplay between God above and man below. Man has a role to play in "awakening" God. The *modus operandi* of the awakening is aliyah, the return to the land. Not all viewed the brothers Rokeah's flight and resettlement in positive terms, feeling they had abandoned their charges. Whilst they prayed at the Kotel, the Jews of Hungary were being destroyed.

Kalonymos Kalman Shapira

We now proceed to the thought of the Piaseczner Rebbe, Rabb. Kalonymos Kalman Shapira, Rabbi of the Warsaw Ghetto. The Piaseczno community dated from the eighteenth century. Prior to the Second World War, the community numbered around 3000. Between 22–27 Jan. 1941, the entire Jewish community were deported to Warsaw and subsequently liquidated. The teachings of Rabb. Kalonymous were rescued from the Ghetto in a milk can. "Sacred Fire" contains his responses. Rabb. Kalonymous himself perished along with his community in 1943. Y*isurin shel ha'Shem* provides the foundation for the role of God within the theology of catastrophe. In the midst of the terrible sufferings of the Ghetto, Rabb. Kalonymos Shapira offered the response that spares God from being the architect of evil and suffering as contingencies of goodness and blessing, namely the *yisurin shel h'Shem*. In a simplified form, *yisurin shel h'Shem*, suffering for God's sake, viz. Israel's suffering, is ancillary to God's. In common with some other responses to the Shoah, Rabb. Shapira is involving the people and God together.

This was not a new concept. Exodus Rabbah 11:5 contends that God participated in the sufferings of the captivity. The midrash to Lamentations (Lam Rabbah 35:4) presents God weeping over the exile of the people and the destruction of the Temple, in the manner of mortals. Prof. Dorothee Sölle has suggested that to generate an authentic response we must attempt to move towards an understanding of God's own pain (Sölle, D., "God's Pain, our Pain: How Theology has to change after Auschwitz", in *Remembering for the Future*, supp. vol. Pergamon, Oxford, 1988). Even in the Warsaw Ghetto, there is nothing but God: no duality, no evil power, no satanic insurrection or forces fighting for supremacy. All is from God, and it is all happening to God. God is at the centre, and he surrounds every event. The Holocaust can be regarded as the material manifestation of God's suffering. Thus it is possible to consider the Shoah (Holocaust) as the outward expression on earth of God's tears, his crying in the innermost chambers of heaven. Jews can find a way to follow God to that innermost place where he hides his face in order to cry. The Zohar insists that God, the Torah and Israel are one. The Final Solution of the Jewish problem by the Nazis was an attack on God. His suffering and their suffering are one and the same.

In the face of unnatural, inhuman, inexplicable evil, rationalism must be destroyed. Finite, human knowledge must be replaced by unquestioning, total immersion in the depths of faith, which is the knowing of God and the essence of the self. Only when abandoned to God and totally immersed in him will the Jews find not only the true relationship but the knowledge of him. When the desire to explain and comprehend evaporates and the capacity to accept have appeared, they will become worthy of miracles. The darkness, suffering, senseless evil and utter godlessness of the times should be understood as a vehicle for prophecy and revelation. God's character could be found in the midst of the darkness. The assault on the Jewish people is in reality an assault upon God himself. The latter thought is consistent with the God-people-land trichotomy that runs as a rich seam throughout the Tanakh. The Piaseczno community, along with the Rebbe, perished in the ghetto in 1943. This brought an end to Piaseczner Hasidism, the community, not being reconstructed following the cessation of hostilities.

Divine suffering – Christian viewpoints

Dorothee Sölle, the radical German theologian mentioned above, argues that the traditional doctrine of an all-loving, omnipotent deity must be modified in the light of the terrible events of the Holocaust. We can no longer hold a belief that God possesses such attributes. Whereas we can conceive of God as all-loving, we cannot conceive of him as all-powerful. Prof. Sölle contends that the only way we can now perceive God is as being alongside the victims and suffering with them. Only in this way does God retain credibility. She regards this position as being represented by such different Jewish philosophers as Elie Wiesel, Abraham Heschel, and particularly Hans Jonas ("The Concept of God After Auschwitz", in Albert Friedlander (ed.) *Out of the Whirlwind*, New York, 1976). She also feels that Dietrich Bonhoeffer came close to this understanding during his imprisonment by the Nazis.

When dealing with God's suffering, Sölle feels that she cannot view the subject within the category of masculinity, and presents God as our Mother, as a necessary contingency of the ability to comfort. God cannot comfort us if she was not bound to us in pain. The fact that Sölle feels the necessity to view comfort as the exclusive realm of femininity could be said to weaken her argument, rather than to strengthen it (Sölle, Dorothee, *God's Pain and our Pain*, in Otto Maduro (ed.) *Judaism, Christianity and Liberation*, New York, 1991).

The Catholic Professor David Tracey was one of the first scholars to emphasise the dangers of the escape from history. Tracey suggests that it is important to rethink anew the reality of suffering in the reality of God's own self as the self who love is. He associates his thought with that of Dietrich Bonhoeffer in the belief that:

> Only a suffering God can help us now . . . God is none other than pure, unbounded love – the God who radically affects and is affected (that is suffers) by the evil we, not God, inflict on God's creation. I believe, therefore, that the unspeakable suffering of the six million is also the voice of the suffering of God. (Tracey, D., *Religious Values After the Holocaust*, Philadelphia, 1982)

Marcus Braybrook, one-time chairman of the World Congress of Faiths, reflecting on the murder of eleven million people by the Nazis, of whom six million were Jews, proposes that the picture of Jesus suffering on the cross serves as a framework for comprehending the suffering love of God in the Nazi era. In common with Prof. Sölle, he believes that to emphasise God's suffering love one must reject the traditional descriptions of God as omnipotent, impassable and omniscient. Braybrook appeals to Psalm 23: 4 and Psalm 139 to affirm that God is with us in our suffering. In the shadow of the Shoah only a suffering God is credible. A God who could have acted and did not do so, is not worthy of worship. The picture of God as suffering love is shaped by an understanding of the death of Jesus. Braybrook continues that as we reject God's omnipotence it follows that prayer does not change God, but changes us. This picture of God also suggests that the future is in the hands of humanity. If we desire to shape a more just and peaceful world, we should imitate God's way of suffering love. (Marcus Braybrook, "The Power of Suffering Love", in Tony

Bayfield and Marcus Braybrook (eds.) *Dialogue with a Difference*, London, 1992)

Braybrook and others reflect Process Theology. The weakness of Process Theology is that it is essentially panentheistic. One doubts, for those unfamiliar with the term, whether Process Theology isn't in fact more philosophically than biblically or confessionally based. Process Theology claims a tradition going back to Heraclitus in the fifth century BCE, but it was the work of the famous mathematician-philosopher Alfred North Whitehead (1861–1947) that brought it to the fore, as he sought a set of metaphysical concepts that would be able to explain all individual beings, from God downwards to the most minuscule form of life. From the 1960s, faced with the waning of liberalism and the challenges of the modern world, the aftermath of the Holocaust and the nuclear threat, Process Theology surfaced again with the writings of John Cobb, Schubert Ogden, Daniel D. Williams and Norman Pittenger. The writers attempted to show that Process Theology offers a view of God dynamically related to human history in continuity with the biblical sources rather than the more traditional Christian [Hellenistic] view of classical theism. The view of God as being timeless, immutable, impassable and omniscient was developed from Hellenistic categories that were at odds with the biblical view of God's love. Pittenger pictured God as the cosmic lover who in Jesus actualised the divine aim. Jesus was the supreme human embodiment of "love-in-action" (N. Pittenger, *Christology Reconsidered* and *Process Thought and Christian Faith*, New York, 1968). Attractive as the idea is of God the suffering lover who seeks to persuade other beings in the direction of love, one doubts whether it is enough to tell the victim of torture, the one whose family was transported and sent to the gas chamber, or the one who must live with the ongoing pain of their personal history that there is a passive fellow-suffering God who understands!

The most helpful suggestion arises from Jurgen Moltmann concerning the categories of omniscience and impassibility. Omniscience implies that God's foreknowledge of human history deprives humans of creative responsibility for the future, whilst impassibility implies that God is detached from human pain. Moltmann avoids the philosopher C. G. Jung's notion that it is not humans who have to ethically improve but it is God who has to ethically improve (*Answer to Job*, New York, 1954) and suggests that a key to understanding is the abandonment of traditional philosophical axioms:

> We must drop the philosophical axioms of the nature of God. God is not unchangeable, if unchangeable means that He could not in the freedom of His love open Himself to the changeable history of His creation. God is not incapable of suffering, if this means that in the freedom of his love He would not be receptive to suffering over the contradiction of man and the self-destruction of His creation. God is not invulnerable, if this means that He could not open Himself to the pain of the cross. God is not perfect if this means that He did not in the craving of His love want His creation to be necessary to His perfection (Moltmann, Jurgen, *The Church in the Power of the Spirit*, London, 1970).

How does a Christian respond theologically to the Holocaust? As in one sense it is an ethical question one is tempted to adopt Aquinas' gloomy dictum that:

> Ethics as a *scientia operativa* does not enjoy simplicity or great certainty because of the multiplicity of contingencies that it must bring into unified consideration. (Aquinas in XII *Libros Metaphysicorium* I.I. lect. ii)

One would boldly suggest that the theological response must, therefore, be outside of ethics or theodicy and that it is necessary to develop a Theology of Catastrophe on the lines suggested above, with the *yisurin shel Ha shem* holding the best suggestion of the place of the divinity. In the meantime, the church should take upon itself the command of Isaiah 40:1f., to comfort God's people who remain his representatives upon the earth and will be major players in salvation's drama at the closing of the age.

A LITURGY FOR YOM HA SHOAH

The liturgy covers all aspects from instigation and promulgation through to collaboration and indifference to Jewish suffering. A plea for strength and courage to face the problems of Christian antisemitism and the bloodstained history of Jewish-Christian relationships is included. The liturgy concludes with a prayer for reconciliation. Throughout there is the theme of the continuity of Judaism and Christianity. Although designed initially for Yom Ha Shoah, it can be used at any time.

Preparation

A table should be set with two plain candles. A bowl of water may be included for symbolic handwashing.

Leader Blessed art Thou O Lord our God, King of the Universe who has brought us to this time. We light a candle of Remembrance for all those who died as victims of hatred without cause. Let us take a moment to remember them.

One or two minutes with a quiet musical background – preferably a Jewish lament.

Leader We are gathered together on this night in memory of those who died in the Final Solution of the Jewish Problem under the tyranny of Nazi Germany. At the same time we remember all those Jewish people – men, women and children – who suffered and died at the hands of Christians as a result of hatred without cause. We pray that the Holy One of Israel in his infinite mercy will grant us a place of intercession for the church, that the hatred without cause will end, that there will be reconciliation between Jew and Gentile and that the church will abandon Replacement Theology and relate in a biblical manner to the State of Israel.

Let us a take a moment to come before the Lord and confess our personal sins, that we might enter the Holy Place with clean hands and a pure heart. Are we in right relationship with God, our spouses, our children, each other and the church we belong to? *At this stage a washing of hands may be appropriate as an expression of clean hands and a pure heart.*

To express our solidarity with the Jewish people we will sing the Shema:

Shema Israel Adonai Eloheynu Adonai echad
Baruch Shem kavod malchuto le olam Va-ed

Leader Why is this night not like other nights?

Congregation Because this night we confess the sin of the church against the Jewish people, we remember their sufferings and declare our intent that the Holocaust and similar events past and present will not happen again.

Congregation We confess the sin of antisemitism in the church from its early days. We refute all antisemitic teaching, all anti-Jewish sentiments, the misreading of Scripture, removing Jesus from his Jewishness, and Replacement Theology. We confess that Christ loved the church and gave his life for those who would be part of it, both Jew and Gentile. We have failed to make Israel jealous and in our history many times the cross of reconciliation has become a sword of destruction. Lord have mercy upon us according to your unfailing love. Amen.

Leader Let us confess our position concerning the Jewish people.

Congregation We proclaim that they have not been rejected, that they have not fallen beyond recovery. (Romans 11:1,11) Theirs remain the adoption as sons, theirs the divine glory, the covenants, the receiving of the law, the Temple worship and the promises. Theirs are the Patriarchs, and from them is traced the human ancestry of Christ, who is God over all, forever praised. Amen.

Leader Praise the Lord.

Congregation The Lord's Great Name be praised forever and to eternity. May the high praises of God be in our hearts and our mouths and may both we and the house of Israel exalt his name together.

Leader Magnified and sanctified be his great name in the world that he has created. According to his will may he establish his kingdom during our life and our days and during the life and the days of the house of Israel. May there be shalom both upon us and upon the House of Israel.

Congregation May there be abundant peace from heaven and well springs of life. May he who makes peace on the high places make unto us shalom and shalom to the House of Israel. Amen.

Worship – A song of peace

Leader We appeal to you, O Lord Most High, to restore the testimony of the church to the Jewish people.

Congregation O good and merciful Father, what can we say, what can we speak, before your face of righteousness and justice? Our needs are many and our wisdom is slender, but our hope is in you. Restore, O Lord, the honour of your name and that of your Son

Yeshua the Messiah of Israel in the testimony of your church. Shame covers us as often as the remembrance of the teaching of Yeshua and your unending love confronts us. No longer let the name of Yeshua bring reproach, but let it be received with joy by your people. Amen.

Leader We acknowledge before your throne of mercy, O Lord, the sin of indifference and ambivalence.

Congregation Forbid it Lord, that, as in times past and particularly in the Shoah, we should stand idly by crowned with indifference as your people suffer. Give us a courageous spirit to stand up against all injustice and antisemitic positions. Forgive all silence where there should have been speech, forgive us for abandoning your children to the flames.

Leader May your loving-kindness and mercy not depart from us. Create in us a heart of love for your people and deliver us from all future reproach.

Congregation Blessed is the man that walks not in the council of the wicked nor stands in the ways of sinners or sits in the seat of scoffers. Let our delight be in you, O Lord, and your Word.

Leader We give thanks that your Word is a lamp to our feet and a light unto our path and we walk in darkness at our peril. Lord, let us be good and faithful hearers and teachers of your Word.

Congregation Lord we acknowledge that your Word is our fence and our safety. Let us walk in the light of your Word and live our lives accordingly. We believe that as faithful students of your Word we will be equipped to deal with antisemitism in the church and the world at large.

Worship – a song of reconciliation

Leader We now turn to specifics and we will respond by repudiating and renouncing the causes of antisemitism and recognising the activities of sin. Inasmuch as it depends upon us we will ensure that such things never happen again.

Leader For the antisemitism of the apologists and Early Church Fathers, the demonisation of the Jews and the charge of deicide.

Congregation We repudiate and renounce this teaching in Jesus' Name.

Leader As for the teaching of contempt.

Congregation. We renounce all blood libels, charges of profaning the Host, and conspiracy theories in Jesus' Name.

Leader As for the demonisation of the Jews.

Congregation We renounce and acknowledge as sin the demonisation of Jewish people. We renounce all negative stereotypes in Jesus' Name. We confess that the Jewish people remain your beloved.

Leader As for the Crusades.

Congregation We acknowledge that the Crusades brought a dark stain to the history of the church when the cross was turned into a sword. We renounce the crusaders' activities as an expression of Christ and his Kingdom. As for all movements that persecuted and destroyed your people in the name of Jesus and his church we acknowledge these as sin.

Leader As for the Office of the Inquisition.

Congregation We acknowledge the persecution of Jews and conversos as sin and renounce the practices of this Office and its inheritance in Jesus' Name.

Leader As for the antisemitism of the Reformation.

Congregation We renounce and repudiate the antisemitism of the Reformation and its ongoing effects.

Leader As for the failure of the church to respond to National Socialism and its international equivalents and for its collaboration in some areas.

Congregation We renounce cowardice and failure to respond to such challenges in Jesus' name.

Leader As for Replacement Theology.

Congregation We renounce and repudiate Replacement Theology as contrary teaching to your Word and your purposes. We confess that the Jewish people are not redundant, cast aside, forgotten, or without hope or purpose. We believe that they have a hope and a future.

Leader We recall the words that remembrance leads to deliverance whilst forgetfulness leads to destruction.

Congregation We proclaim before heaven that is your throne and earth that is your footstool, that as much as it depends upon us we will combat antisemitism in all its forms. We will remember those who have died because of hatred without cause. We pray that, by our endeavours, their flame may not be extinguished, their names that were consigned to ashes and dust will be remembered and be a blessing for the future and their deaths might not be meaningless.

Leader As we have approached your throne of grace and mercy, we boldly request, O Lord our Father, that you will use us to correct the antisemitic ills of the past and use us as instruments of your grace and mercy from this time forth.

Worship – a song of strengthening

Conclusion

Leader We have gathered together today in the presence of Almighty God to state our purpose and intent to depart from the antisemitic inheritance of the church. It is an awesome thing to be in the presence of the living God. We will now light a candle of hope from the candle of remembrance and ask that the symbol of the two candles will remind us of the transaction that has taken place here today.

Aaronic blessing

(May be antiphonal, Hebrew read by leader and English by Congregation.)

> **Y'varekh'kha Adonai v'yishmerekha**
> [May the Lord bless you and keep you.]
> **Ya'er Adonai panav aleikha vichunekka.**
> [The Lord make his face shine upon you and
> show you his favour.]
> **Yissa Adonai panav eleikha v'yasem l'kha shalom**
> [May the Lord lift up his face toward you and
> give you peace.]

The Lord's shalom be upon you, your house, those you love and upon the House of Israel. Amen.

CONFESSION OF FAITH FOR JEWISH CONVERTS OF THE CHURCH OF ANTIOCH

The Antioch Confession below is but one of many such documents requiring Jewish converts to denounce their previous practice. It contains all of the typical antisemitic elements found in confessional statements of its type.

I renounce all customs, rites, legalisms, unleavened breads and sacrifices of lambs of the Hebrews, and all the other feasts of the Hebrews, sacrifices, prayers, aspirations, purifications, sanctifications and propitiations, and fasts, and new moons, and Sabbaths, and superstitions, and hymns and chants and observances and synagogues, and the food and drink of the Hebrews: **in one word, I renounce absolutely everything Jewish**, every law, rite and custom, and above all I reject Antichrist whom all the Jews await in the figure and form of Christ...and if afterwards I shall wish to deny and return to Jewish superstition, or shall be found eating with Jews, or feasting with them, or secretly conversing and condemning the Christian religion instead of openly confuting them and condemning their vain faith, then let the trembling of Cain and the leprosy of Gehazi cleave to me, as well as the legal punishments to which I acknowledge myself liable. And may I be an anathema in the world to come, and may my soul be set down with Satan and the devils. (Assemani Cod Lit)

LIST OF JEWISH OPPONENTS TO MUHAMMAD ACCORDING TO IBN ISHAQ

From the Jews of Banu Haritha, there was Kinana b. Suriya. From the Jews of Banu Amr b. Awf, there was Qardam b. Amr. And from the Jews of Banu 'l-Najjar, there was Silsila b. Barham.

From the Banu 'l-Nadir there were: Huyayy b. Akhtab and his brothers Abu Yasir and Judayy; Sallam b. Mishkam; Kinana b. al-Rabi b.al-Rabi b Abi 'l-Huqayq; Amr b. Jahhash; Ka b b. al-Ashraf, who was from the Tayyi' of the Banu Nabhan clan, and whose mother was from the Banu ;l-Nadir, al-Hajjaj b. Amr, an ally of Ka b b. al-Ashraf; and Kardam b. Qays, also an ally of Ka b.

From the Banu Tha aba b. al-Fityawn there were: Abd Allah b. Suriya al-Awar – there was no one in the Hijaz in his time more learned in the Torah; Ibn Saluba; and Mukhayriq, who had been their rabbi, but later converted to Islam.

From the Banu Qaynuqa there were: Zayd b. al-Lasit – according to some his name was Ibn al-Lusit; Sa d b. Hunayf; Mahmud b. Sayhan; Uzayr b. Abi Uzayr; Abd Allah b. Sayf – according to some his name was Ibn Dayf; Suwayd b. al-Harith; Rifa a b. Qays; Pinhas; Ashya; Nu man b. Ada; Bahri b. Amr; Sha's b. Adi; Shas'b Qays Zayd b. al-Harith; Numan b. Amr; Sukayn b. Abi Sakayn; Adi b. Zayd; Numan b. Abi Awfa; Abu Anas; Mahmud b. Dahya; Malik b. Sayf, whose name according to some was Ibn Dayf; Ka b Rashid; Azar according to some sources; Rafi b. Haritha; Rafi b. Huraymila; Rafi b. Kharfija; Malik b. Awf; Rafi b. Zayd. B. al-Tabut; and Abd Allah b. Salam b. al-Harith who was their rabbi and chief scholar. His name was originally al-Husayn, but when he became a Muslim, the Apostle of Allah gave him the name Abd Allah.

From the Banu Qurayze there were: al-Zubayr b. Vata b. Wahb; Azzal b. Shamwil; Kab b. Asad, who had negotiated a treaty on behalf of the Banu Qurayza which was broken in the Year of the Parties (627); Shamwil b. Zayd; Havak v, Amr b. Sukayna; al-Nahham b. Zayd; Qardam b. Ka b; Wahb b. Zayd; Nafi b. Abi Nafi; Abu Nafi; Adi b. Zayd; al-Harith b. Awf; Kardam b. Zayd; Usama b. Habib; Rafi b. Rumayla; Jabal b Abi Qushayr; and Wahb b. Yahudha.

THE PACT OF UMAR

Abd al-Rahman b. Ghanam related the following:

When Umar b. al-Khattab, may Allah be pleased with him, made peace with Christian inhabitants of Syria, we wrote him the following:

In the name of Allah, the Merciful, the Beneficent.

This letter is addressed to Allah's servant Umar, the Commander of the Faithful, by the Christians of such-and-such city. When you advanced against us, we asked you for a guarantee of protection for our persons, our offspring, our property, and the people of our sect, and we have taken upon ourselves the following obligations toward you, namely:

We shall not build in our cities or in their vicinity any new monasteries, churches, hermitages, or monks' cells. We shall not restore, by night or by day, any of them that have fallen into ruin or which are located in the Muslims' quarters.

We shall keep our gates wide open for passers-by and travellers. We shall provide three days' food and lodging to any Muslims who pass our way.

We shall not shelter any spy in our churches or in our homes, nor shall we hide from the Muslims.

We shall not teach our children the Koran.

We shall not hold public religious ceremonies. We shall not seek to proselytise anyone. We shall not prevent any of our kin from embracing Islam if they so desire.

269

We shall show deference to the Muslims and shall rise from our seats when they wish to sit down.

We shall not attempt to resemble the Muslims in any way with regard to their dress, as for example, with the qalansuwa, the turban, sandals, or parting the hair (in the Arab fashion). We shall not speak as they do, nor shall we adopt their kunyas.

We shall not ride on saddles.

We shall not wear swords or bear weapons of any kind, or ever carry them with us.

We shall not engrave our signets in Arabic.

We shall not sell wines.

We shall clip the forelocks of our head.

We shall always adorn ourselves in our traditional fashion.

We shall bind the zunnar around our waists.

We shall not display our crosses or our books anywhere in the Muslims' thoroughfares nor in their marketplaces. We shall only beat our clappers in our churches very quietly. We shall not raise our voices when reciting the service in our churches, nor when in the presence of Muslims. Neither shall we raise our voices in our funeral processions.

We shall not display lights in any of the Muslim thoroughfares or in their marketplaces.

We shall not come near them with our funeral processions.

We shall not take any of the slaves that have been allotted to the Muslims.

We shall not build our homes higher than theirs.

(When I brought the letter to Umar – may Allah be pleased with him – he added the clause "We shall not strike any Muslim.")

We accept these conditions for ourselves and for the members of our sect, in return for which we are to be given a guarantee of security. Should we violate in any way these conditions which we have accepted and for which we stand security, then there shall be no covenant of protection for us, and we shall be liable to the penalties for rebelliousness and sedition.

Then Umar – may Allah be pleased with him – wrote: "Sign what they have requested, but add two clauses that will also be binding upon them; namely, they shall not buy anyone who has been taken prisoner by the Muslims, and that anyone who deliberately strikes a Muslim will forfeit the protection of this pact."

Translated from al-Turtushi
Siraj al-Mulul (Cairo, 1289/1872), pp. 229–30

ARAB IMMIGRATION 1922–1943

Town or District	Growth from 1922	Growth to 1943	Percentage increase	Type of Area
Jerusalem	28,571	56,400	97%	Heavily Jewish
Jaffa	27,437	62,600	134%	Heavily Jewish
Haifa	18,404	58,200	216%	Heavily Jewish
Hebron	16,650	22,800	26%	Mostly Arab but under Jewish redevelopment
Nablus	15,931	23,300	51%	Mostly Arab but under Jewish redevelopment
Bethlehem	6,658	8,800	33%	Mostly Arab but under Jewish redevelopment
Gaza	17,426	17,045 (1931)	3%	Mostly Arab. No Jewish redevelopment
Beersheba District	71,000	49,000 (1939)	45%	Mostly Arab. No Jewish redevelopment

Town or District	Growth from 1922	Growth to 1943	Percentage increase	Type of Area
Bethlehem District	24,613 23,725 (1929)	26,000		Mostly Arab. No Jewish redevelopment
Hebron District	51,345	59,000		Mostly Arab. No Jewish redevelopment
Nazareth, Beit Shan, Tiberias and Acre	89,600	151,000		Heavy Jewish settlement and rural development
Jaffa and Ramalah District	42,300	126,000		Heavy Jewish settlement and rural development

NB The population of the Beersheba district would have been 89,000 if the average natural birth rate was included. Therefore, in real terms the drop was 39,000 people or 56%. The population of the Hebron district would have been 72,000 if the average natural birth rate was included. Therefore, in real terms the drop was 13,000 people rather than an increase of 7,655. Data extracted from L Shimony, *The Arabs of Palestine*, Tel-Aviv, 1947.

ABBREVIATIONS

b	ben, or bar – son of. (Or ibn in Arabic, meaning son of)
BCE	Before the Common Era
Ber	Tractate Berachot (Talmud)
BT	Babylonian Talmud
c	About
CE	Common Era
CO	Colonial Office
d	Died
FO	Foreign Office
Gen Rab	Genesis Rabbah
MEMRI	Middle East Media and Reporting Institute
PARDES	*The Journal For Biblical and Hebraic Studies*
q	quoted in
r	ruled
R	Rabbi

GLOSSARY

Achund	Islamic Religious authorities
Aliyah	Heb: To go up – used as the term for the return to Israel
Al-Buraq	Arabic name for the Western Wall
Al-Quds	Arabic name for Jerusalem
Bat Kol	Voice from Heaven
Conflate	To add supplementary material or commentary
De-khulakisation	Stalin's removal of petty or small scale farmers with their own holdings in the 1920–30s
Dhimma Dhimmi	The Islamic law concerning people of the book
Eugenics	Human engineering in its early stages. Involved selective breeding, sterilisation and medical experiments
Extant	Still in existence
Galut	Exile
Given	An element of a topic that is generally accepted without question

Gnostic	Heretical teaching offering "secret knowledge". Based in Eastern mysticism and pluralism
Goyim	Heb. term for the Gentiles
Haj	Arabic Pilgrimage (to Mecca or Medina). The title accorded to one who has made the pilgrimage
Haskalah	Heb. term meaning "enlightened"
Haram esh Sharif	Arabic name for the Temple Mount
Haskalah	Jewish intellectual movement in the nineteenth century that advocated secular education, colloquial languages, assimilation and productive work as pre-requisites for emancipation
Hester Panim	Heb. The hiddenness of the face. Sometimes referred to as the "Silence of God"
Historiography	The manner of the way history is written
Internecine	Internal disputes generally of a political nature
Instrumentalism	Where a person or people group are used as a political tool
Kiddush Ha Shem	Heb. Sanctification of the Holy Name
Kotel	Heb: The Western (Wailing) Wall
LXX	The Septuagint. A Greek version of the OT prepared in Alexandria approximately 200 BCE
Manichaean	Pluralistic gnostic thought generally used to describe a view that sees absolute good and absolute evil with no middle ground

Marrano	(Pig) A derogatory term for Jewish convert to Christianity in 15th century Spain
Maskilim	Members of the Haskalah
Menses	The product of menstruation
Minim	Heb. term meaning "heretic". May be applied to Jewish Christians or Christians in general
Mythos	A generally accepted non-verifiable account of the founding of a state or people group. Something that is a myth is not necessarily a complete fabrication: usually it is based upon a real event
Notice	Used to designate a piece of information within a block of text
Polemic(al)	A piece of writing or speech against another, often designed to defame the opponent
Procrustean	From Greek mythology. Either cutting or stretching to fit
Purim	Jewish festival celebrating their deliverance from Haman who attempted to eliminate all the Jewish people in the Persian Empire
Qalansuwa	A conical cap
Responsa	Letters containing answers to questions, mostly on issues of Jewish law
Roma	The main group of European gypsies
Seder	Passover meal
Shia	Sect of Islam
Sitra achra	Heb: the evil impulse
Sunna	Sect of Islam
Sharia	Islamic law
Siddur	Jewish prayer book

Sinti	One of the major groups of European gypsies
Siyata de'shemaya	Heb: Divine assistance
Talmud	Body of Teaching comprising the Mishna and Gemara, commentaries and discussions on subjects that cover all aspects of Jewish life. There are Jerusalem and Babylonian Talmuds completed around 450 and 500 CE respectively
Tanakh	Old Testament
Usury	Lending money at interest – the practice was considered unfit for a Christian
Waqf	Muslim religious endowment
Yishuv	Jewish community of Palestine
Yom ha Shoah	Holocaust Remembrance Day
Ziara	Islamic place of visit
Zohar	Kabbalistic book
Zunnā	A sash or kind of belt

SELECT BIBLIOGRAPHY

Adiv, Udi, *Return*, No. 5, London, December 1990

Arberry, A. J., *Arabic Poetry: A Primer for Students*, Cambridge, 1965

Arendt, Hannah, *Eichmann in Jerusalem*, London, 1963

Ballard, P. Boswood, *Obliviscence and Reminiscence*, Cambridge, 1913

Baron, Salo, *Social and Religious History of the Jews*, New York, 1952 (second edition)

Baron, Salo, Early Approaches to Jewish Emancipation, *Diogenes*, Vol. XXIX, 1960

Barth, Karl, *Verheissung und Verantwortung der Christlichen Gemeinde im Heutigen Zeitgeschehen*, Zürich EV, 1944

Barth, Karl, *The Church and the Political Problem of our Day*, New York, 1939

Bauer, Yehuda, *The Holocaust in Historical Perspective*, Seattle: University of Washington Press, 1980

Bayfield, Tony and Braybrook, Marcus, (eds), *Dialogue With a Difference*, London, 1992

Beck, N. A., *Recognising and Repudiating the Anti-Jewish Polemic of the New Testament*, Toronto, 1985

Benjamin, J. J., *Eight Years In Africa and Asia From 1846–1855*, Hanover, 1859

Berdayev, Nicholai Alexandrovich, *Christianity and Antisemitism*, New York, 1954

Berkowitz, Eliezer, *Faith After the Holocaust*, New York, 1973

Berkowitz, Eliezer, *With God in Hell*, New York, 1979

Berkowitz, Eliezer, "Facing the Truth" *Judaism* 27, 1978

Bethge, Eberhard, *Dietrich Bonhoeffer*, Munich, 1967

Bolles, Edmund Blair, *Remembering and Forgetting: An Inquiry into the Nature of Memory*, New York, 1980

Camon, Ferdinando, *Autoritratto di Primo Levi*, Padova, 1987

Camus, Albert, *La Peste*, Paris, 1946

Cargas, Harry, *Shadows of Auschwitz*, New York, 1992

Carpi, D., "The Mufti of Jerusalem", in *Studies in Zionism*, 7, Spring, 1983

Chalk, Frank "Definitions of Genocide", in *Holocaust and Genocide Studies* vol 4:2, Oxford, 1989

Chalk, Frank and Jonassohone, K., *A Reader in the History and Sociology of Genocide*, Montreal, 1984

Chaney, I. ed., *Towards the Understanding and Prevention of Genocide: Proceedings of the International Conference on the Holocaust and Genocide*, Westview, 1984

Charlesworth J. H. (ed) "Christianity and Judaism: A Historical and Theological Overview" in *Jews and Christians, Exploring the Past, Present and Future*, New York, 1990

Chavel, C., (ed), *Perush le-sefer Kohelet* in *Kitevi Rabbenu Moshe ben Nahman*, New York, 1953

Cohen, Arthur, *Tremendum: A Theological Interpretation of the Holocaust*, New York, 1981

Cohn Sherbock, Dan, *The Future of Jewish-Christian Dialogue*, New York, 1999

Coudenhove-Kalergi, H., *Das Wesen des Antisemitismus*, Vienna, Leipzig and Paris 1929, English translation, London, 1935

Coudenhove-Kalergi, R., in Valentin, Hugo, A. G. Chater, (tr) *Antisemitism*, Uppsala, 1935

Curzon, R., *Persia and the Persian Question*, London, 1892

Dawidowicz, Lucy, *The War Against the Jews, 1933–45*, London, 1975

Dawidowicz, Lucy, *The Holocaust and the Historians*, London, 1981

Dostoevsky, F., *Crime and Punishment*, 1866 (many versions, *eg* Penguin, Heron, etc)

Dostoevsky, F., *The Brothers Karamazov*, 1880 (many versions, *eg* Penguin, Heron, etc)

Eckstein, Yechiel, *What Christians Should Know About Jews and Judaism*, 1984

Eichorn, J., *Repertorium für Biblische und Morgenladische Literatur*, Leipzig, 1777–80

Epp, Eldon J., "Antisemitism and the Popularity of the Fourth Gospel in Christianity", in *The Journal of the Central Conference of American Rabbis*, 22:35, 1975

Erickson, Robert, *Theologians under Hitler*, Yale, 1985

Espina Alfonso de, *Fortalitium Fidei*, Nuremberg, 1485–98

Fackenheim, Emile L. "The Holocaust and Philosophy", *The Journal of Philosophy*, October, 1985

Fant Clyde E. Jnr, and Pinson, William Jnr (eds), *Sermons to Savanarola*, Waco, 1971

Fein, Helen, *Accounting for Genocide*, Chicago, 1984

Fein, Helen, *Genocide: A Sociological Perspective*, London, 1993

Fiddes, Paul, *The Creative Suffering of God*, Oxford, 1988

Frydland, R., *When Being Jewish was a Crime*, Nashville, 1978

Glover, Julian, *Humanity*, A Moral History of the 20th Century, London, 1999

Goldhagan, Daniel, *Hitler's Willing Executioners*, London, 1996

Greenberg, Irving, *Confronting the Holocaust: A Listing of Articles and Books Reflecting the Jewish Religious Responses to the Holocaust in Its Immediate Aftermath (1944–1949)* [Yiddish and Hebrew] Ramat Gan, 1994

Guttenplan, D. D., *The Holocaust on Trial*, London, 2001

Gutteridge, R., *Open Thy Mouth for the Dumb: The German Evangelical Church and the Jews, 1879–1950*, Oxford, 1976

Harff, Barbara and Gurr, Ted R. "Toward Empirical Theory of Genocides and Politicides", *International Studies Quarterly* 37, 3 1988

Halbwachs, Maurice, *On Collective Memory*, Lewis A. Cozer (ed), Chicago, 1992

Hartom, Menarchem Immanuel, "Hirhurimal ha-Shoah", *deot*, 18, Winter 1961

Heer, Friedrich, *God's First Love*, London, 1970

Hertzberg, A., *The Zionist Idea*, New York, 1981

Hillberg, Raul, *The Destruction of the European Jews*, New York edition, 1985

Hirzowicz, Lukasz, *The Third Reich and the Arab East*, London, 1966

Hume David, *Dialogues Concerning Natural Religion*, New York, 1966

Ibn Hisham, *al-Sira al Nahawiyya*, vol 1, Cairo, 1955

Ignatieff, Michael, *Blood and Belonging: Journeys into the New Nationalism*, London, 1994

Jocz, J., *The Jewish People and Jesus Christ After Auschwitz*, Grand Rapids, 1981

Jonas, Hans, "The Concept of God After Auschwitz", in Albert Friedlander (ed) *Out of the Whirlwind*, New York, 1976

Jonathan, I., *European Jewry in the Age of Mercantilism*, Oxford, 1985

Kaplan, Lawrence, "Rabbi Isaac Hutner's Daat Torah Perspective on the Holocaust", *Tradition*, 18, Fall 1980

Katz, Steven T., *The Black Book, The Nazi Crime Against the Jewish People*, New York edition, 1981

Kirschner, Robert (ed), *Rabbinic Responses of the Holocaust Era*, New York, 1985

Laquer, Walter, *The Terrible Secret, The Secret Suppression of The Truth About Hitler's Final Solution*, Boston, 1980

Laquer, Walter, *Israel Arab Reader*, London, 1984

Leibnitz, Gottfried Wilhelm, *Theodicy: Essays on the Goodness of God, the Freedom of Man and the Origin of Evil*, 1710

Lemkin, Raphael, *Axis Rule in Occupied Europe: Laws of Occupation, Analysis of Government and Proposals for Redress*, New York edition, 1973

Levi, Primo, *I sommersi e i salvatori*, Turino, 1988

Levi, Primo, *Se questo e un uomo*, Turino, 1947

Lewis Bernard, *Semites and Antisemites: An Inquiry Into Conflict and Prejudice*, London edition, 1986

Lewis Bernard, *The Jews of Islam*, Princeton, 1990

Lifton, Robert Jay, *The Nazi Doctors*, New York, 1986

Lipstadt, Deborah, *Denying the Holocaust: The Growing Assault on Truth and Memory*, London, 1994

Little, Franklin, *The Crucifixion of the Jews*, New York, 1975

Marr Wilhelm, *The Victory of Judaism Over Germandom*, Vienna, 1873 and 1879

Marrus, M. R., *The Holocaust in History*, Ottawa 1987

Masa, Ephraim Neimark, *'be-eretz ha Kedem, ed a ya'ari*, Jerusalem, 1946

Maybaum, Ignaz, *The Face of God After Auschwitz*, Amsterdam, 1965

Michael, Robert, "The Case of Martin Niemoeller", in *Holocaust and Genocide Studies*, vol 2:1, 1987)

Mayer, Arno, *Why Did the Heavens Not Darken? – The "Final Solution" in History*, London, 1988

Maza, Bernard, *With Fury Poured Out*, New York, 1986

Moltmann, Jurgen, *Answer to Job*, New York, 1954

Morris, Benny, *The Birth of the Palestinian Refugee Problem 1947–49*, Cambridge, 1988

Morris, Benny, *Righteous Victims*, London, 2000

Munsat, Stanley, *The Concept of Memory*, New York, 1967

Müssner, Franz, *Traktat über die Juden*, München, 1979

Nachmanides, *Perush le-sefer Kohelet* in *Kitevi Rabbenu Moshe ben Nahman*, C. Chavel (ed), New York, 1953

Netanyahu, Benjamin, *A Place Among the Nations*, Haifa, 1981

Neusner, Jacob, *Jews and Christians: The Myth of a Common Tradition*, London, 1991

O'Brien, Conor Cruise, *The Siege*, London, 1988

Parkes, James, *Whose Land?* London, 1970

Pearlman, Maurice, *Mufti of Jerusalem: The Story of Haj Amin el Husseni*, London, 1947

Pelican, Jaroslav, *The Preaching of Chrysostom*, Philadelphia, 1967

Piekaz, Mendel, *Hatecuda Ha'hasidit Ha'sifrutit Ha'ahronacal Admat Polin*, Jerusalem, 1979

Pittenger, N., *Christology Reconsidered*, London, 1970

Pittinger N., *Process, Thought and Christian Faith*, New York, 1968

Prittie, T., *Germans Against Hitler*, Boston, 1964

Reuther, Rosemary Radford, *Faith and Fratricide*, New York, 1974

Reuther, Rosemary Radford, *To Change the World*, London, 1981

Robinson, J. A. T., *The Priority of John*, London, 1984

Rosenzweig, Franz, *The Star of Redemption*, London, 1970 edition

Rubenstein, R., "Auschwitz and Covenant Theology", *Christian Century*, 21st May 1969, in reply to Leroy T. Howe, "Theology and the Death Camps", *Christian Century*, 19th Feb 1969

Rubenstein, R., and Roth J., *Approaches to Auschwitz*, London, 1987

Rubenstein, R "The State of Jewish Belief" in *Commentary 42*, August 1966

Runes, Dagobert, *The War Against the Jews*, New York, 1968

Sartre, J-P, *Antisemite and Jew*, (trans) G. J. Becker, Paris, 1948

Sacks, Jonathan, *Tradition in an Untraditional Age*, London, 1990

Sandmel, Samuel, *Antisemitism in the New Testament*, Philadelphia, 1978

Schweid, Eliezer, *Ma'avak ad Shahar*, Tel Aviv, 1990

Segev, Tom, *One Palestine Complete*, London, 2000

Sereny, Gitta *Into That Darkness: From Mercy Killing to Mass Murder*, London, 1974

Shapira, Kalonymous Kalman, *The Holy Fire: The Teachings of Rabbi Kalonymous Kalman Shapira, the Rebbe of the Warsaw Ghetto*, Nehemia Polen (ed), New Jersey, 1994

Shimony, L., *The Arabs of Palestine*, Tel-Aviv, 1947

Simon, Marcel, *Versus Israel: A Study of the Relations between Christians and Jews in the Roman Empire (AD 135–425)* Translated from French by H McKeating, London edition, 1996

Sölle, Dorothee, "God's Pain, our Pain: How Theology Has to Change After Auschwitz", in *Remembering for the Future*, Supp vol, Oxford, 1988

Sölle, Dorothee, "God's Pain and our Pain", in Otto Maduro, (ed.) *Judaism, Christianity and Liberation*, New York, 1991

Stav, Arie, Arabs and Nazism, in *Outpost*, January 1996

Stendahl, Krister, *School of Matthew*, Philadelphia, 1954 and 1968

Tal, Uriel, *Excursus on the Term Shoah*, Ithaca, 1978

Teitelbaum, Y., Ma'amar Shalosh Sh'vuot *in Va-Yoel Moshe*, New York, 1959

Teitelbaum, Y., *Al ha-ge'ulah*, New York, 1967

Tolichus, Otto, *They Wanted War*, New York, 1940

Tracey, David, *Religious Values After the Holocaust*, Philadelphia, 1982

Von Wahlde, U. C., "The Johanine Jews: A Critical Survey" in *New Testament Studies*, 28 January 1982

Watters, M F, *Mufti Over the Middle East*, London, 1942

Wiesel, Elie, *Night*, London, 1981

Wiesel, Elie, *Beggar in Jerusalem*, Avon, New York, 1971

Wiesel, Elie, *Der Prozess von Schamgorod* (The Trial of God), Paris, 1979

Wright, F., *Words From the Scroll of Fire*, Jerusalem, 1994

Wright, F., *The Cross Became a Sword, the Soldiers of Christ and the First Crusade*, Harpenden, 1995

Wright, F., "Early Jewish Christianity – Orthodoxy and Deviancy to the 4thC CE" in *PARDES, The Journal of the Centre for Biblical and Hebraic Studies* I:I and II, 1995–6

Wright, F., "The Priesthood of James the Brother of Jesus" in *Roots and Branches*, Exploring the Jewish Contour of the Christian Faith, Essays in Honour of David Forbes, London, 1998

Wright, F., *Within the Pale*, awaiting publication

Wright, F., *Understanding Ancient Documents*, PARDES Occasional Paper II, 1998

Lecture Papers Quoted

Jacobovits, Immanuel, *Where Was Man at Auschwitz?*, Transcript of a lecture given at Wawel Castle, Cracow, (Poland), 26th Jan 1995

Maritain, Jaques, *Anti-Semitism*, Transcript of a lecture given in Paris on 5th February 1938 at the *Théâtre des Ambassadeurs*, under the auspices of the *Groupes Chrétienté* and later at the Cosmopolitan Club, New York on 14 December 1938, with additions due to the unfolding events in Nazi Germany

Tracey, David, *The Interpretation of Theological Texts*, Unpublished lecture, Indiana University, 1984

General Works of Reference

Encyclopaedia Judaica

The Great Soviet Encyclopaedia and the History of the Great Patriotic War, (1966 edition)

Institute of Jewish Affairs, *Soviet Antisemitic Propaganda: Evidence from Books, Press and Radio*, London, 1978

Istoriia Velikoi Otchestevennoi Voine Sovetskogo Soiwza 1941–1954, Moscow 1962–1965

Simon Wiesenthal Centre Report, 2001

Government Documents

Peel Report, Chapter 9, para 60

Report by His Majesty's Government on Palestine and Trans-Jordan, London, 1937

Documents on German Foreign Policy, 1918–1945, series D 1937–1945, vol V; June 1937–March, 1939, Washington D. C. 1953, Doc. 566

Palestine Royal Commission Report, Cmd 5479, London, 1937

GB, CO, *Palestine Report*, 1937, Colonial No 146

The Palestine Gazette, Extraordinary, No. 723, 30 September, 1937

Official Report, House of Lords, 15 October, 1946, Col 257, HMSO, London

Government of Palestine, *Survey of Palestine*, British Government Printer, *US Department of Agriculture Report*, 1944

Parliamentary Debates, 15 April, 1946

"Not by might nor by power, but by
My Spirit," says the LORD Almighty"
Zechariah 4:6 NIV